AN
INTERMEDIATE
ENGLISH PRACTICE BOOK

By the same author
THE VISUAL ELEMENT IN LANGUAGE TEACHING

AN INTERMEDIATE ENGLISH PRACTICE BOOK

S. PIT CORDER

Langenscheidt-Longman
ENGLISH LANGUAGE TEACHING

Nach dem Urheberrechtsgesetz vom 9. September 1965 i.d.F. vom 10. November 1972 ist die Vervielfältigung oder Übertragung urheberrechtlich geschützter Werke, also auch der Texte dieses Buches – mit Ausnahme der in §§ 53, 54 URG ausdrücklich genannten Sonderfälle – nicht gestattet.

Auflage: 11. 10. 9. 8. 7. | Letzte Zahlen
Jahr: 1986 85 84 83 82 | maßgeblich

© 1960 S. Pit Corder
© 1973 Langenscheidt-Longman GmbH, München
Druck: Druckhaus Langenscheidt, Berlin-Schöneberg
Printed in Germany · ISBN 3 - 526 - 50701 - 5

CONTENTS

§ 1. ARTICLES AND POSSESSIVES 1

The Definite Article and Abstract Nouns. Omission of Definite Article. The Possessive Form. The Double Genitive.

§ 2. SOME AUXILIARIES AND ANOMALOUS VERBS 7

Can. *Couldn't* and *Managed to*. *Can be* + Adjective. *Need* and *Dare*. *Needn't have* and *Didn't need to*. *Mustn't* and *Needn't*. *Must* with meaning of inference or probability. *Shall* and *Will*. *Would* and *Should*. *Would* in hypothetical situations. *Have*.

§ 3. THE PASSIVE VOICE 24

§ 4. RELATIVE CLAUSES 28

Defining and Non-defining Clauses. The Uses of *that*. The Omission of the Relative Pronoun. Relatives in the Possessive form. Relative Adverbs. Non-defining Relative Clauses standing for a sentence. *Whatever, whoever*, etc.

§ 5. WORD ORDER 38

Position and Order of Objects. Substitute Subject, *It*. Inversion of Verb and Subject after certain adverbs. Position and Order of Adverbs. Pre-verb Adverbs. Position and Order of Adjectives. Position of *Both* and *All*. Order of Words in Indirect Questions.

§ 6. INFINITIVES AND GERUNDS 53

Infinitives and Gerunds as Subjects. Gerunds after Prepositions. *Do* + *a lot of* + Gerund. Infinitive as Object. Gerund as Object. Verbs of Sensation. *Be* + Adjective + to-Infinitive. *Be* + to-Infinitive. *For* + Object + Infinitive. Infinitive in place of Relative Clause.

CONTENTS

§7. TENSES OF THE VERB — 73

Simple Present and Simple Past Tenses. Continuous Present and Simple Present. Non-conclusive Verbs. The Future Tenses. *Shall/Will* Future and *Going to* Future. Present Continuous with Future Meaning. Simple Present with Future Meaning. Present Perfect Tense. Simple Present and Present Perfect Tense in Temporal Clauses. The Simple Past Tense. Continuous and Simple Past Tenses. Continuous Past and Simple Past Tense with meaning of Habitual Action. Past Perfect Tense. Simple Past and Past Perfect Tenses in Hypothetical Situations.

§8. CONDITIONAL SENTENCES — 91

§9. PREPOSITIONS — 102

Prepositions of Time. *For* and *Since*. *Under*, *Below*, *Over* and *Above*. *Between* and *Among*. *At* and *In* in Phrases of Place. Prepositions of Direction Towards. Prepositions of Direction From. *In*, *With* and *Of* describing People and their Clothes. Collocations with *At*; with *By*; with *In*; with *On*; with *Out of*. Collocations with the word *Time*. Adjectives followed by *To* and *At*; with *With*, *For* and *Of*; with *From About* and *In*. Verbs followed by *At* and *To*; by *On* and *In*; by *From* and *Of*; by *For*, *With* and *against*. Prepositions at the ends of Sentences and Clauses. *Not until*.

§10. PHRASAL VERBS AND ADVERB PARTICLES — 133

Meanings of the Adverb Particles *Up*, *Down*, *Out*, *Off*, *On* and *Over*. Word Order and Phrasal Verbs. Phrasal Verbs with *Do* and *Make*; with *Come* and *Bring*; with *Keep* and *Let*; with *Get*. Adverb Particles and the Verb *To Be*. Phrasal Verbs which do not have a literal meaning. Words formed with Adverb Particles. Adverb Particles in Imperatives and Exclamations.

§11. PUNCTUATION — 158

Exclamation and Question Mark. The Comma. The Semi-colon. The Colon. The Punctuation of Direct Speech. The Use of Capital Letters.

§ 12. SPELLING 167

The Problem of the Final *y*. The Problem of Doubling Consonants. The Doubling of Final *l*. Words with a Silent *e*. Double Consonants. Plurals. The Spelling of Vowel Sounds. Silent Letters. Words with Greek Roots. The Hyphen.

§ 13. WORD BUILDING 188

The Adjective Suffixes: *-ly*, *-y*, *-ish*, *-like*, *-some*, *-worthy* and *-able*. Negative Prefixes. The Suffixes *-ful* and *-less*. Formation of Comparatives and Superlatives. Compound Adjectives. The Prefixes *Over-* and *Under-*. The Noun Suffixes *-ship*, *-hood* and *-dom*. Noun Suffixes *-t* and *-th*. Agents and people who do things. Feminines. Noun Suffix *-ful*. Verb Suffixes *-en* *-fy*, *-ate*, *-ize*. Verb Prefix *Re-*. Adverb Particles as Prefixes. Prefixes and Verb Roots of Latin Origin. Derivatives. Verb Prefixes *Be-* and *En-*. Noun Suffixes *-al*, *-age*, *-ment*, *-ation* and *-ance*. Modern Derivatives with Latin Prefixes. Compound Nouns.

§ 14. WORDS 214

Verbs and Verbal Expressions. *Become* and *Get*, etc. *Bring, Take, Carry, Fetch. Raise, Rise, Lay, Lie. Say* and *Tell*. Verbs with and without objects. *Wait for, Hope, Expect, Look forward to. Avoid* and *Prevent. Rob* and *Steal*. Nouns. Diminutives. Abbreviations. Collocations. Words with Similar Meanings. *All* and *Whole*. *All, Everybody, Everything. Fairly* and *Rather. Quite.*

§ 15. DICTATION PASSAGES 243

§ 16. PASSAGES FOR COMPREHENSION AND PRÉCIS 248

FOREWORD TO THE STUDENT

THE exercises in this book are meant for all students who have reached the intermediate level of English, and they have been specially designed for those who are preparing to take the Cambridge Lower Certificate Examination in English. I have also tried to include practice in as many language skills as is possible between the covers of a single book.

It is important to understand the difference between exercises and tests. Tests are made up to find out how much you know; exercises are to help you to learn and practise your new knowledge. This book contains exercises, and everything has been done to make them as straightforward as possible; you will not find any 'catches' or special difficulties of the sort that are sometimes put in examination papers. Remember also that exercises are meant for exercise; that is, you are meant to repeat them again and again until you have a mastery of the construction, vocabulary or point of grammar that you are practising. If you are learning a musical instrument or a game like tennis, you have to repeat certain movements over and over again until they are perfect. The same is true when you are learning a language. That is why you should not write down the answers to these exercises in the book itself. If you do, any exercise which has these markings will be of very little use to you any longer.

You will find that some exercises are more difficult than others. Which are difficult and which are easy will, to some extent, depend on what your own mother tongue is. The ones which seem difficult are the ones that you need to practise more often, but you must also make sure that you can do all the other exercises in the book without any difficulty.

Some of the exercises must be written; for example, those in the sections on punctuation, spelling, dictation, précis and comprehension; but the first ten sections of the book should eventually be done orally. You may find that some of the exercises in these sections are too difficult to do in this way. If so, do them in writing first and then repeat them orally later.

SECTION I

ARTICLES AND POSSESSIVES

Exercise No 1. The Definite Article and Abstract Nouns

Abstract nouns in English have no article when used in a general sense, but if they are qualified by a phrase or clause in such a way that their meaning becomes restricted to a particular example, a definite article is needed:

> She loves music.
> He often plays *the* music of Beethoven.

The presence of a qualifying adjective or phrase does not necessarily make an abstract noun particular in sense. Note these examples:

> (*a*) Health is more important than wealth.
> Good health is the right of every man.
> Public health in England is of a high standard.
> *The* health *of the community* is of the highest importance.
> *The* health *he has enjoyed* for the last three years is due to the climate.

> (*b*) Art is long, life short.
> Modern art is difficult to understand.
> Art in France is of a high order.
> *The* art *of Picasso.*
> *The* art *of painting.*
> *The* art *of the XVII century.*

Here are sentences in pairs. The abstract noun in one of them needs an article and the other does not. Supply it where correct:

1. ... Industry is the basis of our economy.
   ... Industry of Sheffield is steel-making.
2. She likes ... modern literature.
   She does not like ... literature of the XVIII century.
3. ... Ignorance is bliss.
   ... Ignorance of these people is astounding.
4. ... Beauty is only skin-deep.
   We were admiring ... beauty of the night.
5. ... Intelligence of these children is very high.
   It requires ... intelligence to understand this problem.
6. ... Public education must be rapidly extended.
   ... Education of little children has been greatly neglected.

7. In mathematics ... accuracy is essential.
   I cannot judge ... accuracy of your calculations.
8. ... Theft, ... murder and ... arson are crimes.
   He was found guilty of ... murder of his sweetheart.
9. He is not a man who likes ... responsibility.
   I am giving you ... responsibility for providing the drinks.
10. Water is necessary to ... life.
    ... Life of these insects is very short.

Exercise No 2. Omission of the Definite Article

English does not use the definite article in certain cases where it is found in several other languages. The principal examples are:

(*a*) Nouns meaning a class of things when used in the plural—

Dogs bark.
Typewriters are useful machines.

(*b*) Uncountable nouns—

Beer is a harmless drink.
He takes sugar in his tea.

But these same nouns are found with an article if they are qualified by phrases or clauses in such a way that their meaning becomes restricted to a particular example of the class or material:

(*a*) *The dogs you keep* are very well behaved.
The typewriters we have in the office are all old.
(*b*) *The beer we drank yesterday* was sour.
The sugar he takes in his tea comes from Jamaica.

The presence of a qualifying phrase or clause does not necessarily restrict the meaning of these words to a particular example:

(*a*) Dogs with long legs run fast. (the class of long-legged dogs)
The dogs with long legs are mine. (not the ones with short legs)
Dogs, which are most useful animals, are found all over the world.
The dogs which are most useful are those which are used by the blind.
(*b*) *Tea without sugar* is undrinkable. (a type of drink)
The tea without sugar is yours. (a particular example)
Sugar made from beet is cheaper. (considered as a class)
The sugar made in Jamaica is more expensive. (considered as a special sort)

SECTION I   ARTICLES AND POSSESSIVES

Put the definite article before the nouns in these sentences where it is necessary:

1. ... Games are good for health.
   He went to Helsinki for ... Olympic Games.
2. ... Cats I breed are all Siamese.
   ... Cats are intelligent animals.
3. ... Sewing-machines have an intricate mechanism.
   ... Sewing-machine you lent me is broken.
4. ... Grass grows everywhere, but ... grass in the valley is the best.
5. ... Money is used all over the world as a means of exchange.
   Have you lost ... money I gave you?
6. ... Oxygen is used in medicine.
   Our bodies use ... oxygen in the air.
7. ... Water is necessary to life.
   ... Water in that basin is not fit to drink.
8. ... Air we breathe is a mixture of ... oxygen and ... nitrogen.
9. ... Pianos are expensive instruments.
   ... Pianos they build in Germany have a high reputation.
10. ... Butter is made from ... milk.
    ... Butter on your plate came from New Zealand.
11. ... Paint I put on yesterday is dry.
    ... Paint helps to protect metal from rust.
12. A shoemaker uses ... rubber and ... leather in his work.
    ... Leather he uses must be of the best quality.

Exercise No 3. The Possessive

The possessive pronoun can replace a noun with a possessive adjective in a sentence where that noun has already been mentioned or is understood:

> This is *my book* = This book is *mine*.
> I've finished *my ink*. Can I use *yours*?

The possessive form of a name or a person can also be used in the same way:

> This is *George's house* = This house is *George's*.
> I know *Mary's husband* but not *Anne's*.

Example:

Rembrandt's pictures are more valuable than *those of Van Dyke*.
= Rembrandt's pictures are more valuable than *Van Dyke's*.

Replace the parts of the following sentences in italics by a possessive word in the same way as in the example:

1. I don't know his name, but I can tell you *what his wife is called*.
2. *The Church of St. Paul* is the finest church in the city.
3. While you are in town, please call at *the butcher's shop*.
4. I've read most of Dickens' novels and some of *those written by Thackeray*.
5. This is my room and that is *occupied by my sister*.
6. The accident was the driver's own fault and not *that of the cyclist*.
7. Whose hat is this? I think it is *the one that belongs to John*.
8. I like Brahms' symphonies but not *those written by Beethoven*.
9. I know the ship's name but not *the name of its captain*.
10. I think that hat is much more stylish than *the one Tom has*.
11. I bought these cigarettes at *the shop of the tobacconist* round the corner.
12. He has been staying for a few weeks at *the house of his uncle*.
13. She prefers my work to *the work my brother does*.
14. That is clearly your responsibility not *that of your employer*.
15. I've read John's letter, but where did you put *the one Mary sent*?

Exercise No 4. The Double Genitive

Look at these phrases:

>A friend of mine (=*one of my friends*)
>A brother of John's (=*one of John's brothers*)
>An acquaintance of his (=*one of his acquaintances*)

This possessive form, sometimes known as the 'double genitive' is common in English when we wish to emphasize the person who possesses rather than the thing which he possesses.

Example:

One of John's friends came to see me yesterday.
=*A friend of John's* came to see me yesterday.

Change the phrases in italics into a 'double genitive' construction in the same way as in the example:

1. It is *one of my habits* to get up early.
2. It was *one of my father's favourite expressions*.
3. It is *one of Mary's weaknesses* to eat too many sweets.

SECTION I ARTICLES AND POSSESSIVES

4. I see that *one of your colleagues* has had an accident.
5. *One of our neighbours* has recently visited Peru.
6. They tell me that *some of the Jones's acquaintances* have been arrested.
7. *Any of your ideas* would be welcome.
8. I seem to remember *one of Graham Green's books* about Mexico.
9. I've seen all John's drawings; now I want to see *one of your drawings*.
10. That was *one of your good suggestions*.

Exercise No 5

Another use of the double genitive is in phrases like these, where there is a word such as *this* or *that* before the noun:

> This idea of yours
> These shoes of Henry's
> That silly old hat of Mary's
> Those dirty hands of yours

This use of the double genitive often shows contempt, arrogance, or a desire to ridicule on the part of the speaker.

Change the phrases in italics into the double genitive form adding the words *this*, *that*, *these* or *those* before it:

> *Example:*
>
> Take *your dirty hands* off my nice clean dress!
> =Take *those dirty hands of yours* off my nice clean dress!

1. *Robert's car* is giving him a lot of trouble.
2. What about *your plans*?
3. Can you remember *Turner's picture* called the 'Fighting Temeraire'?
4. *Your brother* really is an awful nuisance.
5. *Your son's drawings* are remarkably advanced for his age.
6. I wish *Mary's servant* wouldn't always say 'hello' to me like that.
7. *My new shoes* pinch me most painfully.
8. Where did you put *my keys*?
9. *John's latest hobby* takes up all his spare time.

10. Take away *your beastly dog*.
11. I must say, *the butcher's new shop* is really most convenient.
12. *The children's new teacher* is completely ignorant.
13. I'd like to hear *the Jones's new radio*.
14. Have you read *Waugh's latest book*?
15. Would you mind showing me *your old plans*?

SECTION 2

SOME AUXILIARIES AND ANOMALOUS VERBS

Exercise No 6. 'Can'

1. *Can* has the meaning of *ability* or *capacity* (=*know how*):

    I can swim (=*I know how to swim*)

    in the past:

    I could swim well when I was younger.

    We also express this idea:

    I *was able* to swim well when I was young

    if we wish to emphasize the idea of ability.

2. *Can* also has the meaning of *permission* and *possibility* (=*may*)

    We can go as soon as we like

    in the past:

    We *could* go out whenever we wanted.
    =We *were allowed* to go out whenever we wanted.

Put these sentences into the past, using *was able* when the adverb supplied shows that the meaning is *ability* and *could* when the meaning is *permission*:

1. John can visit his club. (whenever Mary let him)
2. She says I can go. (if my father agreed)
3. Mary can cook well. (when she took the trouble)
4. We can see the neighbour's house. (before the trees grew so big)
5. He can play football. (before he broke his leg)
6. His son can do arithmetic. (when he was only four)
7. He can borrow the money. (provided that he promised to repay)
8. She says they can come. (every Saturday morning)
9. He agrees that they can drive the car. (if they were seventeen)
10. I'm sure they can't understand. (because it was too difficult)
11. We can play in the garden. (mother said)

12. They can't talk to each other. (because her father had forbidden it)
13. They can't talk to each other. (because the telephone was out of order)
14. They can buy a new car. (now that they were rich)
15. My father says we can buy some sweets. (because we have been good)

Exercise No 7. 'Couldn't' and 'Managed to'

Look at these sentences:

> The thieves couldn't get into the house last night.
> The thieves managed to get into the house last night in spite of the locked doors.
> The thieves succeeded in getting into the house last night . . .

We do not use *could* with the meaning of achievement of something in the face of difficulties. *Could* only means *possessed the ability*, but it does not mean *achieved something by means of this ability*.

Put these sentences into the affirmative using the adverb expression supplied, changing *couldn't* into *managed to*.

1. She couldn't read 'Othello' in class last night. (in spite of being a foreigner)
2. They couldn't reach the shore when the boat overturned. (although the water was cold)
3. She couldn't finish her book last night. (although it was very long)
4. I couldn't find the money I had lost. (although it was quite dark)
5. He couldn't teach his classes last week. (in spite of a bad cold)
6. He couldn't escape. (although his guards were vigilant)
7. He couldn't climb to the top of the mountain. (in spite of the snow)
8. He couldn't pay all his bills last week. (although he had very little money)
9. The mechanic couldn't repair our car. (although it was badly damaged)
10. She couldn't play in the concert last night. (although she hurt her hand)

11. We couldn't reach the village that night. (although it was a long way)
12. They couldn't go to sleep. (in spite of the noise)
13. She couldn't go out shopping alone when she arrived. (although she knew no English)
14. The student couldn't pass his examinations last year. (although they were very hard)
15. She couldn't reach the telephone. (in spite of her terrible wound)
16. He couldn't cut the grass that afternoon. (in spite of the thunderstorm)
17. She couldn't sew all his buttons on. (in spite of a broken needle)
18. I couldn't persuade him. (although he is very stubborn)
19. I couldn't put it back on the shelf. (in spite of its enormous weight)
20. He couldn't read her letter. (although her writing is practically illegible)

Exercise No 8

Repeat the first ten sentences of Exercise No 7 using *succeeded in* or *was able* in the place of *managed to*. If you use *was able*, you should notice that there is then no idea of difficulty in the achievement:

> 'He *was able* to mend my car last night' means simply that, having the ability, he did so.
> 'He *managed to* mend my car last night' means that it was very difficult, but that in spite of the difficulties he did so.

It is for this reason that the adverb expressions supplied in the exercise all emphasize the idea of difficulty.

Exercise No 9. 'Can be' + Adjective

In the note to exercise No 6, we said that *can* has the meaning of capacity:

> He can swim. (=*he always has the capacity to swim*)

Now look at this sentence:

> He can (could) be very stubborn.

It is clear that in this case he is (was) not always stubborn, but that having the capacity, he is (was) stubborn only on occasions.

The construction *can be* + adjective has the meaning of capacity which is only shown on some occasions.

Change the following sentences into this construction as in the example, omitting the adverbs in italics:

> *Example:*
>
> A visit to a museum is *sometimes* interesting.
> =A visit to a museum *can be* interesting.

1. Little Willie is *sometimes* very annoying, but generally he is a good boy.
2. This drug is *occasionally* useful in the treatment of pneumonia.
3. John is quite amusing *when he wants to be*.
4. It is *sometimes* quite wet here in the month of August.
5. The advice of one's friends is *often* quite useful.
6. *In certain circumstances* it is very dangerous to touch this animal.
7. Mr. Jones is *sometimes* very angry with his children.
8. My grandmother was *sometimes* very strict with us when we were young.
9. It is *often* quite hot in this room when the sun shines.
10. He told me that Mary was *sometimes* very rude. I never found her so.
11. It is *occasionally* very boring to listen to his lectures.
12. All of us are forgetful *at times*.
13. I warn you, that bull is very nasty *if provoked*.
14. Knowing a foreign language is *frequently* of great value.
15. Smoking too much is *often* bad for the health.

Note: The verbs *get, seem, become*, which are all followed by an adjective in the same way as the verb *be*, are used with the same construction:

> It can get very hot in here.
> These animals can become very dangerous.

SECTION 2 AUXILIARIES AND ANOMALOUS VERBS

Exercise No 10. 'Need' and 'Dare'

In the Simple Present Tense *need* and *dare* have both a regular and anomalous form in the negative and interrogative:

> Does he dare to . . .? = Dare he . . .?
> Do you need to . . .? = Need you . . .?
> He doesn't dare to . . . = He daren't . . .
> We don't need to . . . = We needn't . . .

Tail question forms:

> He doesn't need to . . ., does he?
> = He needn't . . ., need he?
> You don't dare to . . ., do you?
> = You daren't . . ., dare you?
>
> *Example:*
> He *doesn't dare* to touch the wire with his finger.
> = He *daren't* touch the wire with his finger.

Reform these sentences in the same way so that *need* and *dare* are used only in their anomalous forms:

1. They don't need to send the letter after all.
2. We don't dare to light a fire among the trees.
3. Do you really need to be so rude to her?
4. Does he dare to show himself in front of them?
5. They don't dare to take the exam.
6. They don't need to tell him they are coming, do they?
7. Why don't you dare to keep a big dog?
8. I don't need to tell you how sorry I am.
9. How do you dare to say such things?
10. Do I need to bring my raincoat with me?
11. I can well imagine that he doesn't dare to wait for them.
12. John doesn't need to cash the cheque until next week, does he?
13. She doesn't usually dare ask him, does she?
14. We don't need to explain it all again, do we?
15. You don't dare to challenge me, do you?
16. Mary doesn't usually need to get up so early on Sundays.
17. Tell the children that they don't need to do their homework.
18. She doesn't need to finish the work today, does she?
19. You don't really need to drive so fast, do you?
20. I bet you don't dare pull his beard.

Exercise No 11. 'Needn't Have' and 'Didn't Need to'

The absence of necessity in the past can be expressed in two ways:

>   (a) I needn't have told him.
>   (b) I didn't need to tell him.

The meaning of these sentences is:

>   (a) I needn't have told him (*but I did and I realize now that it wasn't really necessary*).
>   (b) I didn't need to tell him (*and I didn't tell him because I realized then that it wasn't necessary*).

We can see that in (a) we use the present tense of *need* because it is now, after doing something, that we find our action to have been unnecessary; we use the past tense of *need* in (b) because we realized before doing it that it was unnecessary.

In the following sentences replace the construction *it was not necessary* by *needn't have* or *didn't need to* according to the sense of the sentence:

>   *Examples:*
>
>   *It was not necessary for them to bring* their bathing costumes, as there was no swimming pool when they arrived.
>   =*They needn't have brought* their bathing costumes ...
>
>   *It was not necessary for her to speak* so loud; her audience was much smaller this time.
>   =*She didn't need* to speak so loud ...

1. It was not necessary for me to put on a coat as it wasn't raining.
2. It was not necessary for us to buy more whisky and we were very angry when we discovered it later.
3. It was not necessary for him to speak to her as he had already explained everything to her.
4. It was not necessary for John to telephone Mary; he could have saved himself the trouble.
5. It was not necessary for them to take the examination again as they had already passed it.
6. It was not necessary for you to go there in person and you wasted the whole morning doing so.
7. It was not necessary for the class to repeat the exercise as they already knew it perfectly.

SECTION 2 AUXILIARIES AND ANOMALOUS VERBS

8. It was not necessary for him to turn on the light as the sun was shining brightly.
9. It was not necessary for me to lend him that money after all as I found out later that he was very rich.
10. It was not necessary for me to wear my glasses as I could see perfectly well without them.
11. It was not necessary for us to visit our aunt as, when we got there, she was out.
12. It was not necessary for them to fetch the letters as the postman had already brought them.
13. It was not necessary for him to sell all his valuable pictures, as he inherited a fortune soon after doing so.
14. It was not necessary for the children to go to bed early, as they had rested all afternoon.
15. It was not necessary for you to bring a coat as I could have lent you one.

Exercise No 12. 'Mustn't' and 'Needn't'

Must expresses either of two things: necessity or obligation.

> Necessity: We must take our umbrellas because it is raining.
> Obligation: We must obey our teacher.

If we wish to express the absence of necessity (i.e. that something is unnecessary) we use *needn't*:

> We needn't take an umbrella because it is fine.

Mustn't, on the other hand, expresses an obligation NOT to do something:

> We mustn't disobey our teacher.

Now answer these questions with short form answers in the negative:

1. Must you go home now?
2. Must you hit a policeman over the head?
3. Must you come to the table with dirty hands?
4. Must a man wear a hat in church?
5. Must a lady wear a hat in the street?
6. Must we speak with our mouths full?
7. Must we park our cars in the middle of the street?
8. Must you have a bath before breakfast?
9. Must you drive on the right in England?

10. Must schoolboys talk to each other in class?
11. Must we eat meat for dinner?
12. Must we go by air if we don't want to?
13. Must a man tell lies?
14. Must you lie in bed all day when there is work to do?
15. Must you go to bed at ten o'clock?
16. Must you smoke in the theatre?
17. Must a student neglect his studies?
18. Must you walk about the house without shoes?
19. Must you ever ask a lady her age?
20. Must you go to the office in a dark suit?

Exercise No 13

Add *mustn't* or *needn't* as appropriate in the blank spaces:

1. You ... finish your food if you don't want to.
2. They ... be late at the office or the manager will get angry.
3. John ... forget Mary's birthday.
4. You ... drive fast along this narrow road.
5. You ... drive slowly: it's quite safe.
6. You ... wear an overcoat today: it's quite warm.
7. The doctor said I ... smoke so much.
8. The doctor said I ... take those drugs any longer.
9. The children ... talk so loud, or they will wake the baby.
10. The children ... do their homework today: there is no school tomorrow.
11. You ... walk in the middle of the road: it's dangerous.
12. I ... tell you how foolish it would be to do that.
13. I ... tell you the answer because I promised not to.
14. He ... eat so much: it makes him fat.
15. You ... hurry: there's plenty of time.

Exercise No 14. 'Must' with the Meaning of Inference or Probability

Look at these sentences:

> He must be at least thirty years old.
> What you say must be true.
> He must be a very rich man by now.

SECTION 2 AUXILIARIES AND ANOMALOUS VERBS

Here *must* does not have the meaning of *obligation*. It means that we infer the truth of something for lack of evidence to the contrary. We cannot use *ought to* or *should* in this sense.

Examples:

Surely John *is* older than Mary.
= John *must be* older than Mary.

I suppose he *was* thirty when I first met him.
= He *must have been* thirty when I first met him.

Change the following sentences in the same way, omitting the words in italics:

1. *I suppose* that mountain is about 3,000 ft. high.
2. You live about ten miles away, *I suppose*.
3. *I should think* these ruins are about three thousand years old.
4. Mr. Smith is a rich man nowadays, *I presume*.
5. *Surely* those children over there are playing football.
6. *I think* you are mistaken.
7. *I suppose* the chickens were stolen by a fox.
8. John was working late at the office, *I suppose*.
9. *I think* you were very careless to make so many mistakes.
10. *Surely* he was very busy if he couldn't come to the party.
11. *I should think* the examination was very difficult if none of the candidates passed.
12. *I think* it is going to rain.
13. *I suppose that* they are all going to the concert, since they all bought tickets.
14. *Surely* that is Mrs. Smith I can see over there.
15. The children have had their dinner, *I suppose*, or they wouldn't be so quiet.
16. *I suppose* I was dreaming when I saw her walk in.
17. The Jones family have gone on holiday, *I suppose*, since their house is all locked up.
18. *I think* you are mad to do that.

Exercise No 15. 'Shall' and 'Will'

The tense in English which is formed with *shall* and *will* as auxiliary verbs is used for the future and is called the Simple Future Tense (or *shall/will* future). But because what happens in the future is generally a result of our intention, wish, determination, promise or willingness, it is natural that these words *shall* and *will* usually have some additional meaning beyond the simple idea of the future.

Here are the most important meanings of *shall* and *will*:

1. (a) *Shall* with 2nd and 3rd persons—promise—

    You shall have a reward if you are good. (=*I promise to give you a reward*)
    They shall go to the cinema when they finish their homework.

    (b) Prohibition in the negative (*shall* has heavy stress)—

    You shall not enter the house. (=*I forbid you to enter the house*)
    The children shall not enter the house with muddy shoes.

    (c) Obligation (*shall* has heavy stress)—

    You shall do as you are told. (=*You must do as you are told*)
    He shall come if I order him to.

2. *Will* with all persons: Intention and Willingness (affirmative); Refusal (negative)—

    I will try again if you wish. (=*I am willing to* . . .)
    You will be there at 3 p.m., I suppose. (=*You intend to be* . . .)
    I won't listen to you unless you talk sense. (=*I refuse to* . . .)
    She won't consider coming unless he comes too. (=*She refuses to* . . .)

Now add *shall* or *will*, whichever is correct, in the following sentences:

1. I wonder whether I ... ever see him again.
2. I promise you ... have whatever you want.
3. Nobody ... touch it without my permission.
4. You ... all have a treat if you are good.
5. None of you ... leave the room till it is tidy.
6. I ... not permit that kind of behaviour.
7. ... you lend me your book? You ... have it back in a minute.
8. I ... agree to your proposals on one condition.
9. You ... not prevent me from saying what I want.
10. I'm sorry, but I ... stop taking English lessons next week.
11. I ... go with you if you are frightened.
12. Their teacher insists that they ... do their homework.
13. In spite of what I told him, he ... continue to do it.
14. I'm afraid you ... not like what I am going to say.
15. I ... be delighted to come to your party.
16. All traitors ... die.
17. You ... go when you have finished your work.
18. ... you do it or ... I?
19. If you ... carry the records, I ... carry the gramophone.

SECTION 2 AUXILIARIES AND ANOMALOUS VERBS   17

20. We have told the management that we ... not tolerate such conditions.
21. All right! You ... have what you want.
22. They ... not have any more until they ask properly.
23. I ... meet you again next week, I expect.
24. I ... meet you again if you wish.
25. I suppose I ... not meet you again for a long time.
26. I ... not meet you again in any circumstances.

Note: In conversation both *I shall* and *I will* are reduced to *I'll*. The original difference of meaning between *I shall* and *I will* is gradually disappearing.

In conditional sentences *I shall*, *You will* and *He will* are the usual forms unless there is a strong desire to express the idea of willingness, intention or obligation.

In many cases *I shall*, *You will*, *He will* have little more meaning than just a future:

> I shall be 56 in January next year.
> It will rain later today.
> He will arrive at 3 p.m.

Exercise No 16. 'Shall' and 'Will' in Certain Interrogative Forms and Tail Questions

1. Interrogative forms:

    (*a*) Polite Requests—

    Will you open the door, please? (=*Are you willing to open the door?*)

    (*b*) Offers of Service—

    Shall I help you? (=*Do you wish me to help you?*)

    (*c*) Suggestions—

    Shall we go to the cinema? (=*Do you wish us to go to the cinema?*)

2. Tail Questions with Imperative Forms:

    (*a*) Shut the window, will you?
    (*b*) Let me carry your bags, shall I?
    (*c*) Let's catch that bus, shall we?

Add *shall* and *will* in the correct places in the following sentences:

1. ... we have dinner?
2. Let me show you how to do it, ... I?
3. ... you, please, stop talking?

4. Just come here a moment, ... you?
5. ... I fetch your books for you?
6. ... we buy a new car?
7. Let's go for a walk, ... we?
8. Put it down on the table, ... you?
9. ... I tell him to come again later?
10. Let's order another drink, ... we?
11. ... you repeat that sentence again, please?
12. Have another slice of cake, ... you?
13. ... I bring in the dinner now?
14. Be so kind as to close the window, ... you?
15. ... we have a party and invite all our friends?
16. Just hand me over that book, ... you?
17. Let me give you a hand, ... I?
18. ... you explain that point to me again, please?
19. Let's go and see if we can find it, ... we?
20. For heaven's sake don't let him touch that, ... you?

Exercise No 17. 'Would' and 'Should'

1. *Would* and *should* are the past tense forms of *will* and *shall* used in indirect speech:

    '*I'll* give you some more.'
    He said *he would* give them some more.

    '*You shall* have another if you wish.'
    He said *they should* have another if they wished.

2. Polite requests (*would* with the 2nd person):

    Would you mind opening the window, please?
    Would you be so kind as to come here a moment?

3. Expressions of Desire and Preference (1st Person *should*, 2nd and 3rd person *would*):

    I should like to leave early.
    Would you rather have tea or coffee?
    He would prefer to have coffee.

4. Obligation or showing an assumption (=*ought to*):

    They should be more careful.
    They should be here by now.
    You shouldn't speak so loud in here.
    I should go now, but I don't want to.

SECTION 2 AUXILIARIES AND ANOMALOUS VERBS

5. Hypothetical Situations in 2nd and 3rd persons (see Exercise No. 18).

Add *should* or *would* in the following sentences:

1. I ... prefer not to give any explanation.
2. ... you do me a favour and take this letter to the post?
3. She told him she ... arrive at ten o'clock.
4. On no account ... you ask for more money.
5. ... you mind passing the salt?
6. Mary asked John what she ... do.
7. I doubt whether it ... be any use telephoning them so late.
8. I promised them they ... have ice-cream for tea.
9. This word is wrong. What ... it be?
10. I suppose we ... ask them first.
11. Do you think they ... like to come again next week?
12. What ... you care to drink?
13. ... you stop talking, please?
14. Dinner ... be ready any minute now.
15. He decided that he ... have to work harder.
16. The management told the staff that they ... work harder.
17. It ... be light enough to see by six o'clock.
18. To whom ... I address this letter?
19. I calculate that the plane ... land in about half an hour.
20. He said that the plane ... land in half an hour.
21. These things ... not be here at all. Take them away.
22. She said that they ... all come to dinner and she ... give them a special treat.
23. I don't know whether I ... tell you this or not.
24. According to the time-table they ... arrive any moment now.
25. You really ... not say such things.
26. Do you think he ... mind helping us for a few minutes?

Exercise No 18. 'Would' in Hypothetical Situations

Look at these sentences:

> I wish you would not speak so loud.
> He wishes she would give him an answer.
> If only they would keep quiet for a moment!
> Don't you wish they would explain things a bit better?

Would is used for hypothetical situations after such phrases as *If only*, *I wish*, *We wish*, *He wishes*, etc., when the situation depends upon an effort of will on the part of another person.

Change these sentences as in the example given:

> *Example:*
> I would like you to do as I tell you.
> =I wish you would do as I tell you.

1. John would like his office staff to work harder.
2. I would like you to answer my question properly.
3. The police would like drivers to obey the traffic lights.
4. The Headmistress would like the girls to do their homework more carefully.
5. He hopes the dogs will stop barking at night.
6. I would like everybody to be more polite.
7. Mary would like John to smoke less.
8. Mrs. Jones hopes her maid will do as she is told.
9. I would prefer you not to complain all the time.
10. The children would like their teacher to be less strict.
11. I hope you will try a little harder next time.
12. The gardener would like the dogs to keep off the flower beds.
13. The people would like the government to do something about it.
14. The doctor would like his patients to follow his instructions exactly.
15. Wouldn't you like the others to walk quicker?

Exercise No 19. The Verb 'Have'

The verb *Have* has three principal uses:

1. As an auxiliary verb in compound tenses—

    I have been here all the time.
    He hasn't been there before.
    Have you ever been there?

2. As an anomalous verb (=*possess*)—

    I have three sisters
    Have you any brothers?
    He hasn't any sisters.

3. As an ordinary verb (=*take, get, receive, experience* and in various fixed expressions)—

    He had breakfast at seven o'clock.
    I didn't have any dinner last night.
    Did you have any breakfast this morning?

SECTION 2   AUXILIARIES AND ANOMALOUS VERBS

When *have* is used as an ordinary verb (3) it forms its negative and interrogative with the auxiliary *do*. In other uses it is like other anomalous verbs.

Change these sentences into the negative:

1. They had dinner late last night.
2. He has some money in the bank.
3. He had a wonderful time at the party.
4. They had a game of tennis yesterday.
5. They have seen something unusual.
6. She had her dress altered.
7. The children had their music lesson after all.
8. We had a cup of tea before we came.
9. You have handed in your homework.
10. I have an idea when they will arrive.

Change these sentences into the interrogative:

11. She has someone living with her.
12. She had a shock when she heard the news.
13. The judge had pity on them.
14. He usually has a lot of difficulty in reading her writing.
15. She had a letter from her boy-friend yesterday.
16. John had his tooth out last Saturday.
17. February has thirty days.
18. He had a good reason for what he did.
19. He has something the matter with his legs.
20. Mrs Smith had a baby in the hospital last week.

Note: In modern American Usage when *Have* has the meaning of *possession* it frequently makes its negative and interrogative with *do*.

'Do you have any money on you?'

Exercise No 20. The Verb 'Have' with Other Verb Stems Used as Nouns

A common construction, especially in spoken English, is the verb *have* with another verb stem used as a noun object.

> Compare: I swam yesterday.
> with   I had a swim yesterday.

The second sentence describes a specific action performed once, while the first sentence is much vaguer and could mean *I swam all the time yesterday* or *I swam on several occasions yesterday.*

Now change these sentences from a general to a specific meaning by the use of the construction with *have*:

1. The children rode on an elephant when they visited the zoo.
2. Please let me look at your photograph album.
3. I want to talk with you after dinner, if you don't mind.
4. Would you like to walk round the garden before tea?
5. We shall probably be swimming at the club this afternoon.
6. I think the children ought to sleep this afternoon.
7. Let's borrow Mr. Jones's boat and sail this morning.
8. I haven't drunk champagne for ages.
9. Those two dogs have been fighting for the last ten minutes.
10. John wanted to smoke all through the lecture.
11. All his brothers played the piano so naturally he wanted to try.
12. Shall we dance?
13. It looks to me as though the children need to wash.
14. I'm glad to say that they haven't quarrelled for weeks.
15. If you have a pain, it would be best to lie down.
16. Mary told the children it was too cold to bathe.
17. Old people generally rest after lunch.
18. Taste (this) and see if you like it.
19. They were so tired they simply had to sit down.
20. If this play is to be a success, we must run through (it) in the afternoon.

Exercise No 21. The Causative Use of 'Have' (and 'Get')

Look at these sentences:

    I shall have the barber cut my hair.
    I shall get the barber to cut my hair.

In these sentences both *have* and *get* are used in a causative sense, but only the construction with *get* is current in modern English, while that with *have* is normal in American English. Both these expressions, however, are very common in their passive form:

    I shall have my hair cut (by a barber).
    I shall get my hair cut.

The agent of the passive form is usually omitted if it is vague (i.e. *someone, them, him*) or if it is understood in the meaning of the verb.

Change the following sentences into the passive form, omitting the agent wherever it does not add to the sense:

Example:

We are going to get *them to redecorate our bedroom.*
=We are going to get *our bedroom redecorated.*

1. I am going to have the cobbler mend my shoes.
2. They are going to get an architect to design their new house.
3. She wanted to have a dressmaker alter her dress.
4. We were thinking of getting the gardener to cut the grass.
5. It is about time I got the watchmaker to clean my watch.
6. You really must get someone to test your eyes.
7. I should like to have someone repaint my car, but I can't afford it.
8. Can't you get someone to do the translation?
9. See that you have someone to clean your shoes before you go out.
10. He decided he would have to get someone cut down the trees in his garden.
11. I'm glad to say the Council are having someone to mend the road.
12. Before we leave, we must get the Foreign Office to renew our passports.
13. Have you ever had someone record your own voice?
14. I hope you'll get someone to tune the piano before I come again.
15. Mary decided to have the doctor vaccinate the children.

SECTION 3

THE PASSIVE VOICE

Exercise No 22. The Passive

The passive is often used in English where an indefinite pronoun (such as *on* in French or *man* in German) or a reflexive construction is used in other languages.

It is used more frequently in written English, where it gives an impersonal effect; this is especially so in scientific writing and objective reporting.

A passive sentence which needs an agent with *by* to complete its sense is usually better expressed in an active form.

Examples:

They have decided to increase taxation this year.
=*It has been decided* to increase taxation this year.

Someone has stolen the jewels from the bedroom.
=*The jewels have been stolen* from the bedroom.

Negligence causes many serious accidents.
=*Many serious accidents are caused* by negligence.

Change these sentences into a passive form as in the examples given. The words in italics will be the subjects of the passive sentences:

1. You cannot expect *children* to understand these problems.
2. They announced *the arrival of the next plane* over the loudspeakers.
3. You must understand clearly that this is the last time I shall allow it. (*It must be . . .*)
4. It is high time that I decarbonized *my car*.
5. No one has climbed *this mountain* before.
6. People have expressed *hopes* that the government will act.
7. He disappeared and no one has seen *him* again.
8. Did you grow *these vegetables* in your own garden?
9. People all over the world heard *the Queen's Christmas Message*.
10. They performed *his symphony* for the first time last week.
11. You should have checked *this exercise* before you handed it in.
12. They have proved *all his calculations* wrong.

13. They have decided to open a new branch next year. (*It has been* . . .)
14. You cannot deny that his handwriting has improved. (*It cannot be* . . .)
15. You must never say that he was ungenerous. (*It must never be* . . .)
16. No one has tuned *this piano* for years.
17. Prepare yourself for the worst. (*Be* . . .)
18. I cannot help *it* if he doesn't come.

Exercise No 23

Here are some common passive sentence openings. Complete them:

1. It is generally agreed that . . .
2. It is hoped that . . .
3. It is only to be expected that . . .
4. It is frequently said of him that he . . .
5. It will be remembered that . . .
6. It has been decided that . . .
7. It has often been questioned whether . . .
8. It was widely assumed that . . .
9. It was taken for granted that . . .
10. It cannot be too strongly emphasized that . . .
11. It has been frequently suggested that . . .
12. Never let it be said that I . . .
13. It has now been proved that . . .
14. I thought that it had been clearly understood that . . .
15. No doubt it will be objected that . . .
16. It must be borne in mind that . . .

Exercise No 24

Here is a list of common verbs:

> Promise, give, send, teach, show, lend, allow, ask, tell, call, recommend, •make, offer, refuse, order, pay, deny, prove, answer, appoint.

These verbs often have two objects in an active sentence:

> He gave me the letter.

There are two possible passive forms:

> The letter was given to me.
> I was given the letter.

The second of these two forms is much more common in English.

Example:

> They showed *me* the palace where the king lived.
> =*I* was shown the palace where the king lived.

Change the following sentences into the passive in the same way. The words in italics will be the subjects of the new sentences:

1. They promised *Mary* a new doll for her birthday.
2. Someone will give *you* new instructions before you leave.
3. Did anyone send *you* the photographs which they promised *you*? (2)
4. No one has ever taught *the pupils* to do that exercise.
5. They showed *her* carefully how to do it.
6. The owner himself showed *them* the house.
7. Someone lent *me* two priceless old volumes.
8. They allowed *him* five minutes to get ready.
9. They asked *her* her name at the reception desk.
10. Someone told *the soldiers* to report to the captain.
11. A friend told *me* the latest news this morning.
12. Has anyone ever called *you* a fool before?
13. Her friend recommended *her* a new doctor.
14. They have made *John* manager of the firm.
15. Did they offer *you* the job I told you about?
16. The consular authorities have refused *Dr. Williams* a visa.
17. They refused *us* entry to the meeting because of our opinions.
18. The doctor has ordered *me* a new diet.
19. They didn't pay *the workers* the wages promised them.
20. They were furious when the authorities denied *them* an opportunity of expressing their opinion.
21. They proved *him* to be no better than a charlatan.
22. Did they give *you* enough sugar?
23. Has anyone ever asked *you* to tell of your experiences in Malaya?
24. They answered *me* most rudely in the shop.
25. They offered *me* a much higher salary at the Bank.
26. They appointed *J. Smith and Co.* as auditors to the firm.

SECTION 3   THE PASSIVE VOICE   27

27. Has any other company ever refused *you* a Life Insurance Policy?
28. No one ever taught *me* the rudiments of music.
29. Look what they have given *me*!
30. They must tell *him* that he is not to come here again.

Exercise No 25

Adverbial particles* and the prepositions which follow certain verbs keep their position after the verb in passive sentences:

> I don't like people *looking at* me.
> =I don't like being *looked at*.
>
> They have *turned down* all our suggestions.
> =All our suggestions have been *turned down*.

Change these sentences into the passive in the same way:

1. Look how well they have brought *those children* up.
2. You should look all *these words* up in a dictionary.
3. Now that someone has pointed out *my mistakes* to me, I hope to do better.
4. We must go into *this matter*.
5. Be careful what you say, as they will take down *all your words*.
6. Another company has just taken over *this business*.
7. Scarcity of raw material has brought about *a rise in prices*.
8. You must write off *all those bad debts*.
9. Poor John! A bus ran *him* down.
10. You cannot take *her* in so easily.
11. What has happened has borne out *all my worst fears*.
12. They put down *the bad radio reception* to the sunspots.
13. Have they let off *all the fireworks* yet?
14. You can't catch *me* out as easily as that.
15. They locked *the house* up before they left.
16. Have you washed *all the dishes* up yet?
17. They shared *the money* out long ago.
18. He wishes to see that they have carried out *his instructions*.

* See Exercise No 130 for explanation of Adverbial Particles.

SECTION 4

RELATIVE CLAUSES

Exercise No 26. Relative Clauses—Defining and Non-defining

Defining Clauses are relative clauses which limit or restrict the noun or pronoun to which they refer to a particular type or example. They answer the questions *which?*, *what?* or *whose?*

People are fools.

This is a general statement in which *people* means *all people*:

People *who do such things* are fools.

In this case the relative clause restricts *people* to a particular group only.

Non-defining clauses simply tell us more about the clauses, nouns and pronouns to which they refer. They are much less frequently used in spoken English, where two separate sentences are more usual:

John, *who returned yesterday*, is coming to see me.

is more often expressed thus in the spoken language:

John returned yesterday; he is coming to see me this evening.

Here are some general observations about relative clauses and pronouns:

1. A non-defining clause must be enclosed within commas, as it is really parenthetical:

    George, *whose mother you met*, is not well.

    A defining clause is not enclosed in this way:

    The boy *whose mother you met* is not well.

2. In a non-defining clause the relative pronoun cannot be omitted:

    Mr. Smith, *who(m) you met yesterday*, is a relation of my wife's.

    In a defining clause the relative pronoun is regularly omitted except when it is the subject of a verb:

    The man *you met yesterday* is my father.

3. In a non-defining clause the preposition governing the relative is rarely placed at the end of the clause:

    This is Mr. Roberts, *about* whom I spoke to you.

    In a defining clause the preposition governing the relative is best placed at the end of the clause and the relative can be omitted:

    This is the man I spoke to you *about*.

SECTION 4 — RELATIVE CLAUSES

4. The pronouns *which, who, whose* and *whom* are found in both defining and non-defining clauses.
   The pronoun *that* is ONLY found in defining clauses.

Read these sentences, omitting the relative clause, and then say which contain defining and which non-defining clauses:

1. The man who(m) I met yesterday lent me some money.
2. John, whose wife is ill, cannot come to the party.
3. That is the one which I always use.
4. Where is the hat that I wore yesterday?
5. Here is a comfortable chair, which you can sit on.
6. Here is the chair which is worth £70.
7. Mary is a good typist, who gets £8 a week.
8. Joan is the typist who(m) the manager himself chose.
9. The horse that I selected won the race.
10. Put it on this table, which is conveniently close.
11. This is the company's annual report, of which I spoke yesterday.
12. The answer is -5, which is impossible.
13. Her husband, who is older than she is, is a bank manager.
14. The eldest son, who is in the army, is twenty-four.
15. The son who works in the office is twenty-two.
16. I want to borrow a book that is not too long.
17. He wants to read a book, which is most unusual for him.
18. Lake Windermere, which is 10 miles long, is the longest lake in England.
19. All that I have is yours.
20. This is the best that I can do for you.

Exercise No 27. The Uses of 'That'

That is ONLY used in defining clauses. It is regularly used to refer to both things and people. It cannot be omitted when it is a subject pronoun:

> I want to speak to the girl *that* wrote this letter.
> The book *that* is lying on the table . . .

It is regularly preferred as an object pronoun to *which* and *who(m)*, if it is expressed at all:

> The man (*that*) I met yesterday . . .
> The book (*that*) I am reading . . .

It cannot be used as the object of a preposition. But if the preposition is placed at the end of the clause its use is normal:

> That is the book *about which* I was speaking.
> This is the book (*that*) I was speaking *about*.

We prefer to use it after certain words and constructions:

Only, much, few, little, none, no, all, some, any (and their compounds) and superlatives.

> *Examples:*
>
> I will lend you *the few that* I still have.
> You may keep *any that* you find.
> Is that *the best that* you can do?

Insert the pronoun *that* where it is possible. In other cases use *which* or *who*(*m*):

1. Are these all the exercises ... you have done?
2. Someone ... you all know is coming to dinner tonight.
3. The first thing ... you must do is to have a meal.
4. This is the dog ... I bought last week.
5. These dogs, ... I bought last week, will do tricks.
6. My mother, ... is over sixty, still likes a good walk.
7. The longest walk ... I ever went was over 20 miles.
8. The last time ... I saw him was on Saturday.
9. The girl ... Mr. Jones is going to marry is over twenty-five.
10. Joan, ... Mr. Smith is going to marry, is twenty-six.
11. The man to ... I am sending this parcel is my partner.
12. The lady ... I am sending this letter to is a friend of my wife's.
13. Is that the picture ... you are laughing at?
14. These are the pictures ... they were laughing at.
15. She is the only girl ... he has ever loved.
16. The river ... runs through London is the Thames.
17. The Thames, ... runs through London, is quite wide at its mouth.
18. There is little ... you can do to help him.
19. What you need is a little sugar, ... you can find in the kitchen.
20. The news bulletin ... I heard a few moments ago said that all hope had been abandoned.

SECTION 4 — RELATIVE CLAUSES

Exercise No 28. The Omission of the Relative Pronoun

In defining clauses the relative pronoun is usually omitted if it is the object or if the preposition which governs it is placed at the end of the clause.

Now place a relative in the spaces only where it is necessary:

1. Is this the cupboard ... you keep the linen in?
2. That is the hotel in ... we stayed last summer.
3. Is that the man to ... you lent the money?
4. Mr. Jones, ... is sitting in that corner, is our managing director.
5. The man ... is wearing the bowler hat is our secretary.
6. This car, for ... I paid a lot of money, is now out-of-date.
7. The car ... you can see over there belongs to John.
8. Give me all the money ... you have.
9. Is this the book ... you want me to read?
10. Where is the man ... did that?
11. Bring me the tools ... I shall need for this job.
12. The few ... I've seen were all too big.
13. No one ... has experienced it will ever forget it.
14. The worst ... can happen is already passed.
15. Only I, ... have seen it with my own eyes, can judge.
16. You, ... have never left England, don't know what good food is.
17. Put them down on any chair ... is unoccupied.
18. The place ... we are going to is not far away.
19. The book for ... I am looking has a red cover.
20. The picture ... you are looking at was painted by a friend of mine.
21. The dish ... you have just eaten contained garlic.
22. The food ... is cooked by my wife tastes much better.
23. Much ... has been said is pure nonsense.
24. Find me the man ... said that I was a fool.
25. The pen ... you are using belongs to my father.
26. Bring me any flowers ... you find on your walk.
27. Do you like any of the music to ... you've listened?
28. The noise ... the children made was intolerable.
29. The sound ... woke me up seemed like a shot.
30. Nothing ... I can see resembles what you have described.

Exercise No 29. Relatives in the Possessive Form

The possessive form of the relative pronoun in defining and non-defining clauses is the same: *whose* for persons, often for the names of countries, towns, rivers, etc., but rarely with things, and *of which* with things:

> Scafell, the summit of which is rarely visible, is the highest mountain in England.
> Mr. Jones, *whose* brother you met, is my neighbour.
> The man *whose* skill I most admire is Mr. Wilson.

Add the possessive form of the relative in the places indicated:

1. Mr. Roberts, ... wife died last year, has gone for a long journey.
2. The hill on the top ... you can see a pile of stones is called Beacon Hill.
3. I haven't met Mr. Edwards, ... painting you so much admire.
4. This is Mr. James, the younger of ... sons was hurt in an accident.
5. Yesterday we met a lady ... children go to the same school as ours.
6. There is a lady over there ... age you could never guess.
7. I have two grammars, the more useful ... I intend to keep.
8. Billy is a child ... impertinence is very irritating.
9. The writer ... works I most admire is Mr. X.
10. The Amazon, ... source lies in the Andes, is the world's longest river.
11. 'I love little Pussy, ... coat is so warm.'
12. That was a crime the author ... was never caught.
13. France, ... army has a great tradition, is to reduce her armaments.
14. Let me introduce you to Mr. Jones, in ... hands I have placed the matter.

Exercise No 30

Combine these sentences into one sentence without the use of a relative pronoun:

> *Example:*
>
> I met a *man* yesterday. This is *the man*.
> =This is the man I met yesterday.

SECTION 4   RELATIVE CLAUSES   33

1. These are the things. I spoke about them just now.
2. Here is a story. I want to tell you a story.
3. Now do you see the point? I was trying to make the point.
4. She fell in love with a man. She had never met him before.
5. Here are the exercises. You must do them.
6. These are some flowers. I have been trying to grow them for years.
7. This is a hill. He tried to climb up it last year.
8. What is the word? You want to look it up.
9. Tobacco is a drug. I can't do without it.
10. What is the name of the book? Joan was looking for it.
11. Is that the dish? You asked the waiter for it.
12. Put it back on the pile. You can see it in front of you.
13. Is this the pen? You have been trying to write with it.
14. This is a sort of nonsense. I won't put up with it.
15. Is this the house? You were born in it.
16. Arabic is a language. I find it difficult to learn.
17. What is the name of the man? You are getting married to him.
18. Where are the papers? You wished to show me them.
19. How old is the man? You were telling me about him.
20. Don't buy any of the vegetables. They sell them in the market.

Exercise No 31. The Relative Adverbs

Relative clauses which tell us *where, when* or *why* a thing happened are introduced by the relative adverbs *where, when* and *why*:

> This is the house *where* I was born.
> This is the time of year *when* the flowers appear.
> He could give no reason *why* his sister had left home.

Complete these sentences:

1. This is the place where . . .
2. Can you remember the time when . . .?
3. This is certainly not the reason why . . .
4. Can you point out to me the exact spot where . . .?
5. It was the time when . . .
6. Thursday is the day when . . .
7. Can't you give me an explanation why . . .?

8. These are the cross-roads where . . .
9. You can just see the point where . . .
10. Don't you understand the reason why . . . ?

Exercise No 32

Put the correct relative adverb into the blank spaces in these sentences:

1. This is the point in the film ... we came in.
2. I am asking you the reason ... you did that.
3. This is the field ... we had a picnic last year.
4. Find the place in the book ... we finished reading last time.
5. I have marked the space ... you must sign.
6. We have not fixed the date ... we shall start our holidays.
7. Give me the reason ... you have not done your homework.
8. They showed me the room ... the murder took place.
9. I can't understand the reason ... they have not come.
10. It is past the time ... the children should be in bed.

Exercise No 33. Non-defining Clauses Referring to a Complete Sentence

Look at this sentence:

> He tried to sing at the concert, and it was a disaster.
> =He tried to sing at the concert, *which was a disaster*.

This sort of non-defining clause, which refers to a whole sentence, is quite common in speaking. When you write it you must be careful not to leave out the comma. If you do, the clause changes to a defining type and will then qualify only the noun which comes before it. This may make the whole sentence nonsense.

Change the following sentences in the way shown in the example:

1. I gave my wife a fur coat for her birthday, and it pleased her a lot.
2. I decided not to travel that day, and it was extremely lucky because the train crashed.
3. He passed all his examinations. This made his parents very proud of him.
4. He tried to explain his extraordinary behaviour and it made everybody laugh.

SECTION 4   RELATIVE CLAUSES   35

5. He refused to speak to her; and this made her very angry.
6. He promised to lend me the money. I was profoundly thankful for this.
7. Joan wouldn't let her children go to the pictures. This didn't surprise me at all considering the film that was on.
8. They have decided to stay at home. This, I think, is the wisest course.
9. She told them they were all fools. They replied to this with angry cries.
10. They didn't pay their rent. You can tell by this that they were not satisfactory lodgers.

Exercise No 34

Look at these sentences:

>Give me an example of *the things* you are going to say.
>=Give me an example of *what* you are going to say.

The relative word *what* stands for the words *the thing(s) which* or *that which*. Clauses beginning with *what* are often a form of relative clause.

Replace the words in italics in the following sentences by the word *what*:

1. I shall sell it for *any sum that* I can get.
2. Think carefully about *the thing that* you are going to do.
3. This money is only part of *the sum that* I gave you.
4. After *the thing that* has happened I shall never speak to you again.
5. We shall never again be surprised by *the things that* he does.
6. According to *the facts that* they have told me, they should return in about three weeks.
7. It all depends on *the thing that* you mean.
8. *The thing* she tried to tell him was this: that she was returning to her parents.
9. He bought the car with *the money that* he had in the bank.
10. They disappeared through *an opening that* looked like a door.
11. He was struck on the head by *something that* he thought must have been a stone.
12. Tell me *the plan that* you propose.
13. *The thing that* I don't understand is how they are going to find all that money.

14. Following on *the things* you have just said, I would like to remark that . . .
15. I do not approve of *the things* she has just done.
16. They were terribly sad at *the things that* had happened.
17. This is all quite irrelevant to *the matter that* we are discussing.
18. I must refer you to *the things that* he said yesterday.
19. He doesn't seem at all sorry for *the things that* he has done.
20. It is better to be quite certain of *the things* you think before you open your mouth.

Exercise No 35

Just as *what* means *the thing(s) that*, so:

Whatever = anything that

    We shall eat *whatever* is left over from lunch.
    = We shall eat *anything that* is left over from lunch.

Whoever = anybody that

    Give it to *whoever* asks for it.
    = Give it to *anybody that* asks for it.

Wherever = in, at any place that

    Put it *wherever* you like.
    = Put it *in any place that* you like.

Whichever = any one of several that

    Choose *whichever* of the colours suits you.
    = Choose *any one* of the colours that suits you.

Replace those parts of the following sentences in italics by one of the words, *whatever*, *whoever*, etc.:

1. Put down that book *in any place that* you can find room for it.
2. *Anyone that* is sufficiently advanced can come to my class.
3. You see these books? You may choose *any one of them that* interests you.
4. Her dogs always follow her *to any place that* she goes.
5. Give it to *anyone that* wants it.
6. In spite of *anything that* you may think, I believe it would be best to keep quiet.
7. She says *anything that* comes into her head.
8. You may use it for *any purpose* you like.

9. *The person that* says that is a liar.
10. *Anyone that* comes to see him is welcome.
11. He wrote that letter for *anyone that* cares to read it.
12. I shall buy *anything that* I need for the journey.
13. They offered to play with *anyone that* was willing.
14. Lend him your tools so that he can use *any of them that* he needs.
15. You must do *the one that* is the easier of those two exercises.
16. I shall buy from *anyone that* wishes to sell.
17. Look at the sentences on page forty. Do *any of them that* is marked with a cross.
18. Buy *the one that* is cheapest.
19. I will find you *in any place that* you may be.
20. The beggar sleeps *in any place that* he can find.

SECTION 5

WORD ORDER

Exercise No 36. The Position and Order of Objects

The indirect object usually comes before the direct object:

> We gave *the children* some sweets.
> They sent *him* the rest of the money.
> Mary promised *her sister* a surprise at Christmas.

This order is frequently reversed when

(a) the indirect object is much longer than the direct:

> He will give the book *to anyone who asks for it.*
> They sent the money *to his one surviving relation.*
> Mary promised a surprise *to the children who lived next door.*

(b) we want to emphasize the indirect object for any reason:

> Give the book *to your brother*, not *to me.*
> Send the money *to Edward, or anyone else you like.*

Each of the following sentences has two indirect objects supplied. Read each sentence twice, putting (a) the first object immediately after the verb and (b) the second after the direct object:

Example:

The shopkeeper sold his last matches.
(a) me
(b) a noisy group of schoolboys

(a) The shopkeeper sold *me* his last matches.
(b) The shopkeeper sold his last matches *to a noisy group of schoolboys.*

1. The guide showed the cathedral.
   (a) us
   (b) a group of tourists
2. She is going to send some flowers.
   (a) her mother
   (b) all the girls she was at school with
3. John promised a reward.
   (a) his eldest son
   (b) whoever could find his slippers

4.	They were selling cigarettes.	(a) her (b) all the people in the village
5.	The host offered drinks.	(a) his guests (b) all the guests in the room
6.	Can you recommend a good hotel?	(a) us (b) this party of travellers from Mexico
7.	I have to pay some money.	(a) the plumber (b) the local taxation officer
8.	I don't want to make a loan	(a) anyone (b) a man who has been bankrupt
9.	Mary lent her sewing-machine.	(a) a neighbour (b) the lady who lived next door
10.	John is teaching Spanish.	(a) his children (b) a large class from the University
11.	He told a story.	(a) them (b) all the children who had finished their work
12.	His aunt left a large fortune.	(a) him (b) all her nieces and nephews
13.	He could not refuse a last request.	(a) the dying man (b) those who had served him so long.

Exercise No 37

Here is a list of verbs which often have two objects, but in these cases the indirect object **must** come after the direct:

Explain, describe, announce, confide, entrust, introduce, suggest, propose, say.

Examples:

I am going to introduce you *to some of my friends.*
They announced the arrival of the train *to the people on the platform.*
Please describe his appearance *to me.*

Put the indirect object supplied in the correct place in these sentences:

1. Did you hear what she said? (her friend)
2. She described her symptoms in great detail. (the family doctor)
3. The teacher is going to explain the difficulties. (his students)
4. They announced who had won the race. (a group of spectators)
5. No one likes to entrust a secret. (a complete stranger)
6. The Chairman proposed a new development plan. (the Board of Directors)
7. Can you suggest a good walk? (these young people)
8. He refused to confide his plans. (even his closest associates)
9. She introduced me. (some of her best friends)
10. Please explain where your house is. (the people who are coming to your party)

Exercise No 38. The Substitute Subject 'It'

Look at these sentences:

To speak English well is difficult.
= It is difficult *to speak English well.*

What you mean is not clear.
= It is not clear *what you mean.*

The *it* in each example is called a substitute subject because it replaces the real subject, which is usually an infinitive construction or a noun clause.

Change the following sentences in the same way as in the examples given above:

1. Whether we should accept the money or not is a serious question.
2. That he should say such things is incredible.
3. Where he went to still remains a mystery.
4. That he will return tomorrow seems very improbable.

5. To make fun of her is easy, but to do so is cruel.
6. What they discussed in the meeting is not known.
7. To try and help them seems quite useless.
8. To buy all you can would seem a very good idea in the circumstances.
9. To lend money to that man is generally considered most unwise.
10. To reach the top of that mountain has been found impossible.

Exercise No 39

Example:

It is very surprising to me *that he has not yet arrived.*
=*That he has not yet arrived* is very surprising to me.

Change the following sentences in the same way as in the example:

1. It is perfectly easy to be wise after the event.
2. It was a great experience to shake him by the hand.
3. It is a very serious matter to accept that responsibility.
4. It is clear that he has been most unwise.
5. It is quite a new thing for me to hear him speak French.
6. It will be quite unnecessary for you to bring your own towels to the pool.
7. It has been a great pleasure for me to meet your sister.
8. It is by no means easy to build a wall so that it does not fall down.
9. It seemed the most natural thing in the world to get married.
10. It proved quite impossible to get them to stay.
11. It appears very likely that they will come.
12. It is most unusual to see swallows in the winter-time in England.

Exercise No 40. Substitute Subject 'It' Used for Emphasis

Look at these sentences:

(a) *John* met the new manager.
  It was *John* who met the new manager.

  John met *the new manager.*
  It was *the new manager* (that) John met.

(b) *Yesterday afternoon* John met the new manager in the street.
It was yesterday afternoon that John met the new manager.

John met the new manager *in the street*.
It was in the street that John met the new manager.

We can give special emphasis to any part of a sentence by putting it at the beginning after the words *It is* (*was*). The rest of the sentence then follows as a clause. If the emphasized word is the subject and a person, then the clause starts with *who*.

Example:

It was John who met the new manager.

If *it* stands for the object, the word *that* may be used or omitted to form a contact clause.

Example:

It was the new manager (that) John met.

In all other cases *that* can be used.

Examples:

It was in the street (that) John met him.
It was yesterday afternoon (that) John met him.

In ordinary conversation *that* is often omitted when it is not the subject of a verb.

Reconstruct these sentences in the same way as in the examples in order to put emphasis on the words in italics:

1. I saw him in the street *only last week*.
2. *The doctors* make all the money.
3. No. I've lost *my book*.
4. We met them *in the park*.
5. I hope to go to the theatre *tonight*.
6. He is angry *because you have lost all his papers*.
7. I want to talk *to your brother*.
8. He was looking *for his gloves*.
9. She bought a new dress *to go to the party*.
10. He got lost *later in the evening*.
11. I first got to know them *five years ago*.
12. He made a fool of himself *on her account*.
13. I discovered my mistake *years later*.
14. She gave him the wrong telephone number *by mistake*.
15. She lost her ring *outside in the garden*.
16. You should try harder *for your own good*.

17. *You* are wrong, not me.
18. We punished him *in order to teach him a lesson*.
19. *A large pile of bricks* fell down just now.
20. They have had all the trouble *since they came back*, not before.

Exercise No 41. Substitute Subject 'It' in Questions

The construction practised in the previous exercise is frequently found in questions.

> It was the postman I met at the gate.
> Who was it you met at the gate?
>
> It was at the bottom of the garden I lost my handkerchief.
> Where was it you lost your handkerchief?
>
> But it was only yesterday I telephoned to her.
> When was it you telephoned to her last?
>
> It is because he is very tired that he has stayed at home.
> Why is it he has stayed at home?

Note: the word *that* is more frequently omitted in the question form.

Form the questions to which the words in italics are the answers; the correct interrogative words are given:

1. It was *only last week* that I met her for the first time. (when)
2. It is *three years* since we met. (how long)
3. It's *his dictionary* he's looking for. (what)
4. It was *because he was ill* that he couldn't come. (why)
5. It was *his hat* that he had lost. (what)
6. It is *your answer* that I'm waiting for. (what)
7. It was *your wife* who telephoned. (who)
8. It was *on this very spot* that she died. (where)
9. It is *because he is so young* that he cannot understand. (why)
10. It was *my fault* that the vase got broken. (whose fault)
11. It was *three years* ago he passed his final examinations. (how long)
12. It was *half an hour ago* I saw them last. (when)
13. It is *the meaning of the word* I don't understand. (what)
14. It was *in the Institute* I studied Spanish. (where)
15. It was *the one on the right* that fell and got broken. (which)

Exercise No 42. Inversion of Subject and Verb After Certain Adverbs

Here is a list of adverbs; their meaning is either restrictive or negative:

> Scarcely, hardly, seldom, rarely, little, even less, nor, neither, by no means, nowhere, at no time, never,

and a number of restrictive adverbs made with *only*, such as:

> Only by chance, only then, only today, only yesterday, only with difficulty, only on rare occasions, only by luck.

If any of these adverbs is put at the beginning of a sentence the subject must follow the verb as in a question:

> *Hardly had he finished* when somebody knocked at the door.
> *Seldom have I heard* such a beautiful voice.

If the tense used is Simple Past or Present, we must use the auxiliary verb *do*, just as in a question:

> *Nowhere did he make* a greater impression than in Paris.
> *Little does he realize* how foolish he looks.

Although these adverbs are often used at the beginning of sentences, we can also put them in positions where they do not affect the order of the verb and its subject. (See Exercise No. 43.)

> He had *hardly* finished, when ...
> He *little* realizes how ...

Reconstruct these sentences so that the adverb in italics comes at the beginning of the sentence:

> *Examples:*
>
> I have *never* heard such nonsense.
> =*Never* have I heard such nonsense.
>
> We *seldom* go out in the evening these days.
> =*Seldom* do we go out in the evenings these days.

1. He had *hardly* finished his dinner when the servant came rushing in.
2. You know *little* of what goes on behind the scenes.
3. You know *even less* of what the ministers are thinking.
4. He *not only* showed her how to do it but offered to help her as well.
5. I have *never in all my life* seen such a sight as this.
6. There has *rarely* been such a gathering of celebrities in our house.

7. You could *nowhere* find a better adviser.
8. I heard *only by chance* that his mother had died.
9. We have *seldom* been treated in such a rude way.
10. It has *at no time* been easier to enter a University than nowadays.
11. I *only* learnt the dreadful news *today*.
12. He became confused *to such a degree* that he didn't know where he was.
13. He received a letter a few days ago and did *not* learn *till then* that he had won a lottery.
14. The situation has deteriorated *to such an extent* that something must be done.
15. He did*n't* make *a sound*. (Not a sound . . .)
16. They did*n't* speak *a word*. (Not a word . . .)
17. *And* I could *not* make him see the importance of it. (Nor . . .)
18. *And* she would *not* do as I asked her. (Nor . . .)

Exercise No 43. The Position and Order of Adverbs

1. Most adverbs (and by these we also mean adverbial expressions of more than one word) follow the verb and the object if there is one. You must not put an adverb between the verb and its object.

    I like coffee *very much*.
    She sang the song *beautifully*.

2. If we wish to emphasize how an action is performed, the adverb of manner, **if it is only one word**, is often put between the subject and the verb.

    He *quickly* shut the door when the teacher came in.
    She *slowly* spelled out her name to the shopkeeper.

In these sentences put the adverb of manner before the verb and all the other adverbs at the end of the sentence:

1. She enjoys dancing. (very much)
2. He turned to face his accusers. (slowly)
3. I believe you did that. (deliberately)
4. They seemed to be climbing the mountain. (at a snail's pace)
5. They went out to get some fresh air. (gladly, in the park)
6. They tried to save what was left. (desperately)
7. I believe they will come. (firmly, home)
8. Then stir in the sugar. (gently)
9. He wrote an account of his life. (at sixty)

10. They were dancing together. (all last night)
11. Write these sentences. (in ink)
12. He put the money away. (carefully, in his purse)
13. I heard a cry. (distinctly, outside)
14. They left their books. (thoughtlessly, at home)
15. I remember having heard something like that. (vaguely)
16. We dislike that food. (strongly)
17. The car entered the main road. (at ten miles an hour)
18. I will lend you my pen if you wish. (gladly)
19. You can't want so much to drink. (possibly)
20. You should consider it before you accept. (carefully)
21. He raised the lid. (cautiously, with one hand)
22. You must make up your mind. (definitely, tonight)

Note: Adverbs ending in *-ly* are nearly all adverbs of manner.

Exercise No 44. Pre-verb Adverbs

Here is a list of the most common adverbs which are generally put before the verb:

        Still, just, already, yet.

Adverbs of frequency:

        Seldom, always, often, rarely, sometimes, generally, frequently, usually, never, occasionally.

Restrictive adverbs:

        Partly, largely, in no way, wholly, scarcely, hardly, by no means, only, little.

The correct position for these adverbs is shown in this table:

with different tenses	He He has He will He would	often never rarely sometimes	goes to the cinema gone to the cinema go to the cinema go to the cinema
with anomalous verbs	He can He must	usually hardly scarcely	go to the cinema
in short answers	He He	only always	has can
with the verb *to be*	He is He has		ill been ill

SECTION 5 — WORD ORDER

Put the adverbs supplied into the correct place before the verb in these sentences:

1. We are working on our theses. (still)
2. They have not finished doing their homework. (yet)
3. I have told you a thousand times not to do it. (already)
4. We had come in when the telephone rang. (only just)
5. Her mother approved her choice of husband. (wholly)
6. I shall believe what they say. (never)
7. You will have heard of Mr. Johnson, I suppose. (scarcely)
8. It cannot be explained by his illness. (entirely)
9. They were responsible for the accident. (largely)
10. Have you seen an octopus? (ever) I have. (never)
11. You can excuse yourself for that reason. (hardly)
12. I try to do as much work in the evening as possible. (generally)
13. He comes to see me on Saturdays. (sometimes)
14. He understands the problems we have. (little)
15. He would have been an invalid, had he lived. (always)
16. It is certain that they will succeed. (by no means)
17. I have seen a better one. (rarely)
18. He is to blame for the disaster. (partially)
19. I can understand his suffering. (to some extent)
20. She stays in bed all morning. (frequently)

Exercise No 45

If there are several adverbs in a sentence the usual order in which they follow the verb is:

Manner (*how?*)—place (*where?*)—time (*when?*).

> They have been studying hard at home all day.
> They played football enthusiastically in the rain yesterday.

But there are some variations in this order:

(*a*) If there is a verb of movement, we often put the adverb of place straight after the verb in order to complete its sense:

> They walked *to the theatre* in a hurry last night.
> We flew *to Rome* by B.O.A.C. last summer.

(*b*) We often put adverbs of time right at the beginning of the sentence, particularly if it is a long sentence with other adverbs in it:

> *Yesterday* he unexpectedly flew to Berlin by the afternoon plane.
> *At three in the morning* I heard a loud knock on the front door.

Place the adverbs supplied in the correct place in the sentence:

1. I have been working. (all day, in this room)
2. He was born. (in 1943, in Paris)
3. Take this. (immediately, to your mother)
4. Look! (at this sentence, carefully)
5. Come! (immediately, here)
6. He has loved her. (all his life, fanatically)
7. They were caught. (yesterday, in the rain)
8. You must read your books. (in the library, quietly)
9. They returned. (with their friends, at eleven o'clock, to their hotel)
10. He has been sitting. (for ten minutes, quite quietly, on that chair)
11. They came up. (to the fire, a few minutes later)
12. The goalkeeper remained. (all through the game, lazily, in the goalmouth)
13. He went to fetch his coat. (upstairs, a few minutes ago)
14. The plane arrived. (early, at the airport)
15. I shall meet you. (this evening, at the party)
16. They are going. (for the week-end, to their parents)
17. I said goodbye to them. (regretfully, yesterday, at the station)
18. Let's invite them. (to the theatre, tonight)
19. I have been living. (in Rome, quietly, since 1924)
20. She spoke to him. (quietly, in the hall, after dinner)

Exercise No 46

If there is more than one of the same type of adverb in a sentence then:

(*a*) we usually put the more exact before the more general—

>He was born at 3.42 in the morning on June 24th, 1943.

(*b*) if there are two adverbs of manner, we put the shorter first and often join it to the longer with *and*—

>Press the knob gently with your finger.
>Press it firmly and continuously.

Arrange the adverbs supplied in their correct order after the verb:

1. I shall meet you. (outside the town hall, on the steps)
2. He spoke to the class. (clearly, with deliberation)

3. Take the third door. (upstairs, on the left, in the passage)
4. Hand it to me. (carefully, with your right hand)
5. Put it. (in the dining-room, on the table)
6. She arrived. (this morning, at six o'clock)
7. We should fly. (over Paris, very high)
8. Speak. (with a loud voice, clearly)
9. They are leaving for Italy. (next week, on Thursday, in the afternoon)
10. You must finish your homework. (before midday, tomorrow)

Exercise No. 47

In a passive sentence adverbs of manner are usually put immediately before the past participle:

> That house has been *badly* damaged.

Put the adverbs supplied in their correct position:

1. It was stuck to the page. (firmly)
2. The concert was received. (well)
3. It has been thrown away. (carelessly)
4. She has been restored to health. (completely)
5. He is respected by his colleagues. (highly)
6. The roof has been damaged. (seriously)
7. It has been neglected. (sadly)
8. It must be understood. (clearly)
9. This work must be prepared. (better)
10. The food was served. (beautifully)

Exercise No 48. Position and Order of Adjectives

1. Adjectives usually go before the word they describe:

    A red flag, a clever boy, a new idea.

2. If there are two or more adjectives describing a word, we put the one with the most *general* or *subjective* meaning first and the most specific and objective last:

    A *nice* new carpet, a *fine* old house, a *pretty* yellow flower.

3. If the adjectives are both equally exact, we put the *shorter* first:

    a *quiet* intelligent boy, a *long* interesting book.

4. Two adjectives are often joined by *and* for greater emphasis:

    a dark and stormy night, a new and useful idea.

5. Certain types of adjectives usually come immediately before the word they describe:

>(a) colours: a big *red* book, stylish *black* trousers.
>(b) styles: a tall *gothic* building, a beautiful *renaissance* church.
>(c) nationality: a clever *French* girl, an old *Turkish* carpet.
>(d) nouns used adjectively: a *paper* bag, a *cotton* shirt.

6. Be careful with the adjectives: *old, new, young, sick, poor, rich*.

>a *sick* young boy (=a young boy *who happens to be sick*).
>a *young* sick boy (=a sick boy *who is also young*).

Arrange the adjectives supplied in the correct order before these nouns:

1. a household (well-ordered, quiet)
2. a cup of tea (China, hot, delicious)
3. a girl (poor, defenceless)
4. a farmhouse (Tudor, old, fine)
5. an armchair (luxurious, deep)
6. a lecture (long, technical, boring)
7. clothes (old, useless)
8. a child (weak, pale, sick)
9. a boy (intelligent, active, happy)
10. The news (depressing, recent)
11. a town (industrial, dirty, nasty)
12. pupils (lazy, disobedient, rude)
13. food (indigestible, rich)
14. a servant (elderly, slow, incompetent)
15. water (clear, deep, motionless)
16. a figurine (Japanese, porcelain, delicate, pink)
17. story (incredible, fantastic, ghost)
18. a garden (French, formal, beautiful)
19. a table (fine, oak, old, carved)
20. a hat (broad-brimmed, attractive, Mexican)

Exercise No 49

1. If an adjective, or a participle used as an adjective, is itself qualified by a phrase we must put it after the noun it describes:

>The students, *tired of studying*, went out to play.
>His car, *damaged in an accident*, was no use any more.
>The students *studying Spanish* may come to this lecture.

2. In written English we often put two adjectives joined by *and* after the noun they describe:

> The players, *tired and muddy*, returned from the match.
> The mountains, *tall and majestic*, rose up above the valley.

Put the adjectives supplied in the correct place after the words they describe:

1. The little boy went down the street. (dressed in blue)
2. A bedroom was placed at their disposal. (furnished in the latest style)
3. He received a letter. (written in green ink)
4. He possessed a faith. (deep and unwavering)
5. He inherited a mansion. (ruined past repair)
6. The crowd began to disperse. (drunk and disorderly)
7. A garden lay before them. (filled with flowers)
8. A knife was found among the ruins. (old and rust-covered)
9. The sail was lowered. (torn to shreds by the storm)
10. The house was for sale. (empty and deserted)
11. The cupboard is yours. (standing against that wall)
12. The lecture had ended at last. (long and uninteresting)
13. The workers decided to strike. (dissatisfied with their pay)
14. The breeze revived them. (fresh from the recent rain)
15. Tobacco keeps fresh longer. (sealed in an airtight tin)

Exercise No 50. The Position of 'Both' and 'All'

Both and *all* have two alternative positions in a sentence. Look at these examples:

with compound tenses—

> *Both* my brothers have passed their exams.
> My brothers have *both* passed their exams.

with simple tenses—

> *All* the family enjoyed the picnic.
> The family *all* enjoyed the picnic.

with the verb *to be*—

> *All* my flowers are dead.
> My flowers are *all* dead.

Repeat these sentences putting *both* and *all* into their alternative positions as in the examples given:

1. All his numerous relations were present at the funeral.
2. Both the girls we met last night danced like elephants.

3. All the exercises you have done so far are too easy.
4. All the lights in the town were out.
5. All the beer we bought has been drunk.
6. I suppose all the people you invited will come to the party.
7. Both the letters I got today were sent to my old address.
8. Please tell me when all the children have been inspected.
9. All the lights in the town went out suddenly.
10. All the lights in the town have gone out.

Exercise No 51   The Order of Words in Indirect Questions

Look at these examples:

> '*What are you* doing?'
> He wants to know *what you are doing*.

The Indirect Question is grammatically not a question at all; it does not have an inversion of the verb and subject like the Direct Question. Because there is no inversion we do not need to use the auxiliary verb *do*, which is necessary in a direct question.

> '*When does he* go to bed?'
> I want to know *when he goes* to bed.

Here are a number of direct questions. Make them indirect by using the introductory phrases given:

> *Example:*
>
> (Can you tell me) 'Where did they go?'
> Can you tell me where they went?

1. (I should like to know) 'Where are you going?'
2. (She wonders) 'How often do they visit their friends?'
3. (Tell me) 'What do you mean?'
4. (Have you told her yet) 'How much do you love her?'
5. (Please explain to me) 'How do you perform this operation?'
6. (She wants to ask him whether) 'Can he help her?'
7. (They haven't told me) 'When do they intend to leave?'
8. (He refuses to say whether) 'Will he undertake the job?'
9. (I have no idea) 'Which do you prefer?'
10. (He doesn't know) 'Why did she never come?'
11. (Can you tell me whether) 'Is she married?'
12. (They have just asked me) 'What time does the concert begin?'
13. (Tell me) 'Why have you disobeyed my orders?'

SECTION 6

INFINITIVES AND GERUNDS

English has two verbal nouns, the infinitive and the gerund, where other European languages have one. Students often find it difficult to know when they must use one or the other.

In the constructions practised in this section the *-ing* form of the verb is sometimes a gerund and sometimes a participle. Students do not need to distinguish between them while they are doing these exercises.

Exercise No 52. Infinitives and Gerunds as Subjects of a Verb

Both infinitives and gerunds are used as the subjects of verbs:

> Smoking is forbidden.
> To smoke is forbidden.

In the following sentences change the infinitive into a gerund:

> *Example:*
>
> *To drink* whisky spoils the appetite.
> =*Drinking* whisky spoils the appetite.

1. To blush is a sign of modesty.
2. To read is a good habit.
3. To write with the left hand is more difficult.
4. To climb mountains is good exercise.
5. To eat too much makes one fat.
6. To raise your hat to a lady is good manners.
7. To mend cars is the work of a mechanic.
8. To fly by night is considered perfectly safe nowadays.
9. To spill the salt at table brings bad luck.
10. To drink a lot of water when you are hot is said to be unwise.

Exercise No 53. Infinitives and Gerunds as Objects of a Verb

This is a list of verbs which can have either an infinitive or a gerund as an object:

attempt	bear	begin
continue	dislike	fear
hate	like	intend
love	prefer	omit
propose	start	learn

I cannot bear to eat that stuff.
I cannot bear eating that stuff.

They began to talk.
They began talking.

In the following sentences change the infinitive into the gerund:

Example:

John likes *to go* to the cinema once a week.
=John likes *going* to the cinema once a week.

1. I cannot bear to listen to that awful noise on the radio.
2. Please begin to read, Mr. Jones.
3. He could not continue to speak because of his cough.
4. Do you really dislike to go out in the evening?
5. Of course children always hate to go to bed.
6. He told me he intended to live here till the end of his life.
7. She's the sort of person who likes to cause trouble.
8. I'm sorry that I omitted to tell you the most important news.
9. Which do you prefer to read: novels or biographies?
10. I propose to leave immediately.
11. When are you going to start to take lessons again?
12. Most women fear to lose their good looks.
13. Nobody really loves to work.

Exercise No 54

The infinitive and the gerund are also used as objects of these verbs:

| forget | remember | learn |
| need | regret | try |

but in these cases the infinitive and gerund constructions mean something different.

1. With *remember*, *forget* and *regret* the infinitive refers to an action which takes place after the remembering, forgetting, or regretting:

   Remember to wash your hands.
   I forgot to wash my hands before dinner.
   I regret to inform you that it is impossible.

The gerund refers to an action which took place before the act of remembering, forgetting, or regretting:

   Do you remember washing your hands before dinner?
   I shall never forget washing my hands in that dirty water.
   I bitterly regret having told her that.

SECTION 6 INFINITIVES AND GERUNDS

2. With the verbs *want* and *need* the gerund has a passive meaning:

> My pen needs filling. (=My pen needs *to be filled*)
> My shoes want cleaning. (=My shoes need *to be cleaned*)

3. With the infinitive construction *try* means *to make an attempt*. With the gerund it means *to make an experiment or trial*:

> You must try to understand what I say. (=*attempt*)
> Try adding water to your drink. (=*experiment*)

4. With *learn* the infinitive suggests a certain degree of success, while *learn* with the gerund means no more than *study*:

> She has learnt to cook. (=*now she knows how to cook*)
> She has been learning cooking. (=*she has been studying the subject, but doesn't know how to cook yet*)

Now supply a gerund or an infinitive in the place of the verb in brackets according to the meaning of the sentence:

> *Examples:*
>
> I want (go out) this evening.
> =I want to go out this evening.
>
> She doesn't remember (see) him in the street yesterday.
> =She doesn't remember seeing him in the street yesterday

1. Do you remember (meet) her at my house last year?
2. Please remember (wipe) your feet before coming in.
3. I completely forgot (lock) the front door last night.
4. Don't forget (bring) your bathing suit with you.
5. That was a memorable occasion. I shall never forget (meet) the Prime Minister at your house.
6. These stockings need (mend).
7. Do you really need (buy) all that stuff?
8. We regret (inform) you that your subscription is overdue.
9. I greatly regret (have lent) her my best pen.
10. Do you remember (meet) John in my office last year?
11. She has already forgotten (lend) him the money, since she has offered him some more.
12. Does your car need (wash)? I certainly need (wash) mine.
13. I'm afraid you will regret (have lent) her the money.
14. What's he doing? He's just trying (open) the tin.
15. Just try (be) a little more co-operative.

16. I have been learning (skate) for three years and I still fall down all the time.
17. Although he is only five, he learnt (write) very quickly.
18. The results are very disappointing, I regret (say)
19. You should try (use) petrol, if you can't get it off with water.
20. Try (taste) it before you offer it to your guests.

Exercise No 55. Gerunds After Prepositions

Only gerunds are found after prepositions:

>He is very clever *at breeding dogs*.
>Madame Y was famous *for* always *coming* late.
>Please leave the room *without banging* the door.
>I don't think he is capable *of doing* it correctly.

Complete the following sentences with a gerund after the preposition:

1. They will certainly be angry at our ...
2. Would you be surprised at his ...?
3. They were delighted at ...
4. I do not believe in ...
5. Have you congratulated him on ...?
6. That will depend on your ...
7. You must not insist on his ...
8. You ought to be ashamed of ...
9. She was shy of ...
10. Are you as fond as we are of ...?
11. I'm tired of ...
12. She never goes to a party without ...
13. Try and eat without ...
14. You must apologize for ...
15. Is that the man who was responsible for ...?
16. You'll never learn anything by ...
17. He made his fortune by ...
18. We are going to start the class by ...
19. She caught a nasty cold through ...
20. You can easily open it by ...
21. He was not content with just ...
22. I never have an opportunity of ...
23. She failed all her exams through ...
24. You cannot count on his ...
25. I shall never consent to his ...

SECTION 6 INFINITIVES AND GERUNDS

Exercise No 56. Gerunds After Prepositions

Look at these sentences:

> Before entering the room, he was surprised to hear voices inside.
> After putting the book aside, he fell asleep.
> I met George while walking to the office.
> On my pressing the button there was a loud explosion.

Adverbial phrases of time introduced by one of the prepositions *after*, *before*, *on* or *while* are quite common in written and spoken English.

Put the appropriate preposition before the gerund in these sentences:

1. Never turn on the current, ... making sure that the fuse is in place
2. He was taken to hospital ... being knocked down.
3. She was violently sick ... eating mushrooms.
4. The idea came to me suddenly ... lying awake last night.
5. You should consult his secretary ... disturbing him.
6. The whole room lit up ... his turning on the switch.
7. They all ran in his direction ... hearing the shots.
8. ... considering the evidence carefully, the jury found him guilty.
9. Think what you want to say ... putting pen to paper.
10. You have to get permission ... taking the day off.
11. She burst into tears ... hearing the news.
12. They had a nasty accident ... returning home last night.
13. He suddenly felt faint ... having breakfast and had to leave the table.
14. They all went home ... hearing his speech.
15. He found his spectacles ... looking for something different.

Exercise No 57

Expand this material into complete sentences:

> *Example:*
>
> play at being
> =The children *played at being* robbers all afternoon.

take this opportunity of saying
concentrate seriously on making
insure against our losing

escape from having to
prevent her from calling
accustom the children to being
interested in studying
accused of taking
not approve of Mary's spending
suspect him of taking
live quietly without going
tire quickly of studying
congratulate him heartily on having
pride herself on dressing
discourage them from trying
refrain from asking
unfortunately reduced to eating
not believe in having
beware of using
never think of speaking
make a cake without using
become rich by working

Exercise No 58. Do + a Lot of + Gerund

Look at these sentences:

Mary did a lot of riding when she was young.
I still do a little singing.
He will be doing a lot of travelling next year.

This is a common construction in English when we want to **emphasize the frequency** with which we perform a habitual action.

Change these sentences in the way shown in the example:

Example:

The children *have swum a lot* recently.
=The children *have done a lot of swimming* recently.

1. They drank too much last night.
2. John never gardens much nowadays.
3. They tell me the Jones sisters dance a lot.
4. I practise too little to be any good at tennis.
5. In my job I have to write a lot.
6. Will you walk much during your holidays?
7. When I get to Rome I want to see a lot of sights.

8. We used to run a lot when we were at school.
9. A hundred years ago young ladies were all taught to sing and paint a little.
10. My secretary talks too much.
11. I need to travel a lot in my work.
12. The famous Mrs. Smith-Williams entertains a lot at the Ritz.
13. Do you fish much?
14. Since I sold my wireless I haven't listened in much.
15. The doctor told him he smoked too much.
16. I asked him if he had flown much lately.

Exercise No 59. The Infinitive as Object

Certain verbs only have the infinitive as an object:

afford	fail	pretend
appear	determine	promise
arrange	happen	prove
be bound	hope	refuse
care	hurry	seem
chance	manage	trouble
come	mean	undertake
dare	offer	wish
decide		

He happened to arrive later than we expected.
I think you should arrange to stay there.
She offered to mend his socks.
Don't trouble to ring when you come in.

The following verbs, besides taking an infinitive alone as an object, also take the object and infinitive construction.

ask	intend	love
like	mean	expect
choose	hate	wish
want	beg	

Examples:

I asked to leave. (=*if I might leave*)
I asked *him* to leave. (=*told him to go away*)

My mother liked to sing herself.
My mother liked *my father* to sing.

They all begged to see the photographs.
They all begged *me* to see the photographs.

Make these sentences into an object and infinitive construction by putting the object supplied into the correct position before the infinitive as in the example:

Example:

You surely don't intend to eat all that. (me)
=You surely don't intend *me* to eat all that.

1. She asked to have some tea. (her guests)
2. They are begging to go with the party. (Mary)
3. I didn't choose to help the others. (you)
4. Do you wish to come with me? (your dog)
5. Would you like to learn singing? (your daughter)
6. They hate to do as I ask. (the others)
7. Did you want to eat all those cakes? (the children)
8. They prefer not to go today. (us)
9. I never meant to arrive so soon. (the guests)
10. Did you really expect to become rich? (that man)
11. I don't like to go out so often in the evening. (my wife)
12. Does she really want to do all that work? (her servant)
13. I like to wear nice new clothes. (my secretary)
14. Did you mean to finish the work today? (us)
15. We never intended to spend so much money. (the firm)

Exercise No 60

The following verbs have an object and infinitive construction. They are never used with an infinitive alone.

allow	instruct	press
advise	invite	request
cause	oblige	teach
compel	order	tell
encourage	permit	tempt
force	persuade	warn

They ordered him to leave the room.
We invited them to spend the day with us.
You cannot force him to tell you anything.

Complete these sentences:

1. The government instructed all banks to . . .
2. I strongly advise you to . . .
3. The admiral ordered all the ships to . . .

SECTION 6   INFINITIVES AND GERUNDS

4. The town clerk invited a number of firms to ...
5. You cannot oblige me to ...
6. It is very unwise to force children to ...
7. We should encourage our children to ...
8. Police warned all motorists not to ...
9. I cannot permit you to ...
10. The management requests all guests to ...
11. Would you mind helping me to ...
12. Please tell the others to ...
13. If you pour acid on it, it will cause it to ...
14. She compelled her husband to ...
15. Try and persuade John to ...

Exercise No 61

The verbs listed in the previous exercise are frequently used in the passive with a *to*-infinite:

> Students must be encouraged to read more.
> I have been persuaded to take the family out for the day.
> Passengers are requested to show their passports to the office.
> You are not allowed to bring animals into class.

Change these sentences into the passive construction as in the examples:

Examples:

You must not allow *the children* to eat too much.
=*The children* must not be allowed to eat too much.

They cannot force *him* to if he doesn't want to.
=*He* cannot be forced to if he doesn't want to.

1. We must not allow *the weather* to interfere with our plans.
2. They tempted *me* to try a new drink.
3. They warned *us* not to cross the river by night.
4. Under the new regulations they obliged *everybody* to register at the police station.
5. They do not permit *visitors* to touch the exhibits.
6. You should certainly tell *them* to bring their books next time.
7. They taught *us* all to play football at school.
8. They requested *all the spectators* to leave the stadium.
9. We cannot persuade *him* to leave his dog behind.
10. They invited *us* all to come to their party.

Exercise No 62

Here is a list of verbs which use the object and infinitive construction. In these cases the only infinitives they can have are *to be* and *to have*:

acknowledge	find	believe
guess	calculate	know
consider	maintain	declare
reckon	estimate	take (=*presume*)
see	understand	

Example:

We believe *him to be* the cleverest of them all.
I consider *him to have* the best collection in the country.

In this form the sentences are rather literary and formal. We more often express them in this way in speaking:

We believe *that he is* the cleverest of them all.
I consider *that he has* the best collection in the country.

Change the object and infinitive construction in these sentences into a clause construction as in the example:

Example:

I know *him to be* a man of sense.
=I know *that he is* a man of sense.

1. I guess it to be about 6.20.
2. We estimate it to weigh about thirty tons.
3. Do you suppose this exercise to be too easy for them?
4. Do you believe it to be possible to find a solution?
5. We understand him to be a man of about sixty-five.
6. I've used it and found it to have no value for my purpose.
7. Now that you've explained it I see it to be quite impossible.
8. The engineers think this invention to have great possibilities.
9. The experts consider there to be no danger from this experiment.
10. The doctors declared the patient to be out of danger.

SECTION 6 — INFINITIVES AND GERUNDS

Exercise No 63

The verbs practised in the previous exercise are also frequently used in the passive with a *to*-infinitive:

> *Examples:*
>
> We know *him* to be a man of honour.
> =*He* is known to be a man of honour.
>
> They considered *him* to have more ability than the others.
> =*He* was considered to have more ability than the others.

Change these sentences into the passive form as in the examples given:

1. We know *Mt. Everest* to be the highest mountain in the world.
2. They estimated *the gold mine* to have large reserves.
3. They believed *that book* to be three hundred years old.
4. I understand *Dr. Robinson* to be a very capable surgeon.
5. They found *it* too expensive to buy new machinery for the factory.
6. They have calculated *the sun* to be 93 million miles away.
7. They generally consider *it* to be unwise to go out in the rain without a hat.
8. They declared *the prisoner* to be innocent.
9. People acknowledged *the government policy* to be unwise.
10. They reckoned *George* to be the most capable mathematician among them.

Exercise No 64. The Gerund ('-ing' Form) as Object

The following verbs have a gerund construction. They are never followed by an infinitive:

confess	not help	drop
imagine	excuse	fancy
finish	not mind	prevent
practise	forgive	stop
hinder	pardon	
not bear	not stand	

There are two possible constructions with these verbs:

1. Gerund alone—

   Fancy wearing clothes like those!
   Stop talking!

2. Possessive and gerund—

> I cannot imagine his passing his examinations.
> I could not help his overhearing.

3. Objective case and participle (fused participle construction)—

> We shall never prevent them interrupting.
> Please excuse me coming late.

Generally speaking, people are beginning to prefer the fused-participle construction to the possessive and gerund in spoken English.

> 'You cannot prevent *him* coming.' is more common nowadays than
> 'You cannot prevent *his* coming.'

These constructions are also used after prepositions and other verbs which can take a gerund (see Exercises Nos 53, 55).

Change these sentences from the simple gerund construction to the (*a*) fused participle and (*b*) possessive and gerund construction as in the example by using the words supplied:

Example:

> I remember coming home last night. (you, your)
> =(*a*) I remember *you* coming home last night.
> (*b*) I remember *your* coming home last night.

1. Have you forgotten making that mistake? (me, my)
2. We all love singing that song. (John, Mary's)
3. I'm sorry. I just hate playing that piece. (you, your)
4. We do not permit talking in the library. (people, your)
5. I won't have drinking in my house. (you, his)
6. I prefer travelling by train. It's safer. (my daughter, your)
7. We can't help making a noise. (the dog, his)
8. It's useless trying to go to sleep now. (him, Mary's)
9. Can you understand wanting to climb Everest? (anyone, John's)
10. Can you imagine joining the army? (that boy, Robert's)
11. I wouldn't think of taking that job. (him, my son's)
12. Do you mind trying to mend it? (me, our)
13. I'm not afraid of coming back. (the snake, their)
14. I can't stand drinking that cocktail. (her, my wife's)
15. She will never forgive swearing in her presence. (him, my)

SECTION 6 INFINITIVES AND GERUNDS

Exercise No 65

Only a possessive and gerund construction can follow these verbs:

avoid	delay	put off
consider	deny	risk
defer	enjoy	suggest
postpone		

Make these sentences into the possessive and gerund construction by adding the word supplied before the gerund as in the example:

Example:

I don't enjoy singing. (John's)
=I don't enjoy *John's* singing.

1. I don't deny having gone out on the night of the crime. (his)
2. If you delay leaving, our friends will be disappointed. (her)
3. In no circumstances can we consider going to France for the holidays. (your)
4. Do you really enjoy singing that song? (my)
5. You should really avoid going out with a cold like that. (the baby's)
6. It would be most unwise to risk going down that way. (his)
7. Don't postpone learning the piano till too late. (your daughter's)
8. You mustn't put off going to the doctor any longer. (the children's)
9. I suggest going to that film tonight. (your friend's)
10. I don't want to defer paying until too late. (the firm's)

Exercise No 66. Verbs of Sensation

These verbs use two different constructions:

>See, hear, observe, watch, notice, feel, smell

Although we often use these two constructions as if they meant the same thing, there is really a little difference of meaning between them:

1. Object and infinitive (without *to*)—

    I saw him *cross* the road safely and run away.

    In this case the interest is in the completed action.

2. Objective case and gerund (fused participle)—

    I saw him *crossing* the road amongst all the traffic.

    In this case our interest is in the progress of the action.

Complete these sentences:

1. Have you ever seen her . . .?
2. Please watch me . . .
3. She felt an insect . . .
4. I heard the burglar . . .
5. Who did you notice . . .?
6. She heard the baby . . .
7. The cook smelt the meat . . .
8. The witness denied having seen the prisoner . . .
9. The crowd watched the players . . .
10. I distinctly saw the boy . . .
11. I felt the rain . . . down my neck
12. Have you ever observed a bird . . .?
13. The dog smelt the rabbit . . .
14. He felt a mosquito . . .
15. Did you notice that car . . .?

Exercise No 67

The verbs practised in the previous exercise are frequently used in the passive:

> He was seen entering the house at night.
> A car was heard hooting in the distance.

a following infinitive is complete (with *to*):

> He was observed to put his hand in his pocket and take out a coin.
> Her pulse was felt to beat unevenly.

Complete these sentences:

1. The burglar was seen . . .
2. They were overheard . . .
3. The birds were observed . . .
4. The traveller was seen . . .
5. They have never been heard . . .
6. Have those boys ever been seen . . .?
7. The pain in his leg was felt . . .
8. Has Mary ever been noticed . . .?
9. Mary was watched . . . ing by the children

Exercise No 68. 'Make' and 'Let' with Infinitive (Without 'To')

The verbs *make* and *let* are used with an object and infinitive (without *to*) construction:

>Please let me go now.
>You can't make me do what you want.
>Let him come in now.
>Are you going to make us put on those silly clothes again?

Complete these sentences:

1. Whatever happens, don't let him . . .
2. You won't let Mary . . ., will you?
3. I refuse to make the children . . .
4. Can't you make him . . .?
5. Do you mind letting the dogs . . .?
6. You will never succeed in making the students . . .
7. If you don't let me . . . I shall . . .
8. Please let us . . . for once.
9. John doesn't like making his wife . . .
10. Did you manage to make them . . .?

Exercise No 69. 'Be' + Adjective + 'To'-infinitive

Look at these sentences:

>I shall be delighted to help you.
>They were sorry to hear of his accident.
>He wasn't at all surprised to find that they had gone.

This construction is often used with adjectives having the meaning of pleasure, displeasure, surprise:

>Amazed, sorry, surprised, angry, ashamed, sad, happy, upset, glad, anxious, delighted, shocked, proud, pleased, overjoyed

Change these sentences in the way shown in the example:

Example:

We were pleased *when we saw* that the work had been done.
=We were pleased *to see* that the work had been done.

1. Mary was surprised when she saw them arrive so early.
2. We are proud that we can announce the success of our efforts.
3. They said that they would be pleased if they could deliver the goods next week.

4. She was happy that she was home again.
5. John was angry when he found that the children had broken his pipe.
6. You will be amazed when you hear what I have to tell you.
7. They were shocked when they heard of his death.
8. I should be ashamed if I had to appear in those clothes.
9. They were amazed when they heard the parrot talk.
10. I was very sad when I heard of your wife's illness.
11. Were you upset when you learnt that you had failed?
12. His parents were overjoyed when they saw how well he could swim.
13. I should be glad if I could have your views on this problem.
14. Don't be surprised if you get a letter from me next month.
15. I was delighted when I received your letter.

Exercise No 70. 'Be' + 'To'-infinitive

1. This important construction is used to show commands; it is very often used with indirect speech:

    > All officers are to wear their decorations on parade.
    > Nobody is to touch those things on the table.
    > Mary said that the children were not to go out after tea.
    > I told her that she was to return next day.

2. A subsidiary meaning of the construction is for agreements and plans. If we have made a plan or an agreement, there is always some idea of obligation:

    > Mary and John are to get married in the summer.

Change the following sentences into this construction as in the examples:

Examples:

You *must* come here immediately.
=You *are to* come here immediately.

They said that we *had to* bring our books.
=They said that we *were to* bring our books.

1. All children *must* bring their football boots to school tomorrow.
2. She told him he *had to* do his homework again.
3. The Minister announced that all firms *would have to* pay new taxes.

SECTION 6   INFINITIVES AND GERUNDS   69

4. They *must* not attempt anything so foolish.
5. She asked me what she *should* do.
6. Passengers *must* hand in their passports at the office.
7. All radios *must* be switched off after 10 p.m.
8. She told him that he *must* never speak to her again.
9. No one *may* go into that room.
10. They asked him who they *should* apply to for permission.
11. How on earth *can* we overcome this difficulty?
12. You *must* on no account speak in that way.
13. All drivers *must* show their licences to the police.
14. Where *must* I take these things you gave me?
15. The police have been instructed that they *must not* let anyone through.
16. What *must* be done to save the situation?
17. He wondered where all his friends *could* be found.
18. The meat *should* be served first and then the vegetables.
19. All articles bought abroad *must* be declared.
20. All papers *must* be handed in at the end of the examination.

Exercise No 71. 'For' + Object + Infinitive

Look at these sentences:

> It is most unusual for him to lose his way.
> It takes ten minutes for me to walk to the office.
>
> Can you find a book for me to read?
> There was nothing for the children to play with.
>
> It is too long for me to read this evening.
> Is it warm enough for the children to go out yet?

This construction has a number of different meanings and grammatical uses:

(a) As the subject of a sentence—

> It is not necessary for you to come again.
> =*For you to come again* is not necessary.

(b) With the meaning of result—

> Don't wait *for him to come*. (=*until he comes*)

(c) With the meaning of purpose—

> I have nothing *for you to do*. (=*which you can usefully do*)
> I put it there *for you to see*. (=*so that you could see it*)

(d) With *too* and *enough*—

> It is too hard *for us to understand*. (=*it is so hard that we can't understand it*)
> These apples are not low enough *for us to pick*. (=*they are not so low that we can pick them*)

Change these sentences into this construction as in the examples given:

Examples:

It would be disastrous *if John did that.*
=It would be disastrous *for John to do that.*

This exercise is *so* difficult *that we can't do it.*
=This exercise is *too* difficult *for us to do.*

1. It would be a mistake *if we interfered in the matter.*
2. It is essential *that they pay their own bills.*
3. *The fact that he plays the piano so well* is a great achievement.
4. There are three more items on the agenda *that the board must consider.*
5. Here is something *which you ought to see.*
6. He laid it on the table *so that all could inspect it.*
7. Mother baked a cake *so that all the children could have some for tea.*
8. Why did you choose that book? *Must we read it?*
9. What a foolish thing *it was he did!*
10. She is longing for the moment *when her boy-friend will return.*
11. The car is not ready; *so you cannot drive it.*
12. The car was *so* expensive *that I could not buy it.*
13. Bring your homework *so that I can correct it tomorrow.*
14. Open the door *so that the dog can come in.*
15. We were waiting *until the film began.*
16. Are these shoes big enough? *Can you wear them?*
17. The water is not deep enough. *We can't dive into it.*
18. You had better send it to the museum. *They will identify it there.*
19. He has arranged *it so that they will look after* his house while he is away.
20. Is the soup cool enough? *Can we drink it yet?*

Exercise No 72. The Infinitive in the Place of a Relative Clause

The infinitive can often be used in the place of a clause, particularly if this has future meaning or the idea of obligation:

> I have some work to do. (=*which I must do*)
> He had nothing to say about it. (=*which he could say about it*)

You should note that in this construction the infinitive often has a passive meaning:

> This house is to let. (=*to be let*)
> There is nothing to explain. (=*which needs to be explained*)

Replace the relative clauses in these sentences by an infinitive as in the examples:

Examples:

He gave me a book *which I was to look at.*
=He gave me a book *to look at.*

There are plenty of mountains there *which you can climb.*
=There are plenty of mountains there *to climb.*

1. Is there anything there *that you can see?*
2. He is a man *whom you can trust.*
3. There is no one there *who can help me.*
4. He is not a man *who can be trusted.*
5. I haven't anything *which I must do.*
6. Have you anything *which you ought to declare?*
7. Let's hurry. There is a lot *which must be done.*
8. This is an occasion *which must not be forgotten.*
9. She has no money left *which she can spend.*
10. Don't forget that you have a train *which you must catch.*
11. Please lend me a book *which I can read at the week-end.*
12. There are still a hundred and one things *which must be done.*
13. Would you like something *which you can drink?*
14. She found someone *who was willing to carry her bags at the station.*
15. Can you suggest somewhere *where we can go for our holidays?*

Exercise No 73. The Infinitive in Place of Clauses

The infinitive is often used in the place of a clause beginning with the words *where, when, which, what* and *who*:

> Tell me what to do. (=*what I must do*)
> I can't think who to ask. (=*who I should ask*)
> I don't know where to find it. (=*where I can find it*)
> She doesn't know which to choose. (=*which she ought to choose*)

This construction usually has the meaning of *ought to* or *must*.

Change the clauses in these sentences into an infinitive as in the example:

Example:

You haven't told me *when I ought to come yet*.
=You haven't told me *when to come yet*.

1. I'm going to ask the secretary *what I must do about it*.
2. It is very difficult to know *what we ought to do* in the circumstances.
3. Let's decide *what we are going to play*.
4. Before we start you'd better explain to them *how we have to play*.
5. I can never remember *when I have to press* the button.
6. Have you forgotten *who you must give it to*?
7. Have you any idea *how you must stop the bleeding*?
8. I can't think *what I should make it out of*.
9. Tell them *where they have to put it*.
10. She has just explained to them *what they must mix it with*.
11. The travel agency advised them *which hotel they ought to stay at*.
12. Have you any idea *how long we ought to stay at the party*.
13. I can't make up my mind *whether I should invite them or not*.
14. The Instruction Book advised him *how often he should change the oil in his car*.
15. She couldn't decide *which of them she should keep*.

SECTION 7

TENSES OF THE VERB

Exercise No 74. The Simple Present and the Simple Past Tense

It is important for the student to associate adverbs of time with the tenses with which they are usually used. Very often a student makes mistakes in the use of English tenses because he transfers to English the association of adverb and tense of his own language. This and the following exercises are meant to help the student to establish the correct association of adverb and tense in English.

1. **The Simple Present Tense** is used for permanent truths, habitual actions and states. It is found with such adverbs as these:

    Always, often, frequently, rarely, generally, sometimes, usually

    and such adverbial phrases as:

    Every day (week, month), once (twice, several times) a week (month)

    and time clauses beginning with:

    Whenever, every time that . . .

    Examples:
    She often rests after lunch.
    He visits the hospital several times a month.
    They go to the theatre whenever they can.

    This tense is generally **not** used with adverbs of present time, such as:

    At the moment, at present.

2. **The Simple Past Tense** can also be used for habitual actions and states in the past. When it is used in this way it usually has the same adverbs as the simple present tense:

    Last year I walked to the office every day.
    =Last year I used to walk to the office every day.

    My grandmother always went to Switzerland for her holidays.
    He got angry every time I asked for money.

Put the verbs in brackets in the following sentences into the correct Simple Tense, either Past or Present:

1. He (come) to see me every day last week.
2. We usually (have) breakfast at seven o'clock nowadays.

3. Water always (freeze) at 0 degrees Centigrade.
4. Students frequently (make) mistakes of tense usage when they do this exercise.
5. I (have) my hair cut whenever it gets too long.
6. I (take) my dog for a walk every evening before it died.
7. He (come) to my office whenever he needed money.
8. Last year she (wear) the same dress at every party.
9. Whenever I climb a hill, my car (boil).
10. She (sing) very beautifully before she was married, but nowadays she (not sing) any more.
11. I seldom (see) him at concerts these days. He (go) to them regularly before the war.
12. She cooks very well but her sister (cook) much better when I knew her.
13. Every time he opens his mouth, he (say) something foolish.
14. He occasionally makes a big effort, but usually he (not bother).
15. Whenever I (go) to see him, he was out.
16. In the past men frequently (fight) duels. Nowadays they seldom (do).
17. How often you (go) to the theatre when you were in London?
18. You (play) with dolls when you were a little girl?
19. The ancient Egyptians (build) pyramids as tombs for their kings.
20. When I was young, my father always (give) me some money on Saturdays.
21. If he is wise, a pianist (practise) four hours a day.
22. His parents don't know what to do with that child. He (lie) habitually.
23. My aunt Jane (hate) girls who made up.
24. We all (study) Latin when we were at school.
25. Wood always (float).

Exercise No 75. The Continuous Present Tense and The Simple Present Tense

The Continuous Present Tense is used for actions in progress at the time of speaking. It is usually used without any adverbs of time, because what is happening at the time of speaking is evident and needs no explanation. We do sometimes use these adverbs with this tense:

> Now, at present, at this moment, still

SECTION 7 — TENSES OF THE VERB

The Simple Present Tense is used for habitual actions and states. It is not generally used for actions at the moment of speaking. (But see Exercise No. 76 for exceptions to this general rule.)

Examples:
Joan usually plays tennis every afternoon, but this afternoon she is resting.
She generally cooks on the electric stove, but today she is cooking on the oil stove.

Put the verbs in brackets into the correct Present Tense, continuous or simple:

1. Buses usually (run) along this street, but today they (not run) because it is under repair.
2. John (pass) the post-office on his way to work every day.
3. She usually (sit) at the back of the class, but today she (sit) in the front row.
4. I rarely (carry) an umbrella, but I (carry) one now because it is raining.
5. What you generally (do) for a living?
6. You (enjoy) your English class today?
7. You (enjoy) washing dishes as a rule?
8. We nearly always (spend) our holidays at the seaside, but this year we are going to France.
9. Mr. Jones usually (sell) only newspapers, but this week he (sell) magazines as well.
10. You (wash) your hands before every meal?
11. Mary generally (begin) cooking at 11, but today she came home early and (cook) now, although it is only 10.30.
12. I'm sorry you can't see her. She (sleep) still. She usually (wake) much earlier.
13. Why you (wear) a coat this morning? I never (wear) one till October.
14. Joan still (do) her homework. Her sister, who always (work) quicker, (play) already in the garden.
15. These builders generally (build) very rapidly. They (work) at present on two separate contracts.
16. What (do) you at this moment? If you (not do) anything, please help me.
17. John, who (study) medicine at present, hopes to go abroad after graduating.

18. He generally (come) to my office every day, but today he (visit) his parents in the country.
19. You (watch) television often? The electrician (install) ours at this moment.
20. Mary usually (wear) a hat to go shopping. but today, as the sun (shine), she (not wear) one.

Exercise No 76. Non-conclusive Verbs

There are a number of common verbs which we do not often use in the continuous tenses. Although we may be using them for describing an action at the moment of speaking, we use **the Simple Tense**. The reason why they are generally used in the simple tense is that the actions they describe are ones which cannot be stopped or started at will; they are more or less involuntary actions or states.

These are the principal verbs of this type:

Smell, hear, see, notice (*sensations*)
Think, believe, know, remember, forget, suppose, understand (*mental processes*)
Want, wish, desire, need (*desires*)
Like, dislike, love, hate, detest, prefer, mind (=*object to*) (*likes and dislikes*)
Seem, appear, resemble, look (=*appear*) (*appearance*),
mean, matter, consist of, belong to, contain

Examples:

I hear what you are saying.
I believe he is coming tomorrow.
His behaviour really seems extraordinary.
I don't mind your going if you want to.
What does this box contain?

The following sentences all refer to the present. Put the verbs in brackets into the correct tense, Continuous or Simple Present:

1. You (see) the house on the corner? That is where I was born.
2. You (listen) to what I am saying? You (understand) me?
3. I (notice) Mary (wear) a new hat today.
4. She (not understand) what you (mean).
5. I (need) a new suit. They (offer) special prices at the tailor's this week.
6. You (smell) gas? I (think) the new stove is leaking.
7. Look at Mary! She (drink) up her medicine, but I can see that she (hate) it.

8. John (seem) rather tired today.
9. It still (rain), but it (look) as if it will soon stop.
10. You (mind) helping me a moment? I (try) to mend this table.
11. Ask him what he (want).
12. You (remember) the name of that girl who (walk) on the other side of the street?
13. 'Will you have some whisky?' 'I (prefer) beer, please.'
14. I (suppose) I must go now. My wife (wait) for me at home.
15. You (see) this box? It (contain) matches.
16. These twins, who (resemble) one another so strongly, (study) art at present.
17. After what has happened, you really (mean) to say that you still (believe) him?
18. You (suppose) the children still (sleep)?
19. The train still (stand) in the station. You (think) we can just catch it?
20. I (notice) you (possess) a copy of Waugh's latest book. Will you lend it me?

Note: Students will sometimes hear some of these non-conclusive verbs used in the Continuous Tense. In such cases the meaning of the verb may be slightly different or the speaker may wish to emphasize the temporary nature of the action described. The student does not need to study these uses at this stage.

Exercise No 77. The Future Tenses

English has two principal ways of expressing the future: the tense made with the auxiliaries *shall* and *will*, known as **the Simple Future Tense**, (*I* (*we*) *shall; You* (*he, she, they*) *will*) and the *going to* construction:

> I shall arrive tomorrow, if the weather is fine.
> They will do it next week, if they have time.
> We are going to buy a new car next month.
> John is going to spend his holidays in Italy next summer.

The principal adverbs with a future meaning are:

> Soon, shortly, tonight, tomorrow
> Next week (month, year)
> In a few minutes (days, weeks, months)
> By next week (tomorrow, two o'clock)

The future tenses are also found with clauses introduced by: when, until, as soon as, before, after, the moment that, now that (see Exercise No 82 for the tenses used in these clauses).

In the following sentences change the Simple Future Tense into the *going to* construction as in the example:

> *Example:*
>
> *I shall cut* the grass when the mowing machine is mended.
> =*I am going to cut* the grass when the mowing machine is mended.

1. I don't know how I shall manage without a maid next week.
2. The police will be much stricter with bad drivers in future.
3. I think he will ask for a rise in salary very soon.
4. Do you suppose it will rain before dark?
5. How soon will you be ready?
6. The show will begin in about ten minutes.
7. She will not give another concert this year.
8. The climbing party will try to reach the top tomorrow.
9. He says he will pay me back the week after next.
10. Do you think the government will reduce taxation next year?
11. He says he will call up before six o'clock.
12. Do you think he will get back before dusk?
13. When he has gone I shall tell you a secret.
14. As soon as we have had dinner, we shall play bridge.
15. Now that we have sold our old car, we shall buy a new one.

Note: Although the *shall/will* future and the *going to* future are both perfectly correct in these sentences, they do not always have quite the same meanings. The next exercise will show the difference between them. You should also study Exercise No 15 for the various meanings of *shall* and *will*.

Exercise No 78. The 'Shall/Will' Future and the 'Going To' Future

Look at these sentences:

> I am going to sell my car after Easter.
> =I intend to sell my car after Easter.
>
> Are you going to meet your friends at the airport?
> =Do you intend to meet your friends at the airport?
>
> He says he is going to get up very early in future.
> =He says he intends to get up very early in future.

In these sentences *going to* has the meaning of intention.

SECTION 7 — TENSES OF THE VERB

> It looks as if it is going to be very hot today.
> Do you think the examination is going to be very difficult?
> I'm afraid you are going to have a lot of trouble with him.
> That tree is going to die soon, I think.

In these sentences *going to* suggests that what is to happen is inevitable.

The *shall/will* future does not have the meaning of intention or inevitability to the same degree and for that reason is more often used when circumstances which we cannot control are expressed or implied:

> We shall enjoy ourselves *if the play is good*.
> They'll have an accident *if they're not careful*.
> You'll get bitten *if you play with that dog*.
> *All being well*, we shall arrive tomorrow.
> *Stop doing that* or I shall get angry.
> *Ask John* and he'll give you the answer.

Now compare these sentences:

> I'm going to give you some good advice.
> If you'll listen, I'll give you some good advice.
>
> It's going to rain soon.
> If the wind drops, it'll rain.
>
> You're going to find it very difficult, I'm afraid.
> If you do it that way, you'll find it very difficult.

Change these sentences from the *going to* construction to the *shall/will* future adding the conditions given in brackets:

> *Example:*
>
> That dog is going to get run over. (if it's not careful)
> That dog will get run over if it's not careful.

1. John is going to buy a new car. (only if he has enough money)
2. We are going to visit America this summer. (if we can get a booking on a ship)
3. They are going to build a new bridge across the river. (if they can find the money)
4. New legislation is going to be introduced. (if the Minister approves)
5. Are you going to sell your house? (if you can get a good price for it)
6. He is going to finish his book this year. (given good luck)
7. I am going to have a bath. (if there is plenty of hot water)

8. The dog is going to bite the postman. (unless we stop him immediately)
9. (Unless we hurry) we are going to be late.
10. The children are going to start Latin next year. (if they pass their exams)
11. (Pay me more or) I'm going to stop work.
12. I'm going to see the dentist. (if he's not too busy)
13. The pilot says we're going to land in half an hour. (all being well)

Exercise No 79. The Present Continuous Tense with Future Meaning

The Present Continuous Tense is also frequently used with future meaning. In this use it is associated with adverbs of future time:

> Soon, this evening, tomorrow, next week, tonight, in a few minutes, next summer, later this year (month, week)
>
> *He intends to go* to the cinema this evening.
> =*He is going* to the cinema this evening.

Change these sentences in the same way into the form with the Present Continuous Tense:

1. The Jones family *plan to go* to Italy this summer.
2. *Do you want to go* to the concert tonight?
3. John *plans to sell* his car this week and *to buy* a new one.
4. I must leave immediately, I *hope to catch* a bus in a few minutes.
5. Please wait a moment! I *promise to come* soon.
6. Come and say goodbye. Our guests *have to leave* in a minute.
7. I'm sorry I can't come. I *plan to shop* all morning and *have* lunch in town.
8. We *mean to visit* our friends in London and *spend* the night with them.
9. That new Italian film *is booked to come* to the Regal Cinema shortly.
10. Goodbye! I've *arranged to play* tennis in half an hour.

Exercise No 80. The Simple Present Tense with Future Meaning

The Simple Present Tense is also used with future meaning, but in a much more restricted way, with verbs of *going* and *coming*, such as:

> Go, come, leave, arrive, get, return, set off, take off, embark, sail, fly

In this sense it is used when we are describing activities, planned beforehand (principally travel) in the future and according to a fixed timetable.

Example:

> The 'Queen Mary' *is due to sail* next Friday.
> =the 'Queen Mary' *sails* next Friday.

Change the parts of the following sentences in italics into the Simple Present Tense:

1. When *are* you *due to return* to your own country?
2. I *am due to get back* from New York in a week's time.
3. At what time *is* your plane *scheduled to take* off?
4. The climbing party *plan to set off* at dawn tomorrow.
5. According to the time-table we *are to leave* on Wednesday, *stay* one night in Paris and *return* the following morning.
6. John *is due to get back* to the office on Monday next.
7. The whole company *are due to embark* next Thursday at 7 p.m.
8. ... and the ship *is scheduled to sail* an hour later.
9. The manager *is booked to fly* to Rome very soon for important consultations.
10. I'm sorry to hear you *have arranged to leave* so soon.

Exercise No 81. The Present Perfect Tense

The Present Perfect Tense is a present tense. It is used for an action which began in the past and which has continued up to the time of speaking, or for an action which took place in the past, the results of which we can feel or observe in the present.

It is used with such adverbs as these:

> Now, just (=*this minute*), today, this morning (week, month), still, ever, never, not yet, already, recently, lately

and adverbial clauses and phrases beginning with *for* and *since*. It is not used with adverbs of past time, or clauses introduced by other conjunctions.

Examples:

He has just put his coat on. (=*He is wearing it now*)
Have you ever met Mr. Jones? (=*Do you know him?*)
They have already passed the first examination. (=*They are ready now to do the second*)

The Present Perfect Continuous Tense is used with the same meaning as the Simple Tense and with the same adverbs. This tense is more often used with verbs which have the meaning of prolonged action, such as:

Live, wait, stay, work, read, sleep, study

and with many other verbs when they mean repeated action.

The adverbs used with this tense often have *all* before them to emphasize the meaning of continuous action:

All this morning, all this week, all day, all this year

Examples:

They have been living here since 1954.
I have been waiting for you all morning.
She has been sleeping for three hours now.

Supply the correct form of the Perfect Tense, Continuous or Simple in the place of the verbs in brackets:

1. They just (arrive) from New York.
2. They still (not succeed) in reaching the summit.
3. I this very minute (receive) a telegram from my brother in India.
4. We already (have) breakfast.
5. I now (study) your proposals and regret I cannot accept them.
6. They (live) here since January.
7. We (wait) on the platform since three o'clock.
8. She already (ring) the bell twice.
9. I see you just (have) your hair cut.
10. She (write) letters all morning, but I (not start) to write any yet.
11. The children (sleep) all this afternoon.
12. How long you (stay) in that old hotel?
13. They (work) in the same factory for twenty years now.
14. Since when you (have) that new car?
15. I (knock) on the door for ten minutes now without an answer.
16. They (build) that bridge for over a year and it still isn't finished.

17. I (try) three times and (be) successful only once.
18. How many times you (be) to the cinema this week?
19. He (go) to the dentist off and on for six months.
20. He (take) the exam three times and (fail) every time.
21. William (marry) the eldest Jones girl at last.
22. I (try) to get in touch with you for several days now.
23. She just (spend) three weeks at her grandmother's.
24. He (work) hard on his book for some time and (finish) it at last.
25. You ever (read) 'War and Peace'?

Note: If the number of times an action is repeated is mentioned, the continuous tense is not used:

> I have been telephoning you all morning.
> I have telephoned you *at least four times* this morning.

Exercise No 82 Simple Present and Present Perfect Tense in Clauses of Time

In English we do not use the Future Tense in clauses of time introduced by:

> When, until, as soon as, before, after, now that, the moment that, by the time that

In these cases we use **the Simple Present Tense** or **the Present Perfect Tense**:

> He will come as soon as he has finished his homework.
> He will explain the moment that he gets home.

Both these tenses are used equally often in this way and there is no difference of meaning between them:

> They cannot leave until they have done their work.
> They cannot leave until they do their work.

Repeat each sentence twice: once with the Simple Present Tense and once with the Present Perfect Tense in the place of the verbs in brackets:

1. I shall stay here until you (promise) to do as I ask.
2. When I (hear) from you again I shall let you know.
3. As soon as they (pay) the first instalment, the television set will be delivered.
4. They refuse to give me any more money until I (do) some more work.

5. You will get the doctor's bill as soon as you (get) better.
6. William is to study medicine as soon as he (finish) military service.
7. We cannot wait here until you (make) up your mind.
8. The children are to do their homework the moment they (arrive) back from school.
9. The postman cannot reach the house until the snow (melt).
10. You may not borrow another book until you (return) the one you have.
11. John and Mary are going to the cinema when the children (go) to bed.
12. It will not be possible to finish the experiment until we (get) better equipment.

The conjunctions *after* and *now that* (and *when* with the meaning of *after*) are generally found with the Present Perfect Tense only.

Replace the verbs in brackets with the Present Perfect Tense:

13. Come and see me when you (have) your dinner.
14. He will visit you after he (has) something to eat.
15. After they (write) their letters they are going for a walk.
16. Now that you (leave) school, you must learn to be more grown-up.
17. You will get a higher salary when you (work) for three months.
18. You will never forget it once you (learn) it properly.
19. Now that you (win) the lottery, what are you going to do?
20. Once you (drink) that whisky, you will never want to drink any other.

Exercise No 83. The Simple Past Tense

The Simple Past Tense is used for an action which took place in the past and is complete by the time of speaking. It is used with such adverbs of past time as these:

> Yesterday, last night (week, year), just now (=*a few moments ago*)

adverbs of time with *ago*:

> A few minutes ago, three days ago, a long time ago

adverbial clauses introduced by:

> When, while, until, before, as soon as, after, once, the moment that

SECTION 7   TENSES OF THE VERB   85

Examples:

John arrived last night.
That house was built many years ago.
I waited for three minutes while he finished telephoning.

Supply the Simple Past Tense in the place of the verbs in brackets:

1. The water in the pond (freeze) last night.
2. They (get back) very late last night.
3. I (have) a letter from my wife last week.
4. Last month the cost of living (rise) to a new high point.
5. Last week the government (introduce) new legislation.
6. Yesterday afternoon the police (catch) a thief in the High Street.
7. He (ring) me up just now.
8. It is exactly five years ago today that we (get) married.
9. I (see) the bus pass a few minutes ago.
10. While he was reading in his study, his wife (call) to him to come.
11. As soon as he had opened the door, his dog (rush) out to greet him.
12. He had left before we (have) time to warn him of the danger.
13. The thief had escaped before he (come) into the room.
14. He played poker until the sun (rise).
15. They (not visit) us after we had quarrelled.
16. You (remember) to turn out the lights before leaving the room?
17. It was only last week that I (tell) you not to say that.
18. It is a little over two hundred years since Mozart (be) born.
19. When you last (see) your father?
20. At the end of last year they finally (succeed) in producing the drug synthetically.

Exercise No 84. The Continuous and Simple Past Tenses

The Continuous Past Tense is used for continuous actions in the past about whose beginning and end we are not concerned. It is most often found in compound sentences with another verb in **the Simple Past Tense**, to describe the background against which the Simple Past Tense action took place:

I was reading a book when you came in.

It is often found with adverb clauses beginning with *while* and *when* and other adverbs which show the duration of the action:

All last week, all yesterday, all last night

Supply the correct Tense, Continuous or Simple Past in place of the verbs in brackets:

1. I (wash) my hands when the telephone (ring).
2. She (sit) at the table when the children (come) home.
3. He (watch) television when his friend arrived.
4. What you (do) when I knocked at the door?
5. Mary was sewing while John (mend) the radio.
6. They (study) the same exercise all last week as they were studying this morning.
7. She broke down when she (hear) the news.
8. The children ran away when they (see) the policeman.
9. The bus crashed and some of the passengers (get) hurt.
10. The gardener (dig) in the garden when he found a valuable old coin.
11. She (look) for her pen when she discovered she (have) it in her handbag all the time.
12. I (try) to ring you up all yesterday but your telephone wasn't working.
13. The bus crashed while the driver (look) the other way.
14. Why did you talk to that man while I (wait) all the time?
15. She already (lie) in hospital when her husband heard of the accident.
16. I was thinking about the problem all night, but I never (find) the answer.
17. The aeroplane already (fly) very low when I caught sight of it.
18. Did you see Mr. Jones in the theatre last night? He (sit) in the third row.
19. Her aunt died while she (spend) her holidays in Italy.
20. They all (have) breakfast when I got up.

Exercise No 85. The Continuous Past Tense and The Simple Past Tense (with the Meaning of Habitual Action in the Past)

The Simple Past Tense is used for habitual actions and states in the past (see Exercise No 74). **The Continuous Past Tense** is **not** used with this meaning (see previous exercise):

> She was walking to work when I met her.
> She walked to work every day last year.

Give the correct tense Simple or Continuous Past in the place of the verbs in brackets in the following sentences:

1. My grandmother (walk) in the park every day until she was ninety.
2. My aunt (walk) in the park when I met her.
3. The Jones family (swim) in the sea when it began to rain.
4. The Jones family (swim) in the sea during their holidays.
5. She (cook) dinner when the doorbell rang.
6. She (cook) beautifully before she got married.
7. We (drive) along the river when the car ran out of petrol.
8. Mr. Jones (drive) a Ford all last year; now he drives an Austin.
9. My wife not (wear) stockings very often when we were on holiday.
10. Mary (wear) a new hat when the wind blew it away.
11. You often (play) football at the University?
12. She (play) tennis when she sprained her ankle.
13. Mary always (mend) her stockings until her eyes became bad.
14. The old lady (mend) stockings when the lights went out.
15. She (talk) to her neighbours in French, because her English was so bad.
16. She (talk) to her neighbours when the baby began to cry.
17. My grandmother (bake) the most delicious cakes when I was young.
18. We (fly) over the Alps when we ran into bad weather.
19. John (work) on a new project when the Manager came in.
20. The thief just (get) out of the window when the police arrived.

Exercise No 86. The Past Perfect Tense

The Past Perfect Tense is used for an action which has already begun before another action which takes place in the past. It is generally found:

(*a*) in indirect speech—

'I have finished my work.'
He said that he had finished his work.

'They left about an hour ago.'
He told me that they had left about an hour before.

(*b*) in compound sentences in the past with clauses of time introduced by such words as—

After, before, when, until, as soon as

He returned home after he had left the office.
I had already finished my work before my friends arrived.

Change the following sentences into the past, using the Simple Past and Past Perfect Tenses:

Example:

He wants to know what you did last week.
He wanted to know what you had done last week.

1. He tells me that he has never met you.
2. They want to know what has happened.
3. I know that they haven't been there yet.
4. He says he wasn't present at the meeting.
5. She believes that she put it away in the cupboard.
6. I am told that the plane didn't leave last Tuesday after all.
7. We wonder if he has lost his way.
8. I cannot remember whether he has paid his subscription or not.
9. The students believe that they have already done the exercise.
10. Do you really think that he has been thrown into prison?
11. John wants to know why Mary came home late.
12. He is under the impression that they have made a mistake.
13. She is unable to tell us where she got the money.
14. They tell me they have only once seen her in their lives.

SECTION 7   TENSES OF THE VERB

Exercise No 87

See explanation to the previous exercise.

Put the verbs in brackets into the correct tense, Simple Past or Past Perfect.

1. When he (leave) already, he (realize) he (forget) his wallet.
2. She (burst) into tears the moment he (shut) the door.
3. His finger (begin) to bleed as soon as he (cut) himself.
4. He (lose) his new knife shortly after he (buy) it.
5. He (begin) to read as soon as he (find) the place in his book.
6. The fire (burn) for three hours when the firemen arrived.
7. It already (rain) for half an hour when we (step) out into the street.
8. The patient (die) already by the time the doctor (arrive).
9. When John (enter) the room the thief already (escape).
10. When we (get) home, night already (fall).
11. Until he (explain), the students (not understand).
12. Until the aeroplane (take off), we (can) not hear ourselves speak.
13. Until the gardener (water) the plants, they (not grow).
14. His neighbours (will) not speak to him until he (apologize).
15. They (be) not able to make the pudding until the maid (bring) the eggs.

Exercise No 88. The Simple Past and Past Perfect Tenses in Hypothetical Situations

The Simple Past and **Past Perfect Tenses** are both used to show imaginary or desirable situations in the present and past respectively when the sentence begins with certain verbs or conjunctions:

> I wish John were here now. (*he would know what to do*)
> We all wished John had been at the party. (*he would have known what to do*)

These two tenses are really subjunctive in mood in this use; only the verb *were* with the 3rd person shows the subjunctive form.

The principal verbs and conjunctions which introduce this use of the two tenses are:

> I wish(ed)   I'd rather
> It's high time   as if

and in exclamations:

> if only!   supposing!

Examples:

If only I were rich!
Supposing all of them came!
I'd rather you didn't do that.
He ran as if the devil were after him.
It's high time you washed your hands.

Replace the verbs in brackets by the correct tense, Simple Past or Past Perfect:

1. I wish the children (sleep) longer in the morning; then I shouldn't get woken so early.
2. I'd rather you (not mention) it to them just yet.
3. Mary wishes John (come) back a bit earlier from the office. He's always late for dinner.
4. We all wished we not (stay) to see the end of the film.
5. I wish my car not always (rattle) so much nowadays.
6. I wish the train (not arrive) so late; then I could have got home before breakfast.
7. They now wish they (work) harder at school. Then they wouldn't have failed their examinations.
8. She says she'd rather he (leave) tomorrow instead of today.
9. It's high time you children (know) your tables.
10. Supposing he never (come)! What would happen then?
11. She ran as if she (have) wings on her feet.
12. He looked as if he (not wash) for years.
13. Suppose I (do) what you ask! What would become of me?
14. Suppose I (do) what you asked! What would have become of me?
15. If only we (do) as we were told! This would never have happened.

SECTION 8

CONDITIONAL SENTENCES

Conditional Sentences are conveniently classified into three groups:

GROUP I. Cause and Effect

(a)

If	PRESENT	PRESENT
If	one buys a car,	it costs money.

(b) *

If	PRESENT	FUTURE OR IMPERATIVE
If	**you buy that car,**	**it will cost you £1,000.**
If	**you buy that car,**	**drive carefully.**

(c)

IMPERATIVE	'AND'	FUTURE
Buy a car	and	it will cost you a fortune.

(d)

If	'SHOULD'	FUTURE OR IMPERATIVE
If	you should decide to buy a car,	please tell me.

GROUP II. Hypothetical but Possible

(a) *

If	PAST	CONDITIONAL
If	**you bought a car today,**	**it would cost you a lot of money.**

(b)

If	'WERE TO'	CONDITIONAL
If	you were to buy a car,	it would cost you a lot of money.

* Of all these forms those printed in heavy type are the most common and important.

GROUP III. Hypothetical and Impossible

(a) *

If	Past Perfect	Perfect Conditional
If	you had bought a car a year ago,	it would have cost you much less than now.

(b)

Past Perfect Inverted	Perfect Conditional
Had you bought that car,	you wouldn't have had all that trouble.

Exercise No 89

If	Present	Present
If	water boils	it changes into steam.

Supply the correct tense of the verb in brackets:

(*Note:* In this type of conditional sentence, the *if* can be replaced by *when*.)

1. If you (have) a cold, it (be) wise to go to bed.
2. If people (be) tired, they generally (go) to bed.
3. If you (throw) a stone into water, it (sink).
4. If a man (have) children, he (must) look after them.
5. If you (heat) butter, it (melt).
6. If you (go) to the doctor, you (must) pay.
7. Students (learn) fast, if the teacher (be) competent.
8. Plants (grow) quickly, if you (water) them.
9. I (sing), if I (be) happy.
10. I (can) not understand you, if you (speak) Chinese.

* Of all these forms those printed in heavy type are the most common and important.

SECTION 8 CONDITIONAL SENTENCES

Exercise No 90

Complete these sentences using the same tense sequence:

1. Thin ice breaks if you . . .
2. The flight is generally postponed if . . .
3. People earn a lot if they . . .
4. It is possible to reach it only if . . .
5. People don't understand if . . .
6. Salt dissolves if you . . .
7. They generally play football if the weather . . .
8. She visits her family when . . .
9. I wear a black suit if . . .
10. If people feel ill, they . . .

Exercise No 91

IMPERATIVE	AND	FUTURE
Give us the tools	and	we will finish the job.

Now change the following sentences into this form:

1. If you take away his toys he will cry.
2. If you drive too fast you will get killed.
3. If you say that again, I will hit you.
4. If you listen to me carefully, I will explain.
5. If you turn over the page, you will see what I mean.
6. If you leave them alone, they will come home.
7. If you think of the difficulties, you will realize why progress is slow.
8. If you invest in that business, you will be ruined.
9. If you touch that wire, you'll get a nasty shock.
10. If you go to the doctor, he will give you some medicine.
11. If you look out of the window now, you'll see him walking down the street.
12. If you knock at the door, they will let you in.
13. If you tell me the answer, I will give you a prize.
14. If you move, I'll shoot you.
15. If you give them an inch, they will take a mile.

16. If you follow my instructions, you won't get lost.
17. If you send in this form, we will do the rest.
18. If you give me a pencil, I'll explain how to do it.
19. If he escapes, he will do it again. (Let him . . .)
20. If I have your pen, I'll write the answers. (Let me . . .)
21. If they come, I'll talk to them. (Let them . . .)
22. If we try, we may succeed. (Let us . . .)

Exercise No 92

If	Present	Future or 'Can'
If	he comes	I will speak to him.

Complete these sentences:

1. If they arrive early, we . . .
2. I shan't play tennis today if it . . .
3. It will be your own fault if you . . .
4. If he does that again, I . . .
5. We shall be delighted if you . . .
6. If you don't hurry, you . . .
7. They will pass their examination only if they . . .
8. The bus will arrive in time if the driver . . .
9. If the teacher doesn't explain it to you, how . . .?
10. Will you promise to do it if I . . .?
11. What will happen if I . . .?
12. If you drink too much whisky, you . . .
13. What will he do if . . .?
14. Will you invite him to dinner if he . . .?
15. If I don't find my glasses, I . . .

Exercise No 93

If	Present	Imperative
If	she comes,	give her my love.

SECTION 8 CONDITIONAL SENTENCES

Complete the following sentences:

1. If you ..., tell me.
2. Lend me some, if you ...
3. Don't come if you ...
4. Be careful if you ...
5. If you find any specimens, ...
6. If your friend is there, ...
7. If the shops are open, ...
8. ..., if it's not raining.
9. ..., if you want to know what happens.
10. Let's throw it away, if it ...
11. ..., if you don't want to lose the way.
12. Buy me a pound if ...
13. Let's not go, if it ...
14. Let him come if he ...

Exercise No 94. 'Or Else'

Look at these sentences:

> Say you are sorry, *if you don't, he will* never forgive you.
> Say you are sorry; *or else he will* never forgive you.

The phrase *or else* takes the place of a conditional clause introduced by *unless* or *if not*. It is most frequently used after an imperative, and the whole construction belongs to the first type of conditional sentence.

Change the following sentences into the *or else* construction as in the example:

Example:

If you don't take care, you'll fall.
=Take care, or else you'll fall.

1. Put on your coat. If you don't, you will catch cold.
2. Be careful. If you aren't, you will drop those plates.
3. You must work harder. If you don't, you will fail your examinations.
4. Put that knife away. If you don't, you will cut yourself.
5. Unless you find a seat quickly, there won't be any left.

6. Unless I go now, I shall miss my train.
7. If you don't give me that immediately, I shall get angry.
8. Unless you hurry, you'll be late.
9. If you don't follow the instructions, you will spoil the machine.
10. Drink up your coffee; if you don't, it will get cold.

Exercise No 95

IF	PAST	CONDITIONAL OR 'COULD'
If	they were here	I should speak to them.

Now supply the correct forms of the verbs in brackets:

1. If Mary (see) him, she (be) delighted.
2. If I (ask) you, would you help me?
3. The bridge (collapse) if a heavy car (go) over it.
4. If she (have) more money, she (dress) more fashionably.
5. They (hear) better if you (speak) louder.
6. (Marry) you me if I asked you?
7. He (play) more often if he (have) someone to accompany him.
8. The waiter (serve) you quicker if you (speak) to him more politely.
9. The workers (produce) a higher output if their conditions (be improved).
10. Do you think he (lend) me his clarinet if I (ask) him nicely?
11. If they really (want) to see the house, I (have to) get the permission of the owner.
12. If they really (try), they (can) easily win the prize.
13. He (propose) to her at once if she (give) him any encouragement.
14. This soup (taste) better if it (have) more salt in it.
15. If he (be) a gentleman, he (not say) things like that!

SECTION 8 — CONDITIONAL SENTENCES

Exercise No 96

If	'WERE TO'	CONDITIONAL
	'WERE TO' inverted	
If they were to arrive tomorrow, Were they to arrive tomorrow,		we should be quite unprepared.

Now change these sentences into the *were to* form:

1. If he listened more carefully he wouldn't make so many mistakes.
2. If that man took more exercise he wouldn't get so fat.
3. If I ever heard his voice again, it would bring back many happy memories.
4. Do you think we should speak better if we studied phonetics?
5. It would be easier to read his writing if he wrote in ink.
6. If the lecturer spoke louder, all the audience could hear.
7. If we climbed to the top of the mountain, should we get a good view?
8. He wouldn't put on so much weight if he drank less.
9. I should be ruined if I bought that picture!
10. If you ever met the Queen, how would you address her?
11. If he presented himself before me, I should soon deal with him.
12. If he entered business, he might become a rich man.
13. I should go for a walk if it stopped raining.
14. If I became a great artist, you would probably be as surprised as I.
15. If the plane crashed, we should all be killed.

Exercise No 97

If	PAST PERFECT PAST	'COULD HAVE' 'COULD'
If	they were stronger,	they could lift the table.
If	they had been stronger,	they could have lifted the table.

Complete the following sentences:

1. If I were the Prime Minister, I ...
2. He could buy a new car, if he ...
3. If the motorist had a map, he ...
4. If the carpenter had just two more nails, he ...
5. If I had the time, I ...
6. If he hadn't been ill, he ...
7. They could have passed the examination last time if they ...
8. We could have come with you if we ...
9. If her parents had been richer, she ...
10. If he had come yesterday, he ...
11. If it hadn't rained, we ...
12. If he were more intelligent, he ...
13. If the ground were more even, the plane ...
14. We could see the distant mountains if ...
15. If she practised harder, she ...

Exercise No 98

If	Past Perfect	Conditional Perfect
If	I had known the answer,	I would have told you it.

Supply the correct tense of the verb:

1. It would have been better if they (not come).
2. If he hadn't explained it to me, I never (understand).
3. If I had worked harder in my youth, I (be) a rich man now.
4. He would never have behaved like that if he (have) a good education.
5. They would have done it if they (know) how.
6. The soldiers (fight) better if they had been given clear orders.
7. The dog would have bitten you if it (not be tied) up.
8. We (play) tennis yesterday if it (not rain).
9. If the children had been good, their mother (give) them some cake.
10. If the students (study) harder, they (pass) their examinations.
11. I should never have troubled him, if I (know) he was so busy.
12. He (miss) his train if he (not hurry).

13. If my watch (not stop), I should have been on time.
14. Mary would have been sick if she (eat) all those sweets.
15. If he (fall) overboard, he (drown).

Exercise No 99

Finish these sentences with the same tense sequence as in Exercise No 98:

1. If the policeman hadn't shown me the way, I . . .
2. If you hadn't called me, he . . .
3. If we had lived a century ago, . . .
4. If the window hadn't been open, the thief . . .
5. My mother would have been very angry with me if she . . .
6. The streets would have been full if . . .
7. I should have broken my glasses if . . .
8. The other team would have won the match if it . . .
9. The 'Queen Mary' would have arrived on time if . . .
10. If I had dropped that priceless vase, my wife . . .
11. If the car hadn't broken down, we . . .
12. The pupil would have been punished if he . . .
13. That building would never have been finished if the architect . . .
14. He would never have won his case if his lawyer . . .
15. The burglar would never have got in if . . .
16. Would you have married me if I . . .?

Exercise No 100

Past Perfect Inverted	Conditional Perfect
Had I known,	I should never have gone.

Complete the following sentences:

1. Had he . . ., he would have met her.
2. Had they . . . they would have built a bigger house.
3. Had we . . . we should have caught the train.
4. Had Shakespeare . . ., he would have been very surprised at our actors.
5. Had I . . . he would never have repaid me.

6. Had the jury . . ., they would never have found the prisoner guilty.
7. Had he not . . ., he would never have seen the fight.
8. Had we not worked hard last year, we . . .
9. Had our friends not warned us, we . . .
10. Had the cinema not been full, we . . .
11. Had it not been a hot day . . .
12. Had they not brought their books with them, the teacher . . .
13. Had he lived to see it, my father . . .
14. Had they all done what they said they would, we . . .

Exercise No 101. Mixed Types Using 'Unless'

Finish the following sentences:

1. Unless I am very much mistaken, this . . .
2. He won't answer unless . . .
3. Unless it is very fine, we . . .
4. I can't help you, unless . . .
5. He could never have achieved that, unless his wife . . .
6. I would never take a gun with me, unless . . .
7. The servant would never open the door, unless there . . .
8. I should never have gone to the cinema, unless you . . .
9. We shall never arrive in time, unless . . .
10. Unless you do what I say, . . .
11. Unless he were to do something silly now, I think he . . .
12. They could never understand properly, unless you . . .
13. Your hair will never look nice, unless you . . .
14. Unless you mean to offend your host, you . . .
15. You will never play the piano well unless . . .

Exercise No 102

Complete the following sentences:

1. Supposing you had five minutes to spare, what . . .
2. Provided that you do what I say, you . . .
3. As long as our children are well, what . . .?
4. If only he would study harder, he . . .
5. Suppose you take 3 from 27, what . . .?
6. I shan't mind so long as you . . .
7. If only he hadn't been thinking of something else, the car . . .

SECTION 8   CONDITIONAL SENTENCES

8. Provided he gets the telegram, he . . .
9. Don't worry so long as . . .
10. Supposing you wake up in the night, what . . .?
11. Provided that he has the strength, he . . .
12. If only the concert started earlier, we . . .
13. Supposing you won the lottery, what . . .?
14. So long as we have a servant, we . . .
15. Provided that there is a spare ticket, you . . .

Exercise No 103

'Should' Inverted	Future or Imperative
Should it prove to be true,	I shall sell all my shares immediately.

In such conditional sentences the present tenses *must* and *ought to* are considered as Future in sense.

Now complete these sentences:

1. We shall be forced to act should . . .
2. We must certainly buy some more, should . . .
3. Should he wake up . . .
4. Should there be a seat free, you ought to . . .
5. Should that happen, . . .
6. Should the worst come to the worst, . . .
7. Give it her, should she . . .
8. Tell him to come and see me should you . . .
9. Should the job turn out to be too difficult . . .
10. Should the mountain be too steep, we . . .
11. Should the weather be fine, . . .
12. Take it away from him should he . . .
13. Should the train be late, we must . . .

SECTION 9

PREPOSITIONS

Exercise No 104. Prepositions of Time

Besides those prepositions of time whose meaning is quite clear, such as:

Until, before, after, during

there are a number of others which are often used with other meanings than time and for that reason are often misused:

At, for, in, since, by, from, on

1. *At* is used with an exact point of time, for example: with hours, moments, also with the names of festivals:

   At three o'clock, at this moment, at Christmas

2. *In* is generally used with the Future Tense to show the period within which an action will happen. It is also used with seasons, years, and parts of the day and months:

   In two months' time, in 1958, in January, in the morning

3. *By* is used to show the latest time at which an action will be finished. It is generally used therefore with the Future Tenses:

   He will probably arrive by 6 o'clock.

4. *For* is used with periods of time to show how long an action lasts. It is most frequently used with the Perfect Tense in speaking, but is also found with the other tenses:

   I have lived here for three years.

5. *Since* is used with a point of time in the past from which some action began and continues until the time of speaking. Used with the Perfect Tense:

   I have lived here since 1952.

6. *On* is used with more general points of time than *at*, usually with days and dates:

   On Wednesday, on March 5th, on a Friday afternoon, on his birthday.

7. *From* is used with the starting point of any action in the past or future and is nearly always found with *to* or *till*. Compare it with *since*, which is used only with a point in the past and only for an action which lasts until the moment of speaking.

   He lived in London from 1950 until 1957.
   I shall be at home from 6 p.m. until 9 p.m.

SECTION 9 — PREPOSITIONS

Supply the missing prepositions:

1. I will meet you there ... six o'clock sharp.
2. It will all be over ... five minutes.
3. He has been waiting there ... five o'clock.
4. The swallows gather and leave England ... the autumn.
5. The family are all gathering again ... Christmas.
6. I can't tell you ... the moment but if you will wait I'll let you know ... a few minutes.
7. It has been the same old story ever ... he was a little boy.
8. We have had no rain now ... three months.
9. I'm sorry I can't come as I have an appointment ... Thursday ... 2.30.
10. He still comes to see me ... time to time.
11. I wonder if you could get it done ... tomorrow.
12. She called the police immediately, but ... the time they arrived the thief was miles away.
13. The house should be finished ... next month.
14. Wait a bit! He should be here ... a few minutes.
15. He's been in bed ... the last week.
16. He's been living in his new house ... last week.
17. Everybody buys a new hat ... Easter.
18. They may arrive ... any time now.
19. She always goes to visit her old aunt ... Saturdays.
20. The dinner should be over ... ten o'clock.
21. This contract expires ... December 31st.
22. The applications must be handed in ... December 31st.
23. They have been living here ... 1953.
24. ... six years' time he will be twenty-one.
25. It always gets cool here ... the evening.
26. His father was away on a journey ... the day that he was born.
27. He has been sick ... the day that he arrived.
28. ... January 1st there has been no work done in this factory.
29. I expect him to call me ... any moment.
30. If you can wait, he should be here ... a short time.
31. It is pleasant to go out for a walk ... a fine summer's evening.
32. You don't think he's going to stay ... ever, do you?
33. We are going to try to set off ... daybreak.
34. He has been lame in that leg ... childhood.

35. ... a cold night in January 1942, there appeared at the door of the house six escaped prisoners.
36. I am always in town ... a Saturday morning.
37. He'll be in town ... Monday till Saturday.
38. They come to visit us ... time to time.
39. He has been in hospital ... January.
40. He was in hospital ... January until June.

Exercise No 105. 'For' and 'Since'

These two prepositions used with phrases of time are frequently confused:

1. *For* is used only with periods of time and can frequently be omitted—

    He has lived here for three years.
    He has lived here all his life.

2. *Since* is used with points in time and cannot be omitted—

    He has lived here since 1953.

    Note these two phrases which can easily be confused:

    He has been ill since last week.
    He has been ill for the last week.

Now repeat each of these sentences twice using the phrases of time in brackets and supplying the prepositions *for* or *since*:

1. He has been learning Latin. (years) (the beginning of the year)
2. Mary has been married to John. (twenty-five years) (before the war)
3. They have been away on holiday. (the end of the month) (March 30th)
4. She has been teaching them the piano. (their birthday) (a long time)
5. He has been waiting. (the whole afternoon) (lunchtime)
6. We have been asleep. (the moment we arrived) (all the afternoon)
7. I haven't seen you. (ages) (leaving school)
8. Mary hasn't been to the theatre. (a long time) (her illness)

9. They said they hadn't read the newspaper.	(the last few days) (the beginning of their holidays)
10. She told him she had been in hospital.	(three weeks) (the month before)

Exercise No 106. 'Under', 'Underneath', 'Below', 'Beneath', 'Over' and 'Above'

The prepositions: *under, underneath, beneath, below, over* and *above* are sometimes confused with each other.

1. *Under, underneath, beneath* all have the same meaning basically, but:

   (a) *under* is the ordinary preposition of position—

   There's some dust under the table.

   (b) *beneath* is more often used figuratively—

   She has married beneath her.

   (c) *underneath* is also used as an adverb—

   I found nothing underneath.

2. *Over* and *above* are frequently used interchangeably, but:

   (a) *above* means only *higher than*—

   They saw the snow mountains towering above them.

   (b) *over* means *vertically above*—

   We hung your calendar over the fireplace.

3. In the same way, *below* means *lower than*, and *under* means *vertically below*:

   We could see the valley below us.
   There was snow under our feet.

4. *Under* and *beneath*, *over* and *above* can all be used figuratively:

   He was above me at school.
   I have no power over him.
   He has three men working under him.
   His actions are beneath contempt.

Supply the missing prepositions:

1. First stick a stamp on this receipt and then write your name ... it.
2. Take this contract and sign your name ... mine.
3. He was generally known ... the name of Charles.
4. Mr. Robinson is well-known: he's travelled all ... the world.
5. My hat fell ... a chair as I was leaving the room.

6. I have a nasty cut ... the knee and another ... the foot.
7. He could not make himself heard ... the noise of the engines.
8. ... all, remember this!
9. The dog took the bone and buried it ... the ground.
10. He suffers from arthritis and has been ... treatment for a long time.
11. The maid carefully spread the cloth ... the table.
12. Kingston is ... London, on the Thames.
13. In the fields ... my house, they keep a flock of sheep.
14. It is absolutely intolerable working ... these conditions.
15. She is rather snobbish and doesn't like mixing with people ... her.
16. As usual the dog has taken up his position ... the table.
17. When he reached the top he could see the others still struggling up the path far ... him.
18. I am surprised at Joan. I thought she was ... that sort of thing.
19. He is a despicable man and utterly ... my notice.
20. He has lost all his fortune and finds himself ... the necessity of begging.
21. Before leaving the office she remembered to put the cover ... the typewriter.
22. My house stands a good way ... the village, and it is a hard climb to the shop.
23. The raincoat is rather small and I doubt if you can put it ... your coat.
24. They were standing on the hillside in a line one ... the other.
25. My cabin is a very poor one and well ... the waterline.
26. The children are always climbing ... the wall to steal my fruit.
27. You can't go that way, I'm afraid, as the road is ... repair.
28. The man was led away ... guard.
29. The young shoots appear ... ground in early spring.
30. I was certainly ... the impression that he had arrived.
31. These things aren't cheap. You certainly can't get one ... £5.
32. I'm afraid he can't sign this as he's ... age.
33. I certainly shall not allow such a letter to be sent ... my signature.
34. He has ten men working ... him.

SECTION 9 — PREPOSITIONS

Exercise No 107. 'Between' and 'Among'

1. *Between* is used with:

    (a) two persons or things—
    He stood between his son and daughter.

    (b) any two of a larger number—
    He walked across the garden between the flower beds.

    (c) the speaker and a group—
    Ladies and Gentlemen! Between ourselves, I have . . .

2. *Among* is used with more than two people or things and has a less exact meaning of place:

    Life among the Eskimos.

Supply the correct preposition:

1. Life ... the Arabs has been described by Doughty.
2. I was sitting ... my two sisters when the bell rang.
3. She divided the cake ... her five children.
4. I can't see any difference ... these two books.
5. We spent our last holidays ... the mountains, north of Lake Como.
6. She gave him a pound of apples, but there wasn't a good one ... them.
7. She hid ... the bushes at the bottom of the garden.
8. I've invited John ... others.
9. War has just broken out ... the two neighbouring countries.
10. They can never agree ... themselves. I should punish both of them.
11. That family is always quarrelling ... themselves.
12. Confidentially and ... ourselves, I can't stand her.
13. The railway line runs ... the river and the road.

Exercise No 108. 'At' and 'In' in Phrases of Place

At is used to show the exact point: houses, stations, small villages, etc.; *in* has the idea of within a larger area and is consequently used with bigger towns, valleys, countries.

   Examples:

   I was standing in the street when the storm broke.
   She waited half an hour at the corner of the street.

Supply the missing prepositions:

1. You'll find our house ... the end of the next street.
2. It is strictly forbidden to park ... the middle of the street.
3. Why is it she prefers to sit ... the back of the class?
4. They kept their radio ... the corner of the room.
5. There's a ruined castle ... the top of the hill, and another ... the valley.
6. She lives ... a little house near Manchester. Her children prefer to live ... the town itself.
7. The train arrives ... Waterloo at 6.30.
8. You'll find it much more expensive living ... London than ... Paris.
9. He was born ... Yorkshire and still lives ... Linton, the village of his birth.
10. The runners were all lined up ... the starting point.
11. He is staying ... a hotel ... the middle of the city.
12. She met him ... the front door.
13. ... the southern hemisphere the longest day falls in December.
14. But ... the North Pole the sun never rises on that day.
15. ... Spain and ... some countries of South and Central America they love bull-fights.
16. They now live ... the north of England.

Exercise No 109. Prepositions of Direction Towards

| for | at | to |
| against | | towards |

For is used for direction only when the verb indicates beginning of a movement:

> I left for home.
> They set off for London.

Against has the meaning of pressure or contact:

> She threw it against the wall.
> The crowd pressed against the fence.

At is generally used with certain verbs:

aim at	point at
laugh at	stare at
look at	throw at etc.

It frequently has the idea of aim:

> Throw a stone at the fierce dog.
> Compare: Throw a ball to the children.

Towards has the sense of direction, while *to* generally that of destination:

> They went towards the scene of the crash but were stopped by a policeman.
> They ran to the scene of the crash to see what help they could give.

Supply the missing prepositions:

1. I shall come ... your house at four o'clock.
2. He leaned ... me and whispered in my ear.
3. We shall be leaving ... the country tomorrow at daybreak.
4. They ran ... the accident, pushing him ... the wall as they passed.
5. The train ... Glasgow leaves in two minutes.
6. He aimed the rifle straight ... his enemy.
7. Just throw that book over ... me, I want to look something up.
8. His pupils used to make him so angry that he threw books ... them.
9. Don't laugh ... me, I'm doing my best.
10. Just have a look ... this, if you please!
11. Lock it up so that the children can't get ... it!
12. The 'Mauretania' sails ... New York this evening.
13. It was getting late, so we set off ... home.
14. They were heading ... the north, when the pilot changed course.
15. The country seems to be moving ... war.
16. I shall fight ... this measure until my dying day.
17. They all go most unwillingly ... school in the morning.
18. Just point ... the one you want and I'll get it for you.
19. We were always told as children it was rude to point ... people.
20. Kings used to lead their armies ... the enemy in person.

Exercise No 110. Prepositions of Direction From

| from | of |
| off | out of |

1. *From* is used with the point of departure:

    They ran from the scene of the crime.

2. *Of* is used only in fixed expressions with the sense of *from*:

    Die of, made of, ask of, expect of

3. *Off* has the meaning *from the surface of* and also *down from*:

    Take the book off the table.
    He fell off his horse.

4. *Out of* means *from the interior* and has *into* as an opposite.

    He took his handkerchief out of his pocket.
    She took the parcels out of the car and carried them into the house.

Supply the missing preposition:

1. Take those papers ... the drawer and give them to me.
2. Wipe the dust ... the table.
3. I am trying to wash the stain ... your shirt.
4. He took the toy ... his sister and played with it himself.
5. I would ask ... you that you never do it again.
6. It is too much to expect ... them.
7. Have you heard ... your friends recently?
8. He's a bad rider. He's always falling ... his bicycle.
9. Take your elbows ... the table and sit up.
10. It's difficult to keep the dogs ... the flower beds.
11. She's so attractive he can't keep away ... her.
12. He couldn't keep himself ... falling ... the wall.
13. Please get ... the carpet while I'm sweeping.
14. I borrowed these shoes ... my sister.
15. Poor Mary! She's suffering ... a nasty cold in the head.
16. It's one of those diseases the doctor can't cure you ...
17. They live about a mile ... the centre of the town.
18. The accident happened within a mile ... their house.
19. Wine is made ... grapes and whisky ... barley.
20. This ring is made ... gold and yours is ... silver.

Exercise No 111. 'In', 'With' and 'Of', Describing People and Their Clothes

These three prepositions are frequently used in phrases describing people and their clothes.

1. *In* is used with everything (clothes, jewellery, etc.) actually worn on the body:

    A girl in a red dress.
    A woman in gold earrings.

2. *With* is used with anything which is carried:

    A lady with a black handbag.
    A man with an umbrella.

3. *With* is used for physical features and peculiarities, i.e. diseases:

    A man with red hair.
    A boy with a limp.

4. *Of* is used with permanent qualities of character, and ages:

    A man of violent temper.
    A man of fifty-three.

    Note: *With* can also be used with qualities of character, but in general suggests less permanent conditions:

    A man of common sense.
    A man with common sense.

Now add the appropriate prepositions in these phrases and sentences:

1. A young fellow ... a broken leg
2. A woman ... great wealth
3. An employee ... limited ability
4. A nurse ... uniform
5. Some peasants ... their national dress
6. A porter ... a bundle on his back
7. Soldiers ... battledress
8. An old man ... a red beard
9. An actor ... a wig
10. A young woman ... a wedding ring
11. A young couple ... quiet habits
12. A player ... football clothes
13. Four young men ... pleasant appearance ... grey suits
14. A girl ... about sixteen ... a pearl necklace
15. He is a man ... considerable achievements.

16. A gardener ... a spade
17. A boy ... toothache
18. Can you see that man ... black ... a briefcase?
19. That man ... a bald head and only one arm is an old soldier.
20. That lady ... red ... a shopping basket is my sister.

Exercise No 112. 'At'

This is a list of the principal collocations * with *at*:

at dinner, breakfast, table, etc.	at sight, at first sight
at work, play	at short notice, a moment's notice
at war, peace	
at length, last	at home, church, sea, Mass, school.
at will (=*as one wishes*)	
at a loss (=*not to know how*)	at a pinch
at best, worst, most, least, first	at all events (=*anyhow*)
at this, that (=*whereupon*)	at present
at a profit, loss	at once
at any rate (=*anyhow*)	at all costs
at a time, at the same time	at hand
at times	at ease, rest
	at heart

Now replace the part of these sentences in italics by the correct collocation:

1. He felt perfectly well before dinner, but while *he was eating* he had to retire.
2. I am *unable* to explain where all the money has gone.
3. He called her a liar, *whereupon* she got up and left him without a word.
4. She is only twenty-five. *Anyhow*, that is what she says.
5. Most people find it difficult to read and listen to the radio *simultaneously*.
6. *Sometimes* I think he isn't quite right in his head.
7. I took a dislike to her *from the moment I saw her*.
8. Most people don't like being disturbed *while they are working*.
9. Sweden has not been *fighting* with her neighbours for over two hundred years.

* A collocation is a group of words frequently found together. It often has a meaning that cannot be easily understood even if the meaning of each word in the group is known.

10. If you arrange to sit near the television set you can turn it off *when you want*.
11. *When I looked first* I thought it was a horse, but on approaching I saw it was a mule.
12. What a noise the children make *while they are playing*!
13. Let us see if Philip's able to sit quietly *when he is eating*.
14. I haven't much money on me. I can lend you *not more than £3*.
15. He had been waiting for half an hour when, *finally*, she came.
16. *When you see him first* he would appear stupid, but he's really quite bright.
17. He bought his stock when prices were low and now he's sold it *for more money than he paid*.
18. I must confess that, *on occasions*, he annoys me.
19. He's not really such a bad fellow *basically*.
20. You must act *immediately* if you are to save his life.
21. We must recover the stolen goods *whatever it may cost us*.
22. It is wise to have a doctor *near by* in case of emergency.
23. I suppose we could arrive by six o'clock *with difficulty*, if you wanted us to.
24. The firemen are always ready to leave the station *the moment after they are called*.
25. Are you ever sick *on a ship*?

Exercise No 113

The sentences in the preceding exercise do not include examples of all the collocations listed. Students will now make their own examples of them.

Notice particularly the following points:

1. *At first* and *at last* are not opposites. The correct construction is—

    At first he . . . and *then* (or *finally*) he . . .
    We . . . for a long time and *at last* they . . .

2. *At rest* is not the same as *resting* or *taking a rest*. It means *not moving* and is the opposite of *in motion*.
3. *At a pinch* means *with difficulty* and *by a special effort*.
4. Notice that *at once* and *all at once* are not synonymous—

    Come at once! (=*immediately*)
    All at once the lion sprang. (=*suddenly*)

5. *At a time* and *at the same time* are usually synonymous, but note the special use of *at the same time* (=*nevertheless*)—

   I am prepared to pay the bill, but, at the same time, I feel I ought to point out that . . .

6. *At present* and *presently* are not synonymous—

   He is at present in Plymouth. (=*now*)
   She will come presently. (=*soon*)

7. Notice the construction *to be at a loss to* + infinitive (=*not to know how to*)—

   I am at a loss to understand the purpose of that instrument.

Exercise No 114. 'By'

These are the most common collocations with the preposition *by*:

by land, sea, air	by no means
by ship, plane, car, bus, etc.	by all means
by heart	by rights
by letter, post, hand, cable, telegram	by degrees
by day, night	by the way
by chance, design	by sight, name
by mistake	by surprise
by accident, good fortune, luck	by far
by oneself, himself, yourself, etc.	

Now replace the italicized words in the following sentences with a suitable collocation:

1. Oh dear! I've left my books behind *unintentionally*.
2. A bat is one of those animals that sleep *during the day* and fly *during the night*.
3. *It was lucky that* I met him just outside the station, or I should never have known that he was going away.
4. That knob was put on the machine *intentionally* so that you could switch it off in an emergency.
5. Of course, everybody knows Mr. Jones *to look at*, but I think very few have ever spoken to him.
6. It's nice to meet you, Mrs. Smith; of course, I've known *your name* for a long time.
7. I'm sure you can't possibly carry all that *alone*. Let me help you.
8. The Jones are *much* the richest people in this town.
9. Don't punish him. He only broke that cup *accidentally*.

SECTION 9 PREPOSITIONS 115

10. He was officially informed *through the telegraph* of the death of his father.
11. This is *much* the most difficult of the exercises.
12. It is only *accidentally* that you see me here. I ought to be in the office.
13. This letter isn't for me. It got delivered here *in error*.
14. This exercise is *certainly not* so difficult as it appears.
15. *Certainly* borrow my book if you want to.
16. He should be here already *really*.
17. They told her that the injured child was learning to walk again *gradually*.
18. *Incidentally*, the book you lost was found in the train, and you must go to the office to claim it.

Exercise No 115

Now make your own sentences to illustrate these collocations.

Notice the following points:

by all means = as far as the speaker is concerned, with pleasure—
> By all means borrow that book if you want to.

by rights = if all goes according to plan and calculation—
> They should have arrived at six o'clock by rights.

by the way is an interjection which introduces an afterthought—
> Oh! by the way, before I forget, I brought these . . .

by oneself = alone and without help—
> He was standing by himself in the corner.
> I can't carry that by myself. It's too heavy.

by far is only used with superlatives to intensify the meaning—
> He is by far the most intelligent man I know.

Exercise No 116. 'In'

These are the principal collocations with the preposition *in*:

in common	in love
in fun, play	in need
in a hurry	in itself
in public, private, secret	in other words
in time	in a way, that way, some way, etc.
in debt, difficulties, danger	

in half, pieces, two, etc.
in ink, pencil, paint
in place, cf. out of place
in sight, cf. out of sight
in tears
in all
in any case, that case, some cases
in fact, name
in particular
in a sense (=*understood in one way*)
in short, brief, a word
in all likelihood, probability
in turn, cf. out of turn
in bed
in trouble
in hand
in work, cf. out of work
in the long run
in due course
in the end (=*at last, eventually*)
in general

Now replace the parts of these sentences in italics by a suitable collocation:

1. It's surprising they got married. They seem to have no interests *which they share*.
2. Don't be offended. I only said it *as a joke*.
3. The swimmer was *having difficulties* when they threw him a lifebelt.
4. I suppose he'll pay *eventually*, but it seems a long time to wait.
5. There was nobody *to be seen* when we came round the corner.
6. Her priceless antique vase fell on the floor and was broken *completely*.
7. After the charwoman has dusted my desk, nothing seems to be *where it ought*.
8. He came downstairs *crying* and said that his elder brother had hit him.
9. What you say is, *understood in one way*, true; but I should express it differently.
10. This exercise should be done *with a pen*, but the next one can be done *with a pencil* if you like.
11. What you say is, *taken in one way*, true, but I should be inclined to express it differently.
12. The exercise was full of mistakes, badly written, incomplete, careless; *to express it briefly*, quite useless.
13. If you include the members of the family, there were fifty-two people there *altogether*.
14. *Specially*, I want to impress on you the need for extreme caution.

15. You will not often find a mean man helping anyone *who needs anything*.
16. This exercise is not *inherently* difficult but just needs care and patience.
17. If you go on throwing your money about like that you'll soon find yourself *owing money*.
18. You tell me you are feeling sick. *If that is true*, I should go to bed straight away.
19. We've got to get some more money *by some means or other* if we are going to succeed.
20. He told me that he would *very probably* arrive today.
21. You'll have to finish that *quickly* if you want to catch the post.
22. The workers came to the cashier *one by one* to draw their pay.
23. He's a very naughty boy and is always *being punished* for his mischief.
24. They'll learn Chinese *eventually* if they keep on trying.
25. The doctor said he would attend to the minor casualties *as soon as he could* after treating the seriously wounded.
26. The novel ended happily, and the young couple were married *at last*.

Exercise No 117. 'On'

These are the most common collocations with the preposition *on*:

on fire	on purpose
on business, pleasure, holiday, vacation	on the other hand
	on the contrary
on duty, watch, guard	on the whole
on a visit, leave	on no (my, any, etc.) account
on a journey, one's way	on second thoughts
on sale, cf. for sale	on the average
on foot, horseback	

Now replace the words in italics by a suitable collocation:

1. When you tell him something he always does the opposite *deliberately*.
2. Mr. Smith has had to hurry to town *to do some business*.
3. Colonel Roberts was posted to Aldershot *in the course of his duty*.
4. This student always makes a lot of mistakes. *However*, his writing is legible.
5. If it is a fine morning I always go *walking* to the office.

6. You can, of course, do as you please, but *generally speaking*, I think it would be wiser to postpone it.
7. I met my wife while I was *visiting* London.
8. They have a large stock of watches *to be sold* in that shop.
9. When they got back from the cinema they found their house *burning*.
10. We left two men *guarding*, while we went to fetch the police.
11. Miami is the sort of place you would only think of visiting *if you wanted to enjoy yourself*.
12. The most extraordinary thing happened to me in Teheran *while I was having leave*.
13. I think it is much better to make an early start *if you are going to travel*.
14. It is curious how children always behave much worse when they are *having their holidays*.
15. Señor Alvarez looks a fine figure *when riding*.
16. It's my turn *to do duty* tonight, and I don't feel at all well.
17. I'm quite safe. There's no need to worry *about me*.
18. She told her children that they must not, *whatever happened*, play with matches.
19. *On thinking it over*, I've decided it would be better to travel by sea.
20. They say more boys are born than girls *as a rule*.

Exercise No 118. 'Out of'

These are the principal collocations with the preposition *out of*:

out of breath	*out of doors
*out of work	*out of reach
*out of sight, hearing	out of the ordinary
*out of danger	*out of practice
*out of order, repair	out of date
*out of use	out of the question
*out of place	*out of turn
out of control	*out of stock

(*Note:* Those collocations marked with an asterisk have a phrase of opposite meaning formed with *in* or *within*.)

Now replace the parts of these sentences in italics by a suitable collocation:

1. He has been *unemployed* for some years.
2. We stood waving until the train *could not be seen any more*.

SECTION 9 — PREPOSITIONS

3. The doctor told her that her son was *safe*.
4. I took my watch to the watchmaker because it was not *going right*.
5. This mine has been *disused* for a long time.
6. It is most important that this experiment should not get *so that you cannot control it*.
7. It is a pity not to be *outside* on such a lovely day.
8. The shopman was sorry he could not supply the material as it was *no longer available*.
9. When there are little children about, matchboxes should be kept *where they cannot be reached*.
10. Such a solution *cannot be considered*.
11. Those opinions are now considered *old fashioned*.
12. He ran all the way home and arrived *panting*.
13. They waited until they *could not be heard any more*.
14. Wait! It's my turn. You mustn't play *in the wrong order*.
15. I haven't played tennis for years. I *lack practice*.

Exercise No 119. Collocations with the Word 'Time'

The word *time* is found in a large number of collocations. Here is a list:

at times (=*sometimes*)
at a time (when)
one, two, etc., at a time (=*one by one*, etc.)
in time (=*before the appointed hour*)
in time (=*after the passage of a certain period*)
before my time
at that time (=*then*)
at one time (=*once, but not now*)
behind the times (=*out of date*)
by that time

for a time
once upon a time
to time (=*according to the schedule*) in a general sense
on time (=*punctual*)
time after time, time and time again
in time(s) of
at the time (=*on a particular occasion*)
at the same time
for the time being

Now replace the parts of the following sentences in italics by one of the collocations given above:

1. The train drew into the station *at the scheduled hour*.
2. *Once* I thought I should like to be an engine driver, but I grew out of that.
3. They raised the alarm at half past eleven, but *already* it was too late.

E

4. Yes, I did hear that Dr. Williams had been married, but that was *before I was old enough to understand*.
5. *During a certain period* the two cars were abreast, but gradually one went ahead.
6. War broke out in 1914, but I was only a baby *then*.
7. He made his fortune *during the period when* others were going bankrupt.
8. If you think that, you are hopelessly *out of date in your ideas*.
9. It is very difficult to keep the trains running *according to plan* in the winter.
10. He is still very young. He'll learn to do it *eventually*.
11. It's very narrow. You'll have to go along *one by one*.
12. *Once* there was a poor woodcutter, who . . .
13. I've told you that *repeatedly* and still you don't do it right.
14. *When there's a* drought it is often forbidden to use water for the garden.
15. *Sometimes* I get a curious pain in my leg, doctor.
16. I never thought of it *while it was happening*, but later I realized that I ought to have been more careful.
17. Let's leave the problem *temporarily*; we can return to it later.

Exercise No 120

Now make your own sentences incorporating the above collocations with the word *time*.

> Note especially the difference between *on time* and *in time*:
> (a) *on time* means *punctually* and *according to the timetable*—
>   That bus never arrives on time.
> (b) *in time* means *before something else begins, not necessarily planned*. It is the opposite of *too late*—
>   He did not arrive in time to say goodbye to her.
>   He did not come in time to see his father before he died.

Exercise No 121. Adjectives Followed by Prepositions 'To' and 'At'

Supply the missing prepositions using only *to* or *at*:
1. He is quite blind ... her faults.
2. He is extraordinarily clever ... mimicking others.
3. She, on the other hand, is very efficient ... her work.

4. He is an expert ... making himself understood in foreign languages.
5. Contrary ... my expectations, I quite enjoyed myself at the party.
6. She was standing too close ... the fire and got burned.
7. That fellow's no good ... games at all.
8. He carried out the project which had always been dear ... his heart.
9. We are all very indignant ... the injustice done to him.
10. I'm sorry! I'm very bad ... explaining myself.
11. He's the one who's so very lucky ... cards.
12. That device is entirely new ... me.
13. He's not equal ... the job they've given him.
14. He remained faithful ... his principles in spite of great pressure.
15. The delay proved fatal ... our plans.
16. She was overjoyed ... the prospect of meeting him again.
17. His activities are very harmful ... my interests.
18. The government showed itself hostile ... any progress.
19. She's so terribly cruel ... her dog.
20. I engaged him because he was so prompt ... understanding my instructions.
21. He was heart-broken ... her indifference to him.
22. He doesn't like me although I've always been kind ... him.
23. Yes; he's the kind of person who is always quick ... figures.
24. This is much inferior ... the one I bought last week.
25. You will be liable ... a heavy fine if you do that.
26. This flower is not native ... England.
27. Naturally she was sad ... the death of her parrot.
28. He does his work carefully but he's terribly slow ... it.
29. Who wouldn't be triumphant ... their success in the examination?
30. A dutiful daughter and obedient ... her parents.
31. You shouldn't be surprised ... a thing like that.
32. It should be obvious ... the meanest intelligence.
33. The seeds are peculiar ... this genus of plant.
34. Can't you manage to be a little more polite . . your aunt.
35. He works in a factory. Previous ... that he was in a laundry.
36. I have been truly astonished ... the number of people who believe it.

AN ENGLISH PRACTICE BOOK

37. This is quite irrelevant ... the matter we are discussing.
38. They were shocked ... his apparent lack of appreciation.
39. He was so rude ... her that she never spoke to him again.
40. Sacred ... the memory of Mary Jones.
41. They are very sensitive ... people's opinion of them.
42. I've got one similar ... yours.
43. Subject ... the exigencies of the service
44. The people of this country are very skilful ... making dolls.
45. It's useful ... me to have him about the house.
46. It's vital ... a proper understanding of the problem.

Exercise No 122

Supply the missing prepositions, using *with*, *for* or *of*:

1. Don't be afraid ... the dog! It won't bite you.
2. I can't be angry ... him now that he's apologized ... what he has done.
3. He's far ahead ... the others in arithmetic.
4. You ought to be ashamed ... yourself.
5. Are you aware ... the fact that it is half past ten.
6. I'm sorry. They are simply not capable ... doing it.
7. Don't disturb him! He's busy ... his accounts.
8. He's ambitious and eager ... honours.
9. For goodness sake! Do be careful ... that vase. You could easily drop it.
10. Children must be taught to be careful ... traffic.
11. I am not at all certain ... the date of his arrival.
12. His explanation was not consistent ... the facts.
13. Monsieur X was famous ... his collection of pictures.
14. I was conscious ... a feeling of uneasiness.
15. Kingston lies due west ... London.
16. I'm sorry. I'm not content ... your explanations.
17. The soldier was pronounced fit ... service.
18. Mary was terribly envious ... Joan's new hat.
19. We are all very fond ... going to the theatre.
20. John is very discontented ... his salary.
21. I shall be grateful ... any advice you can give me.
22. This exercise is full ... the most terrible mistakes.
23. Are you familiar ... the works of Milton?
24. The manager is well qualified ... his position.

25. That is something I am profoundly glad ...
26. This chair is not identical ... the one I bought last year.
27. He's a sporting fellow, and always ready ... anything.
28. That student is ignorant ... the first rules of grammar.
29. Your explanation is incompatible ... the story I heard.
30. John, you will be responsible ... providing the drinks.
31. Judges must be independent ... political pressure.
32. I know he's a difficult child, but you must be patient ... him.
33. I am extremely sorry ... the delay, but I was held up.
34. He was jealous ... his brother's good fortune.
35. Comedians are always popular ... holiday crowds.
36. I can't bake a cake as we are short ... eggs this week.
37. His income is sufficient ... his needs.
38. He's always very shy ... approaching his chief.
39. Let us be thankful ... small mercies.
40. It is wise to be sure ... your facts before you speak.
41. One is generally tolerant ... small faults.
42. She is unfortunately devoid ... a sense of humour.
43. They gave him a visa valid ... all countries in Europe.
44. I'm tired ... arguing with you.
45. They proved themselves unworthy ... the trust which was placed in them.

Exercise No 123

Supply the missing prepositions, using *from*, *about*, *on* or *in*:

1. Keep away ... the machine while it is running.
2. He was singularly fortunate ... his choice of wallpaper.
3. He is intent ... attending the football match on Saturday.
4. I am very dubious ... your chances of passing the examination.
5. They are proficient ... the use of their fists.
6. This is quite different ... what I expected.
7. The diet here is deficient ... vitamins.
8. That young man is very keen ... cycling.
9. We are all very enthusiastic ... our next holiday.
10. It was far ... my intention to suggest that he was unintelligent.
11. He was perfectly honest ... his intentions to win the prize at all costs.

12. The secretary was not well qualified ... shorthand.
13. Some people appear completely immune ... this disease.
14. I am very reluctant ... asking him to do this.
15. Our plans must remain dependent ... the weather.
16. Everybody was very uneasy ... the outcome of the negotiations.
17. Of course, you are quite right ... that.
18. He was involved in an accident, resulting ... the slippery condition of the road.
19. The enemy is weak ... artillery.
20. Entomologists are still curious ... the life cycle of that moth.
21. I am not very interested ... the story of your life.
22. Put that cake back in the cupboard, where it will be safe ... the cat.
23. I'm afraid he is quite wrong ... the date of the invasion.
24. His father was very sad ... his son's failure in his final exams.
25. I am extremely doubtful ... the wisdom of pursuing that course of action.

Exercise No 124. Verbs Followed by Prepositions

Supply the preposition *at* or *to* as appropriate:

1. What time did you arrive ... your home?
2. He finds it difficult to accustom himself ... the climate.
3. All the visitors exclaimed ... the beauty of the place.
4. Just glance ... this for me, would you?
5. His debts amount ... a considerable sum.
6. I can only guess ... the extent of the damage.
7. It is useless to appeal ... his better nature.
8. She hinted darkly ... all sorts of wild actions in his youth.
9. If you want permission, you must apply ... the caretaker.
10. He was attached ... the French Army during the war.
11. He is too sick to attend ... his duties.
12. ... what do you attribute your success in life?
13. I'm sure this one doesn't belong ... me.
14. He challenged him ... a game of chess.
15. It is very unkind to joke ... the expense of the disabled.
16. Shall I compare thee ... a summer's day?
17. If you want them to hear, you'll have to knock a good deal harder ... the door.

18. The prisoner was condemned ... penal servitude for life.
19. The fire was confined ... the kitchen regions.
20. I will never consent ... her marrying that man.
21. Just have a look ... this for me, would you?
22. I have been entirely converted ... the use of an electric razor.
23. Employees who have twenty-five years' service become entitled ... a pension.
24. You can safely entrust your little son ... her care.
25. People who heard her voice marvelled ... it.
26. Let's invite them all ... dinner.
27. Listen ... me!
28. Do you object ... my smoking?
29. He peered ... the exhibit on account of his short-sightedness.
30. Such an idea would never occur ... me!
31. The patient is reacting very unsatisfactorily ... the drug.
32. The children peeped ... the guests as they were arriving.
33. I have been reduced ... using oil for lack of fat.
34. The children are playing ... Red Indians again.
35. She has been forced to resort ... all sorts of devices to avoid him.
36. The patient has not responded ... treatment.
37. It is very rude to point ... people in the street.
38. If you'll bring the drinks, I'll see ... the food.
39. They have been subjected ... all sorts of indignities.
40. I refuse to submit ... that sort of treatment.
41. Can you wonder ... it, if they are reduced ... begging.
42. I'm sorry he finally succumbed ... the temptation of stealing.
43. If you want to pass your examination, you'll have to work very hard ... your Latin.
44. We shall never surrender ... that enemy.
45. I don't know him, but he has been staring ... me for ten minutes.
46. I have never subscribed ... the general opinion of him.
47. Turn ... page 22 and start reading!
48. The government has again yielded ... the pressure from outside.
49. She always trusts ... her neighbours to help her.
50. Would you please reply ... my question!

Exercise No 125

Supply the missing preposition, using *on* or *in*:

1. You would be well advised to act ... his instructions.
2. I have never believed ... all their travellers' tales.
3. They quickly took revenge ... those who injured them.
4. The story of this book is based ... the truth.
5. Children delight ... nonsense rhymes.
6. I shall now call ... Mr. Jones to give the accounts.
7. He has been employed ... that job for twenty years.
8. The newspapers failed completely to comment ... the affair.
9. He has been engaged ... illegal practices for a long time.
10. I must ask you to concentrate a bit more ... your work.
11. We congratulate you ... becoming a father!
12. I must consult my lawyer ... certain delicate matters.
13. Biologists have been experimenting ... rats to help them find the answer.
14. They failed ... their attempt to reach the top.
15. We must now decide ... the form of our answer.
16. You must not depend ... me for financial aid.
17. He has drawn ... his vast experience in writing that book.
18. It is essential to economize ... clothes, when you travel by air.
19. He has just embarked ... a dangerous undertaking.
20. Help me ... my efforts to explain this to her!
21. Are these items included ... the bill?
22. I cannot impress ... you enough the seriousness of the situation.
23. He is always intruding ... our privacy.
24. I like to indulge ... a hot bath.
25. Please don't lean your elbows ... the table!
26. It is a mystery to me to know what they live ...!
27. They will be operating ... him tonight.
28. He performs beautifully ... the flute.
29. She is instructing her niece ... the art of embroidery.
30. Play us something ... the piano!
31. I like people who take pride ... their appearance.
32. She prides herself ... her cakes.
33. She doesn't seem to be very interested ... the film.
34. You may reckon ... my co-operation.
35. Do you think that is a very good firm to invest ...?

36. You can rely ... him implicitly.
37. Go away before you get involved ... the argument!
38. I shall be angry, if you persist ... doing that.
39. I have absolutely nothing to talk ...!
40. They all shared ... the happiness at her success.
41. Don't tread ... the grass!
42. We shall now proceed to vote ... the motion before us.
43. I would not advise you to trust ... him.
44. The Persians were always making war ... the Greeks in the old days.
45. At the moment he's working ... a very secret project.
46. He's very unreliable. You can never count ... him.

Exercise No 126

Supply the missing preposition, using *from* or *of*:

1. She accused her servant ... stealing.
2. Teetotallers are people who abstain ... alcohol.
3. Who can I borrow a pencil ...?
4. He carries a gun to defend himself ... unexpected attacks.
5. I am sure your mother would not approve ... that sort of behaviour.
6. I hastened to assure him ... my support.
7. Beware ... the dog!
8. I should demand an apology ... him, if I were you.
9. He is always boasting ... his tennis.
10. There's no need to complain ... the service in this restaurant.
11. That is a matter on which I differ profoundly ... you.
12. His failure has completely discouraged him ... trying again.
13. This dish tastes funny. What does it consist ...?
14. The officer was dismissed ... the service for incompetence.
15. This word is difficult to distinguish in meaning ... the others.
16. The ship was diverted ... its course by bad weather.
17. The prisoner had never been convicted ... theft before.
18. I want to draw some money ... the bank.
19. You can't convince me ... the necessity of that course of action.
20. They did all they could to cure him ... his disease.
21. She has been eliminated ... the tournament.

22. And what result emerged ... your discussions?
23. I despair ... ever teaching them anything.
24. That is something you cannot escape ...
25. I should never dream ... asking him to do it.
26. He refused to hear ... anything against her.
27. You cannot exclude it ... your calculations.
28. I should be glad to hear ... them, if you know anyone who can help me.
29. Some of these imports are exempt ... duty.
30. His bad leg hinders him ... taking part in the games.
31. He dislikes to be reminded ... his part in the affair.
32. His youth effectively prohibits him ... participation in the matter.
33. You'll have to paint it to protect it ... the weather.
34. He very soon repented ... his impetuosity.
35. I cannot get rid ... this cough.
36. The whole place smelled ... tobacco smoke the next morning.
37. I don't think he will ever recover ... his wife's death.
38. I have long suspected him ... criminal tendencies.
39. It would be wise to refrain ... comment at this stage of the proceedings.
40. What do you think ... this?
41. After breaking the egg, separate the white ... the yolk.
42. She tires very quickly ... all her friends.
43. I must warn you ... the dangers you will meet on the way.
44. She is not the one to shrink ... her duty, however unpleasant it may be.
45. Poor old Mrs. Smith, she has suffered ... rheumatism for forty years.

Exercise No 127

Supply the missing prepositions, using *for*, *with* or *against*:

1. How do you account ... this terrible state of affairs?
2. Let me first acquaint you ... the facts.
3. I'm afraid I'm strongly prejudiced ... him.
4. You can even insure ... loss of income!
5. Who, may I ask, are you supposed to be acting ...?
6. He has been afflicted ... a nervous tic ever since his accident.
7. I don't agree ... you when you say that.

8. She has come to assist ... the spring cleaning.
9. I think you should apologize ... your outrageous behaviour.
10. He was charged ... a whole series of crimes.
11. Go in through that door and ask ... Mr. Johnson.
12. Whatever else I've done, you can't blame me ... that.
13. All of us protest most emphatically ... new regulations.
14. I shall communicate ... you again in due course.
15. You can't compare his work ... mine!
16. It is useless trying to compete ... the world's champion.
17. The prisoner begged ... mercy.
18. This type of work calls ... the most painstaking care.
19. In order to comply ... the regulations, please fill in this form.
20. It doesn't take people long to start reacting ... a government they've just chosen.
21. His explanations conflict ... the facts.
22. How much do they charge ... pencils in that shop?
23. People don't often rebel ... their chosen leaders.
24. I'm afraid you have confused me ... my sister.
25. I would like to exchange my old car ... a new one.
26. This ship requires considerable modifications to fit it ... tropical conditions.
27. His behaviour contrasts most unfavourably ... that of his brother.
28. I feel I should warn you ... using that gun.
29. The whole people is grieving ... the loss of its beloved leader.
30. I'm sorry. I simply cannot cope ... all this work.
31. This exercise is intended ... advanced students.
32. He has been corresponding ... an eminent scientist for years.
33. We are all disgusted ... his atrocious behaviour.
34. And now we will finish ... a song.
35. Conquered peoples have a natural desire to rise ... their rulers.
36. We ought to begin ... the easiest exercises.
37. For years she has been longing ... this day.
38. Do you mind giving me some help ... the washing-up.
39. She is in mourning ... her mother.
40. Hope ... the best and prepare ... the worst.
41. Wise people provide ... a rainy day.
42. Be careful that dog doesn't get infected ... rabies.
43. I do wish you wouldn't interfere ... me.

44. They all set off to search ... the lost member of the party.
45. The whole population was threatened ... extinction.
46. Oil won't mix ... water.
47. I'm looking ... some papers I mislaid.
48. History is the story of the struggle ... power.
49. He had it from his wife and refused to part ... it.
50. In this exercise we are substituting a preposition ... a blank.
51. I think it is useless to struggle ... fate.
52. He is adequately provided ... the necessities of life.
53. Permit me to thank you ... your assistance.
54. Rubber solution is used ... sticking patches on tyres.
55. There they are, quarrelling ... each other again.
56. Doctors are in the forefront of the fight ... disease.
57. Vote ... Smith!
58. It is impossible to reason ... a man of his mentality.
59. If you want to marry her you have to reckon ... her father.
60. I should be satisfied ... half the sum.
61. How long have you been waiting ... your friend to come?

Exercise No 128. Prepositions at the End of Sentences and Clauses

It is normal and correct usage to put prepositions at the end of certain constructions:

(*a*) Questions

What are you looking at?

(*b*) Relative Clauses

This is what I am looking for.

(*c*) Passive Sentences

He was well looked after in hospital.

Supply the prepositions at the end of these sentences:

1. What is your dress made ...?
2. What do you cut up bread ...?
3. What did you do that ...?
4. What are you sitting ...?
5. Where are you going ...?
6. What on earth are you talking ...?
7. What are you going to wrap the fish up ...?

8. Where have all those letters come ...?
9. Who were you sitting ...?
10. What are you shooting ...?
11. Is that the man you were speaking ...?
12. This is the picture we were looking ...?
13. The chair I was sitting ... broke.
14. I have just found the money I was looking ...!
15. Now you can see the lake we have just walked ...
16. Yesterday they blew up the bridge we came ...
17. They have just lost the toys they were playing ...
18. You can scarcely see the route they climbed ...
19. But this is the shop we've just been ...
20. Thank you for sending on the books I left ...
21. Have you any idea what this is made ...?
22. We don't like that subject referred ...
23. They tell me it's a good firm to work ...
24. You can tell that his clothes are badly looked ...
25. I don't think that subject has ever been talked ...
26. Here's the man that book was written ...
27. Can you tell me, please, who that letter has been passed ...?
28. Never in my life have I been spoken ... in that manner.
29. I can assure you that my jokes are always laughed ...!
30. She certainly manages to get herself talked ...
31. The results of the examination were not to be wondered ...

Exercise No 129. 'Not Until'

> He didn't leave until three o'clock. (=*He left at three o'clock but not before*)
> She didn't understand until I explained it to her. (=*She only understood when I explained it to her*)

This construction with a negative verb and the word *until* is often a difficult one for students; since in other languages the same idea is usually expressed by some other means. In German, for example, *Sie ging erst um drei Uhr weg*.

Now change the following sentences in the same way:

1. They will come when they are called, but not before.
2. I managed to do it when you had explained how.
3. They took a liking to the beer as soon as they tasted it.
4. I shall go to bed as soon as I have finished my work.

5. The maid will open the door when she knows who knocked.
6. John woke up when he heard the alarm clock.
7. We will only leave when the other guests have gone.
8. He arrived on Wednesday morning.
9. John got back from the office very late last night.
10. The bus only leaves when all the places are taken.

This construction is also found with a substitute subject construction with 'it'.

> It was only on Wednesday that I saw him again.
> =It was not until Wednesday that I saw him again.

Now change these sentences in the same way:

1. It was when I paid the money that they handed over the papers.
2. It was at three o'clock that they finally arrived.
3. It was when he saw his mother that he realized how old she had become.
4. It was when they tasted the soup that they found the cook had forgotten the salt.
5. It was when she had read the first chapter that she found that she had read the book before.
6. It was when it was quite dark that they left their hiding-place.
7. It was when he came up close that he saw what had happened.
8. It was when the children had finished their homework that they were given supper.
9. It was only on that Sunday morning that John finally made the discovery.
10. It was in the seventeenth century that women first appeared on the stage.

SECTION 10

PHRASAL VERBS AND ADVERB PARTICLES

Exercise No 130

Phrasal verbs are a type of compound verb made up of a simple verb and an adverb particle:

    To switch off   To take away

1. The principal adverb particles are:

about	before	forward(s)	past
above	behind	in	round
across	below	inside	through
along	between	off	under
around	beyond	on	up
away	by	out	upwards
back	down	outside	
backward(s)	downward(s)	over	

2. With the exception of *out, away, back, backwards, downwards* and *forwards*, these particles have the same meaning as their corresponding prepositions.

3. It is useful to distinguish between the adverbial and prepositional use of the particles because the intonation of the sentence is different:

    He took three hours to climb *up*. (adverb)
    He is climbing *up* the mountain. (preposition)

But notice that in such sentences as this next one, *up* is an adverb in both cases in spite of its position. (See Exercise No. 137 for word order with adverb particles):

    He is counting his money *up*.
    He is counting *up* his money.

4. When used with verbs of movement, with or without objects, there is generally no difficulty in understanding the meaning of the phrasal verb if the meaning of the adverb particle is known:

They	go come jump walk swim hurry run	in out away back down up off

I	turn put bring throw carry push lay	something	in out back off away up on

Supply a suitable adverb particle in the following sentences:

(*Note:* In this exercise several different particles may be equally suitable.)

1. Ask Mr. Roberts to bring ... my book when he has finished with it.
2. Just carry these sheets ... to the bedroom for me, will you?
3. You mustn't throw those papers ...
4. Time for bed, children! Put your toys ...
5. We watched the soldiers marching ...
6. Put the tray ... on the table, please.
7. If you walk ... slowly, you'll see what they're doing.
8. Send the letter ... by the first mail.
9. The farmers haven't got their crops ... yet.
10. Help me to get this box ... on to the top of the cupboard.
11. He walked rapidly ... in the opposite direction.
12. Pass the butter ... to me, please.
13. It's too high. You can't jump ...
14. Run ... to the shop and get a pound of sugar.
15. The opening is too narrow to carry the sofa ...
16. Once it's stuck ..., it's very difficult to get ...
17. The children have scratched all the paint ...
18. It's very late. We must be getting ...
19. If you push him ..., he'll drown.
20. Turn the handle ... and then pull.
21. Take this nasty soup .... I won't have any soup today.
22. The bridge looks very narrow. Do you think we can drive the car ...?
23. I was walking ... quite happily when I met a friend.
24. They watched a squadron of planes flying ...
25. That river looks too wide to swim ...
26. Here is the ballot box. Drop your voting paper ...
27. The keyhole is very small. Can you see ...
28. This dress is too tight. I can't get it ...
29. Throw it ...! It's no use any longer.
30. Tear ... the end of the envelope.

SECTION 10   PHRASAL VERBS

Exercise No 131. 'Up'

Apart from its general meaning of *in an upward direction*, the particle *up* has several other meanings:

1. With verbs of movement, *approach*—

    I dashed up to him and shook hands.

Note that in these cases *up* is frequently followed by the preposition *to*. The phrase *up to* means *as far as* and is a compound preposition.

Using these verbs, complete the following sentences:

    run up   rush up   drive up
    walk up   go up   swim up
    sail up   march up   come up

1. He ... his car right up to the front door.
2. The liner ... up to the dockside under its own steam.
3. He watched the soldiers ... right up to the gate of the barracks.
4. He ... up to the front door and rang the bell.
5. I ... up to him and told him just what I thought of him.
6. While he was waiting, two men ... up to him out of breath.
7. The fishes ... up to the bait but did not bite.
8. If you want to see better, you'll have to ... up a bit closer.
9. My two dogs ... up to me as I opened the garden gate.

2. *Completion*—

Compare:

     You'll never get rich if you don't *save*.
     They have *saved up* enough money to go for a holiday.

In the second example *up* implies that the saving is complete enough for a definite purpose.

Using these verbs, complete the following sentences:

    finish up   tear up   cut up   *pack up   *tie up
    drink up   save up   fill up   *wrap up   use up
    burn up   wake up   shut up   *button up   sweep up
    dry up   wash up   *wind up   *do up

(*Note:* the verbs marked with an asterisk form their opposites with *un-*, e.g., *untie*, *undo*, etc.)

1. ... up your milk, children!
2. I can't write any more. I've ... up all my paper.
3. Don't forget to ... the clock up before you go to bed.
4. All the trunks are ... up ready for the journey.
5. Who has ... up all the paper and scattered the pieces on the floor?
6. People generally don't enjoy ... the dishes up after a meal.
7. The water supply ... up during the hot summer.
8. ... up onions makes one cry.
9. John always ... up at five o'clock in the morning.
10. The gardener spent the afternoon ... up all the dried leaves.
11. I shall get married when I have some money ... up.
12. You must ... up the parcel carefully if you don't want the contents to get broken.
13. ... up these forms for your visa application!
14. The children ... up their coats in the cold wind.
15. They have ... up their house and gone away.
16. ... up your shoes!

Exercise No 132. 'Down'

Apart from its general meaning of *in a downward direction*, *down* has these other meanings:

1. *Completion of destruction—*

   Someone has watered down all the whisky, it's undrinkable.

Using these verbs, complete the following sentences:

burn down	cut down	fall down	knock down
pull down	tear down	tone down	break down

1. They are ... down all the old houses in our street.
2. The rioters ran through the town ... down all government posters.
3. If no repairs are done to these houses, they will ... down of their own accord.
4. He's a big strong man and you won't be able to ... him down easily.
5. I'm sorry to see that they have ... down all the beautiful trees in this street.

6. It took a long time to ... down the enemy's resistance.
7. Old St. Paul's was ... down in the Great Fire of London.
8. I think you ought to ... down your speech a little.

2. *Writing—*
   The reasons have all been set down clearly in this article.

Using these verbs, complete the following sentences:

> set down   get down   write down
> put down   copy down   take down

1. You must all ... down what I have written on the blackboard.
2. He spoke so quickly that I couldn't ... all he said down.
3. ... down the names of all those who come late.
4. What you say may be ... down and used in evidence against you.
5. I want you to ... down his exact words.

Exercise No 133. 'Out'

Apart from its general meaning of *from the interior to the exterior*, the particle *out* has several other meanings:

1. *Clearness and loudness* with verbs of speaking, writing, drawing—
   Please copy out this article before lunch.

Using these verbs, complete the following sentences:

> shout out   call out   draw out   copy out
> speak out   shriek out   write out
> read out   mark out   set out

1. The reasons have all been clearly ... out in his book.
2. The headmaster ... out the names of the winners.
3. ... out this passage to the whole class, please.
4. You cannot prevent me by threats from ... out.
5. As they arrested her she ... out that she was innocent.
6. They were ... out the football pitch when it began to rain.
7. You must ... me out a map if I am to find my way.
8. These exercises must be ... out again. They are all wrong.
9. Your writing is so bad that I must ask you to ... all this out again.

2. *Sudden action—*

> War has broken out between those two countries again.

Using these verbs, complete the following sentences:

> burst out   break out

1. A fire ... out last night in the centre of the city.
2. An epidemic of measles ... out in the school last month.
3. He ... out into a fit of coughing.
4. The child ... out that she hadn't done it.

3. *Disappearance, vanishing—*

> I am going to rub out all the words on the blackboard.

Using these verbs, complete the following sentences:

> turn out   rub out   die out   fade out
> give out   go out   wash out   put out
> wipe out   wear out

1. I'm afraid that these stains on your shirt will never ... out.
2. Radio reception was bad and the programme simply ... out.
3. His strength ... out and he fell to the ground exhausted.
4. My shoes are quite ... out. I must take them to the shoemaker.
5. What time did the lights ... out last night?
6. ... out your cigarettes. Smoking is forbidden.
7. The teacher ... out what he had written on the blackboard.
8. The enemy were ... out to the last man.
9. Many good old customs are ... out nowadays.
10. Remember to ... the lights out when you leave the room.

4. *Distribution—*

> Mr. Jones, will you hand out the textbooks, please.

Using these verbs, complete the following sentences:

> hand out   give out   share out   pay out   divide out

1. The insurance company ... out more than £3 million last year in claims.
2. Little Margaret ... all her chocolates out among her friends.
3. I haven't any more books to ... out. You'll have to share.
4. The examiner ... out the papers at the beginning of the exam.

5. The government have ... out their reasons for the change of policy.
6. Mary ... out the cake equally among all the children at the party.

5. *Extension and projection*—
   The policeman put out his right hand to stop the traffic.

Using these verbs, complete the following sentences:

stick out   pull out   jut out   hang out
hold out   point out   stretch out   reach out

1. Rude children ... out their tongues.
2. I would like to ... out the advantages of my system.
3. The population ... their flags out to celebrate the return of their victorious army.
4. ... the elastic out to its fullest extent before you let it go.
5. The foundations of the bridge ... out into the river.
6. He ... out his hand to receive the gift.
7. Poor fellow! His ears ... out too much.
8. I don't ... out any hope of his recovery.
9. There is no room in these seats to ... your legs out.
10. If you ... out your hand as far as you can, you should be able to touch it.

Exercise No 134. 'Off'

Apart from its general meaning of *from the surface or top of*, the particle has these other meanings:

1. *Detaching, disconnection, departure, disappearance*—
   The aeroplane took off at six o'clock.
   He shook the ants off his sleeve.
   Peel off the outer skin before you eat them.

Using these verbs, complete the following sentences:

set off   cool off   hurry off   turn off   give off
push off   die off   fly off   switch off
pass off   drive off   go off   wear off.

1. We proposed to ... off at daybreak.
2. Why are you ... off in such a hurry? There's plenty of time

3. This stove takes a long time to ... off.
4. All the flowers in this bed have ... off during the dry season.
5. He jumped into the car and ... off into the night.
6. The birds all ... off at the sound of the gun.
7. The doctor assured her that the pain would ... off.
8. He listened to the instructions and then ... off.
9. He ... off without a word to anyone.
10. Don't forget to ... the stove off before you leave.
11. The effects of this drug take some time to ... off.

  2. Same as previous but with the additional idea of *down to the ground*—

    He was sitting on the wall, but fell off and broke his leg.

Using these verbs complete the following sentences:

jump off	fall off	step off	slip off
blow off	knock off	tumble off	get off

1. Take this tram and ... off at the third stop.
2. Get onto this horse and see that you don't ... off.
3. Pin it up on the board or it will get ... off by the wind.
4. While walking along the bank, he ... off and fell into the water.
5. He stopped his horse, ... off, and opened the gate.
6. His glasses got ... off in the struggle.
7. He was learning to ride a bicycle but was always ... off.

Exercise No 135. 'On'

Apart from its general meaning of *on the surface of*, this particle *on* has two other meanings:

  1. *Progression and continuation*—

    You must carry on with your work till the teacher returns.

Using these verbs, complete the following sentences:

read on	get on	carry on	go on
come on	drive on	walk on	hurry on
keep on			

1. Please ... on working until you've finished.
2. ... on with your work!
3. ... on! Follow me! I know the way.
4. The driver of the bus ... on so as not to be late at the terminus.
5. The traffic policeman told the chauffeur to ... on.
6. You should ... on until you see the big white church on your right.
7. Please ... on, gentlemen. I shall be with you in a moment.
8. You are to ... on to Chapter 3 for your homework.
9. Must I really ... on reminding you to bring your books to class?
10. The train didn't stop at the station but ... right on.

2. *Attachment or connection* (compare *off*)—
   She sewed on all his buttons for him.

Using these verbs, complete the following sentences:

stick on	pin on	hang on	tie on
screw on	nail on	fasten on	fix on
put on	switch on	turn on	sew on

1. Just help me to ... this picture on the wall.
2. If it won't ... on with glue, you'll have to ... it on.
3. They ... the medal on.
4. Here are the luggage labels. You should ... them on before you leave.
5. ... the radio on. I want to hear the news.
6. Put the bath-plug in before you ... the water on.
7. His buttons were ... on with very poor cotton thread.
8. ... your coat on. We're going for a walk.
9. The notice board had been ... on and they needed a hammer to get it off.
10. Isn't there a hook for me to ... my hat on?
11. When you've taken your medicine, ... the top of the bottle on again.

Exercise No 136. 'Over'

Apart from its general meaning of *from one side to the other* the particle *over* has the meaning of:

Consideration and inspection.

Using these verbs complete the following sentences:

> think over, look over, read over, talk over, go over

1. I have been ... over what you told me last night.
2. ... the instructions over carefully and then do the exercise.
3. We must ... the matter over together before we make any decision.
4. Kindly ... these notes over and tell me what you think of them.
5. He ... the new recruits over and decided that they were a poor lot.
6. The headmaster always accompanies parents who come to ... over the school.
7. Let's ... over these together, shall we?

Exercise No 137. Word Order and Phrasal Verbs

(*a*) If the phrasal verb has no object the adverb particle follows the verb directly:

> He set *off* for London.
> They ran *away* to the river.

(*b*) If the phrasal verb has a pronoun object the adverb particle must follow the object directly:

> He gave it *away*.
> She took them *off*.

(*c*) If the phrasal verb has a noun object the adverb particle may go before or after the object:

> He took his gloves *off*. =He took *off* his gloves.
> She gave her money *away*. =She gave *away* her money.

If the object is long and would separate the verb from its particle too much, then we prefer to put the particle directly after the verb:

> He gave his watch *away*.
> He gave *away* his watch with the luminous numbers and a second hand.

Repeat these sentences, transferring the adverb particle to its position after the object:

1. Put up your hands.
2. The shooting during the night woke up the watchman.
3. The workmen have been pulling down that building all week.

4. Don't take off your coat. It's too cold. We're putting on ours.
5. The cook has heated up some soup for your supper.
6. Hold out your hand and I'll put something in it.
7. It's much better to keep down your head while they are shooting.
8. They were just lifting up the lid of the chest when I came in.
9. Have you thought over the matter?
10. Did you write down those difficult words?
11. Would you mind sticking on these labels for me?
12. Please rub out what you've written on the blackboard.
13. The thief knocked down the policeman in his headlong flight.
14. I must ask you to read out that piece again. I didn't hear.
15. She gave away all her money before she died.

Now repeat the exercise replacing the noun objects by pronouns.

For example:

    No. 1   Put up your hands. = Put them up.

Exercise No 138. Word Order

Sometimes in narrative writing the adverb particle comes at the beginning of the sentence. This gives a useful liveliness to the sentence. When this construction is used:

(*a*) There is an inversion of verb and subject when the subject is a noun—

    Down came the wall with a crash. (= The wall came down with a crash)

(*b*) There is no inversion when the subject is a pronoun—

    In he came all covered with snow. (= He came in all covered with snow)

Now put the adverb particles in these sentences at the beginning and make any other necessary changes to the order of words:

1. The Christmas pudding came in and everybody started clapping.
2. There was a gust of wind and his hat blew off.
3. He slipped and all the books he was carrying fell down.

4. He made a slight movement and the deer ran away over the hills.
5. He gave it a push and it fell out through the window.
6. They waited five more minutes and the whale came up again.
7. He jumped down and disappeared round the corner.
8. He'd already spoken for an hour and he went on for another whole one.
9. The crowd was thick but they struggled on till they came to the front.
10. They had warned him a hundred times that it was dangerous, but he fell in just the same.
11. You go out! I can't do with you here.
12. We thought we had got rid of them, but they came back nevertheless.
13. They came along until they were opposite the grandstand.
14. They went off without a word of thanks.
15. The captain called for 'hard aport' and the great ship swung round.

Exercise No 139

Here are some phrases with verbs and adverb particles. Give an expression which has the opposite meaning:

Example:
To let a dress out.
Opposite: To take a dress in.

to take one's hat off
to take out your handkerchief
to take down a book from the shelf
to let the cat out
to keep the cold out
to switch the radio off
to push someone away
to take his plate away
to knock a pile of bricks over
to sit up in bed

to hand out the books
to cool the engine off
to stick a label on
to pin up a notice
to hold one's hand up
to stick out your tongue
to walk up to the door
to give something away
to pull the house down
to jump over the stream
to get up from one's chair
to pull the stamp off
to push the knob in

to lift up the cover
to open up an office
to get on a bus
to pay some money in

to get down from your horse
to crawl under
to fall over
to bend down

Exercise No 140. Phrasal Verbs with 'Do' and 'Make'

Note these special collocations:

to do away with	(=*to abolish*)	to make up	1. (=*use cosmetics*)
to do up	1. (=*to fasten,* cf. *undo*)		2. (=*invent*)
			3. (=*complete*) (=*compensate*)
	2. (=*to redecorate a house or room*)	to make up for to make out	1. (=*discern*)
to do someone in	(=*to kill*)		2. (=*prepare in writing*)
to do a room out	(=*to sweep and clean*)	to make off (with)	(=*go away (with)*)
to be done for	(=*useless or broken*)	to make up to	(=*flatter*)
to do with	(=*manage with, be glad of*)	to make over	(=*transfer property*)
to do without	(=*to manage without*)		

Now add the correct particle* in the following sentences:

1. We still need two men to make ... the team.
2. Men don't like girls who make ... too much.
3. Please make ... the bill and I'll pay it immediately.
4. Robert, do your shoes ... before leaving the house.
5. Can you lend me your pen? Mine's done ...
6. You'll have to work specially hard to make ... for the days you were away sick.
7. It's an interesting old document but there are a lot of words I can't make ...
8. She can't do ... her hot-water bottle on these cold nights.
9. He broke into the house and made ... with all the silver.
10. Make ... your mind. We can't wait here all day!

* In this and the following exercises the particle may sometimes be an adverb and sometimes a preposition:

Take your hat off. (adverb)
Take it off your head. (preposition)

11. Get out of here or I'll do you...!
12. Our business could do ... another £5,000 capital.
13. I have my room done ... once a week.
14. The enemy patrol made ... without firing a shot.
15. Look! There he is making ... to her again. He's wasting his time.
16. It's about time we had the bedroom done ...
17. He made his fortune ... to his son before he died.

Exercise No 141.   Phrasal Verbs with 'Come' and 'Bring'

Note these special collocations:

to bring about	(=*to cause to happen*)	to come by	(=*obtain by doubtful means*)
to bring in	(=*to introduce*)	to come upon	(=*discover unexpectedly*)
to bring off	(=*to succeed against difficulties*)	to come across	(=*meet unexpectedly*)
to bring round	(=*to revive someone*)	to come about	(=*to happen*)
to bring round	(=*to bring to a place nearby*)	to come in	(=*to enter*)
to bring on	(=*precipitate*)	to come off	(=*to take place, succeed*)
to bring up	(=*educate*)	to come round	1. (=*to revive*) 2. (=*to visit someone who lives nearby*)

Now add the correct particle in the following sentences:

1. I think she has brought ... her children beautifully.
2. I want an explanation of how this disaster came ...
3. The government has brought ... new measures to combat inflation.
4. He really is an extraordinary man. He's brought the deal ... in spite of everything.
5. The cold weather has brought my rheumatism ... again.
6. When is the first performance of your new play coming ...?
7. May I ask how you came ... my pencil?
8. It took him a long time to come ... after the operation.
9. A new series of regulations came ... last week.
10. The archaeologists came ... a tomb of the sixth century A.D.

11. Can you imagine who I came ... while I was in Paris?
12. They worked for three hours to bring him ... after the accident.
13. The dry weather has brought ... a water shortage in the country.
14. Bring your friend ... to see me whenever you like.

Exercise No 142. Phrasal Verbs with 'Keep' and 'Let'

Note these special collocations:

> to keep up with   (=*to remain abreast of*)
> to keep in with   (=*to remain on friendly terms with*)
> to let on   (=*to reveal a secret*)
> to let up   (=*to relax*)
> to let off   1. (=*to cause to explode*)
>   2. (=*to excuse*)
> to let oneself in for   (=*to commit oneself to*)
> to let someone down   (=*to fail to keep an agreement with*)

Now add the correct particle in the blank spaces in these sentences:

1. We carry an umbrella to keep the rain ...
2. Let's shut the window. It'll keep the cold ...
3. Don't let the dogs ... or they'll make the carpet dirty.
4. Children love letting ... fireworks.
5. I wish you wouldn't keep ... talking. It disturbs me.
6. It's most important to keep ... with your neighbours.
7. You must walk slowly if you want the children to keep ... with you.
8. Keep ... the grass!
9. Mary let ... a cry when John stepped ... her toe.
10. If you behave like that you are letting yourself ... for trouble.
11. I advise you to keep ... from that man. He's a pickpocket.
12. The police blocked the road and let nobody ...
13. The police lined the route of the procession and kept the crowd ...
14. Please let me ... I promise not to do it again.
15. John is getting so fat that Mary has to let ... all his trousers.
16. He promised to deliver the stuff today and has let us ... again.

Exercise No 143

The verb *get* combines freely with adverb particles to make phrasal verbs used with or without an object:

> I can't get my shoes off.
> Please get off the grass.
> Get the table out of my way.
> He quickly got out of the way.

Note these collocations:

to get on	(= *to make progress*)
to get on with someone	(= *to be on friendly terms with*)
to get over	1. (= *to recover from an emotion or illness*)
	2. (= *to surmount a difficulty*)
to get down	(= *to put on paper*)
to get at someone	(= *to approach with the intention of influencing improperly*)
to get at	(= *to reach*)

Now complete these sentences with the correct particle:

1. Get ... from that wall; you might hurt yourself.
2. Please help me to get these things ... on to the top of the cupboard.
3. She got ... her car and drove away.
4. I can't find out where the water is getting ... the roof.
5. I want to get ... from the office early today.
6. They built the wall especially high so that the little boys couldn't get ...
7. He will never get ... the death of his wife.
8. He hasn't started to get ... since he left hospital.
9. It's a good idea to get ... with your neighbours.
10. Be quiet! I want to get ... with my work.
11. He helped her get ... from her horse.
12. I don't know how I shall ever get ... all this work before the end of the month.
13. The story has got ... that she left him.
14. Please show me where we have got ... in the reading book.
15. If you want to see the master, you'll have to get ... the servants.
16. What time do you have to get ... to the office?
17. I don't like lending him books. I never get them ...
18. Lock the door carefully so that the dogs can't get ...
19. You're tall. Can you get ... that lamp high on the wall?

SECTION 10 PHRASAL VERBS

20. Get ...! You're holding everyone up.
21. If you think you can get ... with that sort of work, you're mistaken.

Exercise No 144. Adverb Particles with the Verb 'To Be'

Adverb particles are often used with the verb *to be*. In such cases they may have their ordinary literal meaning, but certain particles form collocations whose meaning is not literal. Here is a list of the most important examples of particles with the verb *to be*:

to be
- at something (=*engaged in doing something*)
- back (=*to have returned*)
- around / about (=*to be somewhere in the immediate neighbourhood*)
- along (=*to arrive when expected*)
- out
  1. (=*not to be considered*)
  2. (=*not at home*)
- out for (=*trying hard to win or get*)
- on (=*to take place (used of performances of all sorts)*)
- over (=*finished (used of performances of all sorts)*)
- through with (=*to have finished with*)
- off
  1. (=*to leave; to start on a journey*)
  2. (=*cancelled; not to take place*)
- up to
  1. (=*engaged in some activity, usually mischievous or illegal*)
  2. (=*capable of*)
- up
  1. (=*finished (used only of time)*)
  2. (=*not in bed*)
  3. (=*happening, usually something bad*)
- behind with (=*to be in arrears with*)
- down (=*written down*)

Explain the meaning of these sentences to show that you understand the meaning of the adverb particle in them:

1. Our time is up at six o'clock.
2. What are the children up to now?
3. What were you all at when we arrived?
4. The film we want to see isn't on tonight.
5. He's not very far on with his work.
6. She was glad when her children were back.
7. Ring again later, please: John's not back yet.
8. The cost of living is up again.
9. You may not believe it, but it's down here in black and white.
10. I'm sorry. The party's off because of the rain.

11. Madam is out. She will return at six o'clock.
12. What's up?
13. Mr. Jones isn't in on Thursdays.
14. The class is over.
15. You can have this book when I'm through with it.
16. The time is past when one could do that sort of thing.
17. Are the children about anywhere?
18. The family will be away until January.
19. He's all out for the prize.
20. What time are you off tomorrow?
21. We can't do it after all. It's quite out.
22. You'll find the gardener somewhere around.
23. Till what time are you generally up in the evening?
24. She's never down till half past nine in the morning.
25. I'll be along about three.
26. I'm afraid none of you are up to doing this exercise.

Exercise No. 145

Phrasal verbs which do not have a literal meaning (1):

ask out	(=*invite*)	call on	(=*visit a person*)
break down	1. (=*weep*)	call at	(=*visit a place*)
	2. (=*have mechanical trouble*)	call off	(=*cancel*)
		carry out	(=*execute*)
break off	(=*stop suddenly*)	carry on	(=*continue*)
break up	1. (=*destroy*)	carry over	(=*transfer*)
	2. (=*finish school*)	carry off	(=*achieve triumphantly*)
call up	(=*summon, or telephone*)	cut down	(=*reduce*)
		cut out	(=*eliminate*)

Supply the particle in the following sentences:

1. He has had to cut ... smoking since his illness.
2. His car broke ... when he was only half way home.
3. Call me ... when you are ready to leave.
4. He carried his performance ... triumphantly.
5. You must carry ... my instructions to the letter.
6. When you have added it all up, carry the sum ... to the next page.
7. Carry ... reading where you left off last time.
8. We shall have to call the party ... if it rains.

SECTION 10 — PHRASAL VERBS

9. He called ... my house on his way past.
10. When do the children break ... for the Christmas holidays?
11. We shall have to cut ... our expenses this year.
12. He broke ... in the middle of a sentence, when she came in.
13. If you need any help, just call ... us.
14. She broke ... when she heard the news.
15. The ice on the lake breaks ... in spring.

Exercise No 146

Phrasal verbs which do not have a literal meaning (2):

draw on	(=*approach*)	fall to	(=*begin to do something*)
draw up	1. (=*prepare a document*)	fall upon	(=*attack*)
	2. (=*stop a vehicle*)	fall in with	1. (=*meet by chance*)
drop off	(=*diminish*)		2. (=*agree*)
drop out	(=*withdraw*)	go in for	(=*take up a hobby or career*)
fall off	(=*diminish*)		
fall out	(=*quarrel*)	go off	(=*explode*)
fall through	(=*not to succeed*)	go out	(=*become extinguished*)

Supply the particle in the following sentences:

1. John's youngest son is going ... for medicine.
2. When the whistle blew, they all fell ... with a will.
3. All our carefully laid plans have fallen ...
4. The wind fell as night drew ...
5. Unfortunately the champion had to drop ... of the race at the beginning.
6. Attendance at class has fallen ... badly this term.
7. Few people can live together without falling ... sometimes.
8. The incidence of the disease has dropped ... considerably recently.
9. The policeman signed to the driver to draw ... at the side of the road.
10. They fell ... their enemies and vanquished them.
11. I have asked my lawyer to draw ... a contract between us.
12. I will gladly fall ... with any plans you may make.
13. Luckily the bomb that fell near our house never went ...
14. Don't let the fire go ... while I'm away.
15. We fell ... with a group of gypsies on the way.

F

Exercise No 147

Phrasal verbs which do not have a literal meaning (3):

give out	(=*fail*)	run down	1. (=*become exhausted*)
give up	1. (=*surrender*)		2. (=*to speak ill of*)
	2. (=*renounce, stop*)	to be run down	(=*in poor health*)
give away	(=*make a present of something*)	set about	(=*begin to*)
		set up	(=*establish*)
give in	(=*yield*)	set out	(=*expose to view*)
leave off	(=*stop*)	set on	(=*attack*)
run out of	(=*have no more*)	set down	(=*write*)
set to	(=*begin*)		

Now supply the correct particle in these sentences:

1. They have set ... a branch of their business in our town.
2. He has failed so many times and yet he won't give ...
3. Please continue this exercise where you left ... last week.
4. I want these facts clearly set ..., so that anyone can understand them.
5. Our stocks have run ... and not been replenished.
6. The besieged garrison refused to give ...
7. How long is it since you gave ... smoking?
8. My Aunt Jane is very run ...
9. It was most embarrassing. We ran ... of whisky half way through the party.
10. They asked him to set ... his ideas before he left.
11. I suppose we had better set ... our packing, as we leave tomorrow.
12. You can't expect someone who is always running ... her friends to be popular.
13. They put food before the men and told them to set ...
14. She gave ... all her old clothes before leaving the country.
15. As they were returning home they were set ... by robbers and wounded.
16. His reserves of energy gave ... as he neared the end of the course.

SECTION 10 — PHRASAL VERBS

Exercise No 148

Phrasal verbs which do not have a literal meaning (4):

take to	1. (=*begin to like*)	take over	(=*assume responsibility*)
	2. (=*develop a habit*)	turn out	1. (=*produce*)
take off	(=*make fun of*)		2. (=*result*)
take in	(=*deceive*)	turn up	(=*appear unexpectedly*)
take after	(=*resemble*)		
take up	1. (=*interest oneself in, study*)	turn in	(=*go to bed*)
	2. (=*occupy*)	turn down	(=*reject*)
take on	(=*accept*)	turn out	(=*eject*)

Now supply the correct particle in these sentences:

1. He was turned ... of his house for not paying his rent.
2. He has recently taken ... going for long walks in the evening.
3. You can't take me ... as easily as that with your stories.
4. John has just taken ... the family business from his father.
5. Her brother turned ... last night. They thought he was in France.
6. Her daughter has taken ... dancing this term.
7. They have taken ... more work than they can conveniently do.
8. The travellers turned ... the moment they arrived in the village.
9. This factory turns ... 100 new cars a day.
10. That boy is always taking ... his teacher's manner.
11. We shall have to move the wardrobe. It takes ... too much space.
12. You know I don't really take ... her very much.
13. They have turned ... our offer of financial aid.
14. The cake turned ... a great success.
15. Little Robert takes ... his father in appearance.

Exercise No 149

Phrasal verbs which do not have a literal meaning (5):

put out	(=*extinguish*)	wear out	(=*to become useless*)
put off	(=*postpone*)	show off	(=*make a foolish show*)
put up	(=*offer and take lodging*)	stick up for	(=*give support to*)
		back up	(=*support*)
to be put out	(=*embarrassed*)	bear out	(=*give proof of*)

pass off	(=*disappear*)	look up	(=*search for information*)
put up with	(=*tolerate*)		
hold up	(=*delay*)	catch up with	(=*reach a moving object*)
find out	(=*discover*)		
put off	(=*repel*)	hold out	(=*endure*)
write off	(=*cancel debts, etc.*)		

Now supply the particles for these sentences:

1. They have had to put the football match ... because of snow.
2. She was very put ... when he spoke to her like that.
3. A large part of their capital was written ... last year.
4. His shoes are quite worn ...; he'll have to get a new pair.
5. Would you stick ... for me if I refuse to do as he asks?
6. Everything you say bears ... my original opinion.
7. Put ... the stove when you have finished cooking.
8. The symptoms of the disease passed ... slowly.
9. I absolutely refuse to put ... with that sort of conduct.
10. The delegates put ... at the best hotel in town.
11. If you run, you might just be able to catch ... with him before he gets there.
12. If you don't know her number, look it ... in the directory.
13. Have you found ... the time of your train yet?
14. The defenders held ... for three days before giving in.
15. I must confess that his appearance puts me ...
16. The member was constantly holding the proceedings ... by his interruptions.
17. I hope you'll back me ... when I tell him what I think of him.
18. There is nothing I dislike more than children who are continually showing ...

Exercise No 150

Adverb particles are often found with nouns or adjectives made from verbs. Sometimes they come before the noun or adjective and sometimes after it. In this exercise the particle comes before like a prefix:

An *outbreak* of measles (cf. Measles *broke out* in the school)

Supply the adverbial particle as a prefix in these sentences:

1. The bridge could not withstand the ...rush of the flood waters.
2. He struck his brother in an ...burst of rage.

3. He has been an ...cast all his life.
4. The ...going Minister had an interview with the President.
5. It was his extravagance which caused his ...fall.
6. I'm going to the station on the ...-chance of meeting him.
7. He's a very ...spoken young man.
8. A miserable ...trodden people they are!
9. My ...come has not increased for three years.
10. The doctors were surprised at the rapid ...set of the disease.
11. These ruins were a temple in ...gone days.
12. She dropped a coin into his ...stretched palm.
13. We couldn't go out because of the ...pour.
14. The ...lay on new equipment is too great for us.
15. To abandon his home and family was a considerable ...-heaval for him.
16. She met his proposal with ...cast eyes.
17. The government's new measures caused a widespread ...cry.
18. There was a serious ...break of fire in the town.
19. He stood with ...lifted arms.
20. She is feeling very ...cast since she heard the news.
21. The centre-forward delighted the ...lookers with his skill.
22. The ...coming traffic was held up by the accident.
23. They are building a new ...-pass road round the town.
24. The ...look is very disturbing.
25. ...put has risen considerably since they installed the new machines.
26. The ...take of students has been raised in the last few years.
27. The chimney is blocked and the smoke can find no ...let.
28. I must explain my reason at the ...set.

Exercise No 151

In this exercise the particle follows the noun or adjective and is usually joined to it by a hyphen. Since this type of compound noun is usually of more recent origin than the type practised in the previous exercise, some of the examples are still rather colloquial.

Supply the particle in the following sentences:

1. Our plans have suffered a serious set...
2. I hear they had a terrific set-... last night.
3. This organization seems to have a very curious set-...
4. He is always surrounded by a lot of hangers-...

5. We keep hearing reports of the most extraordinary goings-... at the Jones's.
6. The plane crashed immediately after take-...
7. I find it a very useful stand-... in case of emergency.
8. We gave our friends a wonderful send-...
9. They considered it a come-... to live in such a small house.
10. The whole scheme proved to be a wash-...
11. The prisoner made good his get-...
12. They gave the new minister a good write-... in the papers.
13. It is a very serious draw... to have too little money.
14. These pots are a throw-... from the factory.
15. The younger son always wears his elder brother's cast-... clothing.
16. You can't imagine the mix-... there was when we arrived.
17. She gives all her worn-... clothing to the maid.
18. If you go, it's entirely your own look-...
19. We'll give the new play a run-... tomorrow night.
20. We ought to give it a good try-... before we buy it.
21. Those children need a good talking-...
22. There has been no dropping-... in the quality of our product.

Exercise No 152. Adverb Particles in Imperatives and Exclamations

Adverb particles are often found in imperative and exclamatory sentences. Some of these exclamations have no verb. In these cases some verb or other is understood. The object of this verb is preceded by the preposition *with*:

>   Throw the government down. = Down with the government.
>   Take your coat off.   = Off with your coat.
>   Go away.   = Away with you.

Explain in what circumstances you would use or hear the following:

Get out!   Shut up!   Get on!   Sit up!
Look out!   Run along!   Wake up!   Turn it off!
Go away!   Come along!   Hands up!   Lights out!
Hands off!   Throw it away!   Down tools!   Time's up!
Put it down!   Eat up!   I'm off!   Hand it over!
Out with it!   Be off!   Turn over!   Give it me back!

Up with the workers!	It's all over!	Down with them all!	Off with his head!
Get along with you!	Carry on! Out with your books!	On with the next number!	Away with them!

Exercise No 153

Adverb particles are often found in pairs forming adverbial phrases or, sometimes, adjectives.

Make suitable sentences incorporating the following to show their meaning:

to and fro	up and down	back and forth	in and out
off and on	through and through	down and out	over and over
up and up		out and out	on and on
backwards and forwards		up and about	by and by

SECTION 11

PUNCTUATION

Exercise No 154. Exclamation Mark and Question Mark.

Question Marks are used after direct questions. They are not used after indirect questions, which are not questions at all, grammatically speaking:

'What time is it?'
but: 'Please tell me what time it is.'

Exclamation marks should not be used too much in English. They are properly used only after real exclamations and sometimes after short and peremptory commands:

'Oh dear! What am I going to do?'
'Get out! I don't want to see you again.'

Supply the exclamation marks or question marks where necessary:

1. 'What a hot day. Let's stay at home.'
2. 'How silly of him. I do wish he'd listen to what I say.'
3. 'What on earth is this.' 'I've no idea.'
4. 'Hullo. I am glad to see you.'
5. 'No matter. He'll come when he can.'
6. 'How many have you. What. Twenty-three. Oh well. The more the merrier.'
7. 'Hush. Do be quiet.'
8. 'A nice mess you've made of it.'
9. 'What do you think you're doing.'
10. 'How late you are. Where have you been.'
11. 'Good Lord. This isn't what I wanted at all.'
12. 'Who's there. Oh, it's only you.'
13. 'Congratulations. When are you getting married.'
14. 'Many happy returns. I hope you have a lovely birthday.'
15. 'Can I borrow your bicycle.' 'No, certainly not.'
16. 'This isn't much use, is it. Can you give me another.'
17. 'He asked them where they were going.'
18. 'Don't do that, please.'
19. 'What. Not arrived yet. What shall we do.'
20. 'They wanted to know who he was.'
21. 'Bother. I've lost my pen.'
22. Dear Sir, I have to thank you for your letter of . . .

23. 'Bad luck. Are you going to try again.'
24. 'Shut up. I can't hear what they're saying.'
25. 'What a nuisance it's lost. We shall have to get another one, shan't we.'

Exercise No 155. The Comma (1)

Commas are used to separate a non-defining relative clause from the rest of the sentence. A defining clause is not separated in this way. (See Exercise No 26.)

>   It is years since I read Ivanhoe, which is my favourite novel.
> but: What was that novel you were reading yesterday?

Some of these sentences contain non-defining clauses. Enclose them in commas:

1. I haven't seen my brother John who is in Paris for six years now.
2. My daughter Anne who is a nurse is getting married soon.
3. He is going to Paris where he has an office.
4. That is the house which we live in.
5. He was riding a bicycle which was remarkable considering his age.
6. Have you met Mr. Smith who is our new manager?
7. This is the knife which I use for cutting the flowers.
8. This is my garden which I am very proud of.
9. Tell us a story which we haven't heard.
10. George who is a great fisherman is coming to stay with us.
11. Let me introduce you to Mr. Roberts whose recent book was so successful.
12. There's a river over there where we always bathe.
13. Do you know the river Dee where we often bathe?
14. This is something we don't speak about.
15. He likes Botany which he's always talking about.

Exercise No 156. The Comma (2)

When a subordinate clause of any sort comes before the principal clause, we separate it with a comma:

>   When you are ready, we shall go.
>   If you can't understand, tell me.

Place commas in the following sentences, where necessary:

1. When he comes give him my love.
2. I shall tell you as soon as I know.
3. Stay here while I go and fetch them.
4. Before he came we were all perfectly satisfied.
5. You should have seen the mess after the firemen left.
6. Where were you when the lights went out?
7. Bring your music so that we can play together.
8. Wherever you go you see these new cars.
9. If I were you I shouldn't do that.
10. Although I was tired I didn't go to bed.
11. I shall have a word with him when he arrives.
12. As soon as you hear let us know.
13. Were I his brother I should help him.
14. Be that as it may I shall not change my mind.
15. You may use it provided that you give it back to me.
16. Because you are rich there is no need to give yourself airs.
17. He will punish her if she speaks again.
18. Until you consent I shall continue to bother you.
19. He went to a restaurant to have dinner because his wife was away.
20. Buses stop in different places in order that people may get off.
21. It is not wise to go there unless you are armed.
22. I shall stay as long as it is necessary.
23. You had better follow where I lead.
24. When the meeting was over they all streamed out into the street.
25. Whichever you choose you must look after it well.

Exercise No 157. The Comma (3)

Commas are used to separate off the following from the rest of the sentence:

(*a*) Absolute constructions—

Dinner over, they rose to go back to the sitting-room.

(*b*) Phrases in apposition—

Mr. Jones, *the Mayor of Casterbridge*, said . . .

(*c*) Adjectival phrases made with participles when they are non-defining—

The speaker, *getting to his feet*, began to . . .

Place commas where necessary in the following sentences:

1. Jones softly opening his door peered out into the street.
2. The game being over all the spectators returned home.
3. Turning my head I could see the captain approaching.
4. Joan came in and seeing us all playing cards went out again.
5. The table made of the best mahogany was a wedding present.
6. These and I may say many others are quite useless.
7. The prisoner found guilty on both counts was led away to prison.
8. This bread untouched by hand in its manufacture is no more expensive than the other.
9. Mary surrounded by her admirers was enjoying herself to the full.
10. I shall give it to him or failing that send it to him.
11. And they supposing the news to be true threw down their arms and ran.
12. Mrs. Jones my next door neighbour went on holiday last week.
13. This as you can see is the last one.
14. Robert the youngest of the family was sent to Africa.
15. John refused and whether you believe it or not so did Mary.
16. I cannot pay more nor whatever you say can the others.
17. They went out for a walk but the weather turning cold they returned earlier than they had intended.
18. The sun having set a light breeze came up.
19. The soldiers footsore and weary soon fell asleep.
20. The motor once stopped was difficult to start again.

Exercise No 158. The Comma (4)

Commas are used in lists of all sorts:

>I shall need a hammer, a saw, some nails, and a piece of wood.

except where the words are arranged in pairs joined by *and* or *or*:

>We wash our hands with soap and water.
>By car or bus, by rail or air, they all came to the capital to see the coronation.

Place the commas in the following sentences:

1. Having put on his coat straightened his tie and dusted off his shoes John was ready for the party.

2. I have never been so angry frustrated and disappointed in my life.
3. Whether you travel by sea air or rail you must leave on the sixth.
4. Standing or sitting eating or drinking sleeping or waking my dog is the handsomest of them all.
5. Slowly carefully and with infinite caution he raised the cover.
6. Cups saucers plates dishes all were broken with a sickening crash.
7. And the life of man solitary poor nasty brutish and short.
8. Everybody including judge jury public and lawyers listened to the prisoner with attention.
9. She bundled all her books papers magazines and letters into the drawer.
10. Nearer and nearer louder and louder and always more insistent came the sound.

Exercise No 159. The Comma (5)

(*a*) These words are usually enclosed in commas if they come in the middle or at the end of a sentence:

> too, however, nevertheless, though, of course, then—
>
> We, *however*, have never made that mistake.
> You, *too*, can have a car like the Jones's.

(*b*) If adverbs or adverbial expressions are placed in an unusual position in the sentence they are enclosed in commas:

> His brother has, *since his wedding*, not been seen at the club.
> They tried, *in spite of my advice*, to climb the mountain.

(*c*) Other adverbs which qualify the whole sentence:

> He has, *oddly enough*, never spoken about it again.
> =He has never spoken about it again, *which is very odd*.
>
> She has, *to my surprise*, married him after all.
> =She has married him after all, *at which I am very surprised*.

Place the commas in the following sentences:

1. I however have never seen him.
2. They all nevertheless agreed to his proposal.
3. Here now is the answer.
4. What then must I do if that is no use?
5. Where for heaven's sake are you going?

6. That in brief is the plan gentlemen.
7. He was naturally very upset when he heard the news.
8. You must of course ask your mother's permission before you go out.
9. My brother has a car and I have one too.
10. I bought it yesterday. I've decided I don't like it though.
11. He decided understandably that it would be wiser not to do it.
12. My wife has for a long time been wanting me to buy her a fur coat.
13. They have quite unjustifiably closed all the schools.
14. This for what it is worth is my plan.
15. The maid without her mistress's permission took the afternoon off.

Exercise No 160. The Semi-colon

The semi-colon is a lesser stop than the full-stop. It is used between grammatically complete sentences and is not followed by a capital letter. It is often found before such connective words as: *and, but, or*:

> He also told me about his aunt; but that is another story.

It is used to separate sentences which are closely connected in thought, where a full-stop would be too complete a break:

> The family is going for a picnic; father carries the rugs; mother, the food; and the children, the rest of the things.

Replace the full-stop by a semi-colon, where it seems better:

1. I want a new dress. Then I want a new handbag. And last of all, a new hat.
2. Firstly, you should listen carefully. Then you should write down what you hear.
3. Never listen to his tales. Don't believe what he says. And always distrust him.
4. They came. They looked at the house. And they went away.
5. It was fortunate for us we brought our coats. Fortunate also that we did not go far.
6. He frequently had toothache. So frequently, in fact, that he was forced to visit a dentist.
7. She arrived late. This did not surprise us as she was always late.

8. A man has called to see you. He is waiting in the next room.
9. I dislike people who talk all the time. Such people bore me.
10. Mr. Roberts is a rich man. You will find him generous, though.

Exercise No 161. The Colon

The colon is used to introduce:

(*a*) a list—

These are the things we shall need: a flask of coffee, some sandwiches, and some fruit.

(*b*) an explanation—

The reason he gave was this: he had not properly understood the instructions.

(*c*) an amplification—

You must consult a good dictionary, such as: the Oxford, Webster's or Chambers's.

Place colons in these sentences where they are necessary:

1. The problem is this which comes first, the hen or the egg?
2. It can be reduced to three simples rules if the light is red, you stop; if green, you go; if amber, you wait.
3. The past tense and past participle of go are 'went' and 'gone'.
4. 'This,' said the doctor, 'is what you must do eat less and give up smoking.'
5. This is what I want a girl who can answer the telephone and take messages.
6. I also want a boy to run errands.
7. He answered the question in this way if it were possible he would do it.
8. Send me all you have the grammars, the dictionaries, the readers.
9. He said he would send us all the books he could spare.
10. To operate the telephone lift the receiver and put in the coin.

Exercise No 162. The Punctuation of Direct Speech

1. The actual words of Direct Speech are a sentence and must be punctuated as such, with capital letters, commas, question and exclamation marks:

He said, 'Why did you do that, when I'd told you not to?'

SECTION 11 — PUNCTUATION

2. The introductory words, such as:

   he said, he asked, cried John

   whether at the end, middle or beginning of the sentence must be separated from the actual words spoken by commas if no other stop is used:

   'Where did they go?' he asked.
   'What on earth,' I asked, 'did they reply?'
   'Follow me!' cried their leader.

3. The actual words of direct speech are enclosed in inverted commas including all the necessary punctuation marks described in (1). The words of each fresh speaker should start a new paragraph:

   'Not a whisper!' she murmured.
   'Are you sure?'
   'Absolutely. Why?'
   'I just wanted to know,' he said.

Punctuate these sentences:

1. Never he said I shall never agree to that
2. What on earth he asked are you doing
3. It only costs $2\frac{1}{2}$ pence he said would you like one
4. Give it to me immediately he demanded no she replied I refuse
5. Would you if I asked you he asked lend me your car
6. I'll see you later then not too late please she asked
7. I'll see you later he said and put down the receiver
8. Good Heavens no she cried that's quite impossible
9. Can you believe it said Joan he actually asked me to marry him
10. When now where to my house all right if you wish he agreed

Exercise No 163. The Use of Capital Letters

Capital letters are used:

(a) At the beginning of a sentence—

   ' Come here! I want to speak to you.'

(b) For names of people, places, rivers, etc.—

   George, London, the Ganges

(c) For nations and adjectives of nationality—

   France, a Frenchman

(d) For names of days, months, festivals and historical eras—

    Monday, January, Christmas, the Middle Ages

(e) For titles of people and names of things when referring to unique examples—

    a mayor *but* the Mayor of Casterbridge
    the Holy Grail, the Golden Fleece

(f) For titles of books, plays, works of art—

    Measure for Measure, Gone with the Wind, the Mona Lisa, the Inferno, the Fifth Symphony

Put capital letters in the correct places in the following sentences:

1. the day after christmas, george called on the mayor.
2. you can cross the thames at westminster to visit the houses of parliament.
3. i started to learn german in january last year.
4. robert wanted to become a colonel before his brother, the major.
5. is sir william a knight or a baronet?
6. the swiss have been expert watchmakers since the middle ages.
7. kings and queens are mortal; so are emperors and empresses.
8. othello, the moor of venice, is a play of shakespeare's.
9. kant's critique of pure reason is one of the great philosophical works of the last century.
10. thomas is flying to rome by b.o.a.c. on the thursday after easter.

SECTION 12

SPELLING

Exercise No 164. The Problem of the Final 'y'

RULE 1: The final *y* of a word changes to *i* before any ending except *-ing*, if it is preceded by a consonant:

    cry—cr*y*ing—cr*i*ed, happ*y*—happ*i*ness

RULE 2: The final *y* remains unchanged before any ending, if it is preceded by a vowel:

    stay—sta*y*ing—sta*y*ed, pa*y*—pa*y*ment—pa*y*able

Now write the present and past participles of the following verbs:

multiply	obey	employ	marry
terrify	pray	bury	delay
enjoy	dry	fry	try
play	pry	modify	supply
qualify	study	destroy	reply
stray	display	sway	annoy
convey	deny	betray	purify
hurry	rely	spray	ally

Exercise No 165

Add the endings given to the following words:

merry-ment	pay-ment	boy-ish	grey-er
enjoyable	funny-ly	enjoy-ment	carry-age
marry-age	joy-ous	employ-ment	beauty-ful
plenty-ful	faulty-ly	glory-ous	dry-ly
body-ly	sleepy-ness	pay-able	pray-er
cloudy-ness	ignominy-ous	fury-ous	annoy-ance
jolly-er	merry-ly	multiply-cation	thirty-eth
bury-al	study-ous	betray-al	lay-er
try-al	salty-ness	greasy-ness	rely-able
sixty-eth	jolly-est	ally-ance	vary-able
sticky-est	vary-ous	joy-ful	victory-ous
undeny-able			

EXCEPTIONS: daily, gaily, said, paid, laid, shyly, slyly

Exercise No 166

RULE 3: When making plural or adding the ending of the third person singular of the Simple Present Tense:

(a) The *y* preceded by a consonant changes to *i* and adds *-es*—

stud*y*—stud*ies*, cr*y*—cr*ies*

(b) The *y* preceded by a vowel letter remains unchanged and adds *s*—

bu*y*—bu*ys*, ke*y*—ke*ys*

Now make these words plural:

monkey	supply	cry	reply
turkey	chimney	day	donkey
fury	valley	story	storey
baby	body	glory	joy
folly	dormitory	victory	sympathy
aunty	way	laboratory	jelly
berry			

Exercise No 167

Read the rule for the preceding exercise.

Now give the third person singular of the Simple Present Tense of these verbs:

multiply	bury	play	reply
betray	rely	cry	fly
pray	stray	solidify	deny
employ	buy	modify	try
hurry	worry	enjoy	supply
sway	annoy	jelly	display
marry	stay	qualify	terrify
fry	dry	convey	

Exercise No 168. The Problem of Doubling Consonants

RULE 4: Words of one syllable that end in a consonant preceded by a single vowel letter, double the consonant before an ending beginning with a vowel letter.

dro*p*—dro*pp*ed, shi*p*—shi*pp*ing, lu*g*—lu*gg*age

SECTION 12 SPELLING

Now add the endings indicated to the following words:

big-er	beg-ar	run-ing	hot-est
win-er	rob-er	hid-en	rid-ance
rub-er	sit-ing	let-ing	whip-ed
hum-ing	shrug-ed	slam-ed	nag-ing
pat-er	wet-est	step-ing	bet-ing
sag-ed	hat-er	fit-est	pot-er
run-er	bat-ing	war-ior	sun-y
mud-y	up-ish		

Exercise No 169

RULE 5: Words of more than one syllable follow Rule 4 only if the word is accented on the last syllable.

permít—permitted, occúr—occurring, forgót—forgótten—but: díffer—dífference, wóman—wómanish

Now add the endings indicated to the following words:

admit-ance	regret-able	commit-ed	prosper-ous
begin-ing	offer-ed	happen-ing	visit-or
confer-ed	omit-ed	enter-ing	murder-er
loyal-ist	consider-ing	repel-ant	inter-ing
pardon-able	upset-ing	compel-ing	

Exercise No 170

RULE 6: If the word already ends in two consonants, or a consonant preceded by two vowel letters, the consonant does not double before any ending.

fast—fastest, weep—weeping

Now add the endings indicated to the following words:

sweet-en	cheap-en	boil-ing	wood-en
gold-en	rot-en	hot-er	long-est
root-ed	feed-ing	bud-ing	set-ing
seat-ing	bet-ed	beat-en	fall-en
wait-er	sweat-er	rid-en	read-ing
rip-ing	reap-ing	lean-est	thin-est
wit-y	part-ed	last-ing	fast-er

EXCEPTION: wool—woollen

Exercise No 171

RULE 7: Words of one syllable and written with one vowel letter do not end with the single consonants -s, -f, -c, -l, -z

    miss, cliff, pull, jazz

EXCEPTIONS ARE: this, his, if, bus, us, has

Now add the extra consonants where necessary:

impel-	wel-	kis-	fiz-
whiz-	fel-	if-	hel-
buz-	stif-	barrel-	pil-
rebel-	bel-	peril-	damsel-
parcel-	compel-	mis-	morsel-
kernel-	kennel-	sel-	jewel-
stil-	instil-	distil-	this-
fil-	fulfil-	analysis-	feel-
stuf-	staf-	leaf-	

Exercise No 172

RULE 8: Words of one syllable with one vowel letter cannot end in -c alone but require -ck:

    luck, back, sick; but: music, cupric, etc.

Words of one syllable with two vowel letters cannot end in -ck, but require -k alone:

    leak, steak, beak, look, etc.

Now add -c, -ck or -k on the following words:

wea-	wi-	wre-	lo-
fantasti-	pri-	tri-	see-
li-	ro-	roo-	kno-
la-	pani-	froli-	coli-
toni-	too-	boo-	emphati-
sto-	publi-	plasti-	fro-

Exercise No 173

RULE 9: Words of one syllable and one vowel letter never end in a single -l; words of one syllable but two vowel letters never end in -ll.

    Example: still, stall, steal, steel, stool

SECTION 12   SPELLING   171

Now add another *l* where necessary:

fil-	feel-	pil-	peel-
refil-	tal-	avail-	appal-
travel-	appeal-	seal-	sil-
until-	tassel-	pul-	repel-
til-	pool-	wel-	fulfil-
bowel-	vowel-	towel-	duel-

EXCEPTION: pal

Exercise No 174. The Doubling of 'l'

RULE·10: Words of more than one syllable that end in one vowel letter and *l*, even if the accent is on the first syllable, double the *l* before an ending beginning with a vowel.

quarrelled, marvellous ; but: realize, appealed

Now add the endings indicated to the following words:

appal-ed	jewel-er	duel-ist	cancel-ing
repeal-ed	rebel-ious	steal-ing	bedevil-ed
snivel-ed	impel-ed	unfeel-ing	befoul-ed
repel-ant	libel-ous	travel-er	drivel-ing
fulfil-ed	tunnel-ed	avail-able	fulfil-ment
pedal-ed	fail-ure	disembowel-ing	rail-ing

(American usage has the single *l* in all cases.)

Exercise No 175. Words with a Silent 'e'

RULE 11: Words which end with a silent *e* drop the *e* when they add an ending beginning with a vowel.

live—living, continue—continuing

EXCEPTIONS: seeing, agreeing, guaranteeing, saleable

Write the present and past participles of the following verbs:

prize	love	continue	incline	rhyme
tire	dine	mine	save	vote
name	fire	smile	revile	behave
abate	shame	hope	cope	fare
confide	praise	raze	blaze	face
	rake	use	rage	

Add the endings indicated to the following words:

write-er	wire-y	praise-worthy	behave-iour
wise-ly	nine-ty	move-ment	love-able
noise-less	noise-y	hope-less	continue-al
tire-some	love-ly	shame-ful	raze-or
abate-ment	remove-al	arrive-al	dispose-al
please-ure	inflate-ion	hygiene-ic	believe-able
use-ful	move-able	compose-ition	catalogue-ed
save-iour	revolve-ed	fertile-ity	

RULE 12: Words ending in -ce and -ge retain the silent e when adding endings other than those beginning with -e or -i.

        change—changing—changeable

Add the endings indicated to the following words:

advantage-ous	service-able	manage-ed	manage-able
replace-able	grace-ious	peace-able	irreduce-ible
age-ing	age-less	trace-ing	embrace-ed
judge-ment	enlarge-ment	engage-ing	disparage-ment
spice-y	entice-ing	conduce-ive	knowledge-able
courage-ous	replace-ing	outrage-ous	indulge-ent
abridge-ment	plunge-ing	arrange-ing	

Exercise No 176. The Silent 'e' (contd.)

The effect of the silent *e* is in most cases to lengthen the vowel before it or to make it into a diphthong:

        bad—bade [a → ei], met—complete [e → i:], sit—site [i → ai],
        rod—rode [o → ou], jut—jute [ʌ → (j)u:]

Now read these words in pairs and then the teacher will dictate selected examples:

rid	ride	mad	made	rob	robe	mull	mule
bit	bite	fad	fade	cock	coke	cut	cute
rim	rime	bad	bade	Jock	joke	luck	Luke
chid	chide	lack	lake	rod	rode	jut	jute
win	wine	back	bake	nod	node	hum	fume
rip	ripe	rag	rage	Dom	dome	stun	tune
pin	pine	stag	stage	con	cone	cup	dupe
lick	like	wag	wage	hop	hope	cub	cube

SECTION 12 — SPELLING

sit	site	pal	pale	drop	rope	tub	tube
rib	tribe	jam	James	doss	dose	sun	prune
pip	pipe	sham	shame	loss	close	dun	dune
whip	wipe	dam	dame	dot	dote	run	rune
hid	hide	pan	pane	mop	mope	buck	fluke
trip	tripe	can	cane	shot	quote	smut	flute
hiss	wise	man	mane	moll	mole	cull	yule
pill	pile	cap	cape	lot	smote	hull	rule
mill	mile	tap	tape	toss	hose	suck	puce
dim	dime	gap	gape	rot	wrote	duck	duke
slim	slime	mass	maze	pop	pope	slut	lute
		crass	craze	doll	dole	us	use
		glass	glaze			fuss	fuse
		rat	rate				
		fat	fate				

Exercise No 177

(There is no need for the student to understand the meaning of the words in this exercise: the teacher will dictate the following lists:)

rid	write	sin	pipe	time
side	bit	dine	whip	dim
ridding	bitten	dinner	dipping	slimming
bided	written	liner	ripen	mimed
bid	whiten	mined	wiped	lime
hidden	writ	sinned	sip	swimming
hat	bad	ham	ban	chap
rate	shade	blame	caned	tape
dated	faded	ramming	canning	happen
batting	ladder	tamed	waned	gaped
fated	adding	stammer	sane	apple
latter	made	shame	planned	shaped
scot	God	top	mob	rock
wrote	mode	slope	globe	stroke
potted	dodder	hoped	robed	pocket
quoted	boded	stopping	robbing	stoked
rotting	sodden	open	probing	cock
smote	strode	hopper	throbbing	stocking

fuss	tube	puce	huge	rude
ruse	hub	truck	bug	mud
abused	rubbing	luckless	hugging	rudder
hussy	cubed	truce	lugger	budding
truss	tubing	reduced	deluge	crude
using	cub	stuck	refuge	deluded
let	scene	eke	grebe	
replete	men	treck	red	
better	these	them	aesthete	
obese	web	theme	set	
less	telling	convened	effete	

Exercise No 178

In some exceptional words the silent *e* does not have the effect of lengthening the vowel:

Arrange these words in two groups: (*a*) those with long vowels and (*b*) those with short:

give	rose	done	drive	love
wine	shone	live	tome	behave
have	above	game	glove	become
wave	one	some	derive	shave
dove	rove	forgive	come	tone
gone	surface	drove	preface	handsome
alive				liver

Exercise No 179. The Ending '-le'

The common ending *-le* lengthens the vowel before it in the same way as a silent *e* if there is only one consonant before it: bridle [ai]. The vowel remains short if there are two consonants: riddle [i].

The teacher dictates these words to the students:

sickle	dribble	able	ripple	duple
tickle	scribble	nipple	cycle	buckle
bubble	bible	apple	sidle	idle
people	tackle	feeble	staple	bottle
struggle	eagle	beetle	title	little
ogle	goggle	doodle	haggle	needle
kettle	fiddle	wheedle	rattle	

Exercise No 180. Double Consonants

In some languages, notably Spanish, the double consonants in Latin words have been reduced to only one:

Attention (English and French)—atención (Spanish)
Possible (,, ,,)—posible (,,)

Write these words adding a second consonant in place of the dash, where it is necessary:

a–bandon	a–cident	a–dept	a–dhere	a–fection
a–bominable	a–cent	a–crobat	a–dition	a–fair
a–breviate	a–cept	a–bundant	a–dress	a–firm
a–bolish	a–commodate	a–cumulate	a–djust	a–dore
a–curate	a–company	a–chieve	a–dmire	a–dverse
a–cess	a–cording	a–cademy	a–dmit	a–dopt
a–count	a–gravate	a–lone	a–ltogether	a–ford
a–flict	a–genda	a–larm	a–lteration	a–monia
a–far	a–gression	a–legiance	a–lways	a–lthough
a–liance	a–lready	a–lmighty	a–fraid	a–griculture
a–lure	a–low	a–lmost	a–natomy	a–petite
a–munition	a–nounce	a–pear	a–proximate	a–pology
a–paratus	a–postle	a–pendix	a–mount	a–pointment
a–partment	a–plaud	a–peal	a–range	a–sent
a–tach	a–tain	a–tempt	a–rouse	a–semble
a–tend	a–titude	a–tom	a–rest	a–sign
a–tribute	a–trocious	a–sure	a–rithmetic	a–sume
a–stonish			a–rable	
e–clipse	e–conomy	e–centric	e–ditor	e–ducate
e–fect	e–ficient	e–fort	e–lephant	e–molument
e–say	e–sence	e–stablish	e–state	e–steem
di–satisfy	di–sappear	di–service	di–sown	di–sability
di–minish	di–sapprove	di–sengage	di–spatch	di–sease
di–sect	di–similar	di–splay	di–splease	di–solve
di–stribute		di–suse		
i–legal	i–literate	i–lusion	i–lustrate	i–dle
i–gnite	i–gnorant	i–magine	i–mitate	i–mature
i–mediate	i–mense	i–moral	i–mune	i–mortal
i–nedible	i–nelastic	i–nequality	i–nocent	i–numerable
i–noffensive		i–norganic	i–resistible	
i–ritate	i–regular	i–rony	i–relevant	i–responsible

po–litical	po–lice	po–lute	po–lygonal	po–sess
po–sible	po–sitive	po–sition	po–sessive	

o–bvious	o–bliterate	o–bedient	o–bscure	o–casion
o–cupation	o–cur	o–cean	o–fend	o–ficial
o–mission	o–nion	o–portune	o–pose	o–pinion
o–press	o–ptician			

su–bstitute	su–btract	su–cess	su–cumb	su–mary
su–mit	su–perb	su–port	su–plement	su–pose
su–rety	su–preme	su–render	su–rvey	su–rvive
su–ply	su–den			

Exercise No 181. Plurals

Words ending in *-f* and some ending in *-fe* make the plural by adding *s* or by changing the *-f* to *-ve* before the plural ending.

    Thie*f*—thie*ves*   grie*f*—grie*fs*

There is no rule and both types of plural are equally common.

This is a list of the common examples of this kind of word. Write them in the plural:

wharf	leaf	wife	knife	loaf
roof	proof	belief	hoof	reef
sheaf	chief	brief	life	half
calf	strife	self	relief	gulf
shelf	wolf	safe		

Exercise No 182

Words ending in *-o* in English are all words borrowed from other languages. Some make their plurals with *-es* and others with *-s*. Generally speaking the words which are commoner and are no longer recognized as foreign use the ending *-es*:

    Potat*o*—potat*oes* but stud*io*—stud*ios*

Write the plural of:

volcano	tomato	potato	photo	piano
solo	hero	allegro	cargo	echo
oratorio	octavo	halo	negro	radio
ratio	shampoo	tango	kangaroo	memento
mosquito	torpedo			

SECTION 12   SPELLING   177

Exercise No 183

Words ending with the sounds [s], [z], [ʃ] and [ʒ], [tʃ], and [dʒ] add the extra syllable [-iz] when spoken in the plural. This is written *-es* when the word does not end in the letter *e*.

    Match—matches *but* judge—judges

Give the written plurals of these words and then pronounce them:

match	judge	garage	crash	latch
hitch	face	rage	box	axe
gas	edge	buzz	dish	patch
ledge	success	image	annexe	index
baggage	polish	varnish	smash	splash
fish	cabbage	recess	appearance	reverse
bunch	prefix	thickness	paradox	bridge

(*Note:* The formation of the third person singular of the simple present tense follows the same system.)

Exercise No 184. The Spelling of Vowel Sounds

The teacher will dictate the following lists, each having one vowel sound but using most of the possible spellings of that sound:

(i) [iː]	(ii) [e]	(iii) [aː]	(iv) [o]	(v) [oː]
key	friend	guard	pot	abroad
leave	bet	father	yacht	ward
queen	stead	harm	cauliflower	port
ceiling	said	branch	cough	shore
steep	well	demand	cross	call
piece, peace	bread	aunt	common	sword
field	any	drama	laurel	laundry
grieve	Thames	draught	knowledge	law
sea, see	says	clerk	sausage	brought
knee	deaf	heart	cloth	source
shield	breath	can't	Moll	water
teeth	threat	glass	doll	floor
beast	leisure	staff		caught
seize	weapon	half		George
mean	bury	rather		bald
people	Leonard	laugh		talk

(i) [iː]	(ii) [e]	(iii) [aː]	(iv) [o]	(v) [oː]
wreath	many	Derby		force
feel		vase		door
week, weak				sore
reach				pour, paw

(vi) [u]	(vii) [uː]	(viii) [ʌ]	(ix) [əː]	(x) [ai]
hook	mood	tongue	fir, fur	die
book	ruse	flood	turn	liar
soot	lose	mud	fern	buy, by
pull	loose	study	heard, herd	child
wolf	tomb	love	burn	mind
could	two	does	courtesy	defy
woman	Ruth	country	journey	rye
should	through	punish	work	eye, I
foot	youth	glove	third	climb
butcher	whom	mother	colonel	aisle, isle
cushion	truth	come	her	height
push	shoe	money	earth	why
bullet	do	London	sir	sight, site
bosom	wound	onion	earn	rise
wool	brood	other	worm	guide
hood	whose	worry	journal	guy
bull	move	flourish	bird	sign
pudding		blood		
bush		couple		
good		enough		

(xi) [ei]	(xii) [ou]	(xiii) [eə]
say	goal	air, heir
jail (gaol)	toll	where
eight	boat	fair, fare
reign, rain	both	layer
angel	brooch	pair, pear
date	comb	care
Cambridge	smoke	prayer
chamber	bowl	dare
gauge	glow	swear
break, brake	so, sew, sow	their, there

(xi) [ei]	(xii) [ou]	(xiii) [eə]
they	bold	wear
grey	most	chair
halfpenny	road, rode	share
veil, vale	folk	stare, stair
danger	whole, hole	mayor, mare
wait, weight	soul, sole	bare, bear
raise	owe	
ache		

(*Note:* The thirteen vowels and diphthongs practised here do not represent all the vowel sounds found in English, but only those which cause difficulties in spelling.)

Exercise No 185

The spelling *ow* has two distinct pronunciations which are often confused: [au] and [ou]:

    how [au]—mow [ou]

Divide these words into two groups according to their pronunciation:

drown	row	allow	glow
brow	blow	low	sow
bow	crow	gown	now
follow	throw	slow	flow
show	hollow	cow	vow
brown	fellow	crown	bestow
fowl	below	clown	snow
frown	bowl	owl	crowd
grow			

Exercise No 186

The following lists of words represent two vowel sounds: [o:] and [ə:].

    word [ə:]—more [o:]

Divide them into two groups according to their pronunciation:

worth	courtesy	journey	work
worse	source	pour	colonel
worm	port	wore	floor

sword	more	worst	torn
course	storm	north	cork
	world	forth	fourth

Exercise No 187

The following words represent two vowel sounds [o] and [ʌ].

    gone [o]—done [ʌ]

Divide them into two groups according to their pronunciation:

some	son	one	cover
common	cloth	wrong	Monday
above	pot	colour	bomb
love	blood	come	doll
across	glove	London	shove
rot	upon	shop	dove
tongue	thorough	brother	cough
donkey	honey	gong	none
monkey	among	mother	

Exercise No 188. Long and Short 'i' Sounds

The following words all have the short *i* sound [i].

Write the word which corresponds to them having the long *i* sound [i:]

ship	whip	dim	sick
kill	hip	dip	sin
did	wit	lip	pill
kin	hid	fit	hit
will	hill	bid	flit
sit	pick	rid	slip
rip	bit	lick	mill

Exercise No 189. Long and Short 'i' Sounds and the Effect of the Silent 'e'

Here are three lists of words which differ in the following way:

List (*a*) long *i* sound [i:]; List (*b*) short *i* sound [i]; and List (*c*) lengthened vowel as a result of the silent *e* [ai].

SECTION 12   SPELLING   181

The teacher will dictate a word from any one list and ask the class to write the corresponding word from the other two lists.

Example:

The teacher says, '*whip*'. The student writes, '*weep*' and '*wipe*'.

List A	List B	List C
weep	whip	wipe
deem	dim	dime
wheat	wit	white
peel	pill	pile
keen	kin	kine
heed	hid	hide
wheel	will	while
bead	bid	bide
seat	sit	site
peak	pick	pike
read	rid	ride
reap	rip	ripe
beat	bit	bite
leak	lick	like
meal	mill	mile
speak	spick	spike
peep	pip	pipe

Exercise No 190. Long and Short 'u' Sounds, (u) and (u:)

The spelling *oo* represents two different sounds [u] and [u:],

    boot [u:]—foot [u]

Divide the following words into two lists to show that you know which word has the long sound and which the short:

soothe	book	cook	stoop
loot	fool	food	roof
good	room	smooth	boon
tool	wood	mood	soot
shook	moon	look	goose
tooth	took	pool	cool
spoon	shoot	hood	wool
		hook	

Exercise No 191. The Sounds of the Spelling 'ea'

The combination of letters *ea* has a number of pronunciations. Two of these are sufficiently common to be considered regular.

[i:] heat [e] head

The following list of words contains only those which have these two pronunciations. Divide them into two lists according to the pronunciations shown above:

wheat	seat	sea	lead
read	dead	pea	stead
deaf	weapon	clean	bean
dread	dream	lean	league
breast	breath	breathe	steal
dreamed	leaped	leaned	bread
	heap	treat	threat

(*Note:* The words: 'great', 'steak', 'break' are exceptional, with the vowel sound [ei].)

Exercise No 192. The Sounds of the Vowel Letter 'u'

The vowel letter *u* in a syllable closed by a consonant has the pronunciation [ʌ], but a certain number of common words with this spelling have the sound [u].

Divide these words into two groups, those having the sound [ʌ] and those the sound [u]:

push	pull	butcher	rush
gull	hutch	cushion	bull
Russian	dull	budding	pudding
bush	full	hush	lucky
sugar	Sunday	bullet	bulletin
fulfil	funny	pulpit	pulse
pussy	fussy	put	but

Exercise No 193

The spellings *ou* and *oa* produce two distinct vowel sounds [o:] and [ou].

loaf *and* soul [ou]
broad *and* thought [o:]

SECTION 12 — SPELLING

Divide these words into two groups having the same sound. Both spellings are found with both pronunciations.

soar	foal	float	boar
though	road	goal	moan
board	source	goad	mould
goat	hoarse	mourn	hoard
court	shoal	pour	roar
ought	shoulder	boulder	load

Exercise No 194. Words with Syllables Closed by 'r'

The vowel sounds [ə:], [a:] and [o:] are often found with *a vowel letter + r* spelling.

[ə:] is regularly represented by the spelling *-ir*, *-ur* and *-er*:

> fir, fur, stern

[a:] by the spelling *ar*:

> far

[o:] by the spellings *-or(e)*, *-oar* and *-our*:

> for, oar, four

(There are, however, spellings with *r* which have irregular pronunciations.)

1. Make these words into three lists representing the vowel sounds [ə:], [a:] and [o:]:

first	third	girl	more
star	Derby	door	fur
heard	heart	soar	court
ward	earth	warn	war
shore	clerk	pearl	warm
earn	journey	work	courtesy
firm	far	burn	worm
world	word		fir
turn	worst		

The diphthongs [iə], [eə] and [uə] are found only in words with *vowel letter(s) + r* spelling.

G

2. Divide these words into three groups so that each group has the same vowel sound:

hear	hair	where	ear
beard	fear	here	air
tier	beer	bear	mere
doer	austere	steer	stair
bare	their	clear	cure
poor	share	pear	fewer
sure	endure	peer	bluer
pare	there	stare	dear
truer			

(*Note:* An alternative pronunciation of the [uə] diphthong in many words is [o:])
(See also Exercise Nos 184.)

Exercise No 195. Silent Letters

Some of these words begin with a silent *k*. Say which (some exist with and without silent *k*):

–nave	–need	–nead	–net	–nife
–night	–nought	–nit	–neat	–nob
–nub	–nock	–now	–nuckle	–nickel
–new	–newer	–nell	–not	–naked
–nickers	–nib	–nymph		

Some of these words end with a silent *b*. Say which:

lam–	dram–	gum–	rum–	thum–
bom–	com–	drum–	rim–	lim–
jam–	clam–	clim–	cram–	succum–
groom–	num–	slim–	slum–	wom–
hum–	dum–			

Some of these words have a silent *l* in place of the dash. Say which:

a–mond	wa–k	sta–k	sa–mon	shou–d
ba–ke	cou–d	revo–ke	ha–f	pa–m
sha–m	psa–m	ca–m	ra–m	sa–fe
fo–k	yo–k	co–ke	ta–k	ha–m
beha–ve	beha–f	cha–k	ha–ve	wou–d

SECTION 12 SPELLING

Some of these words have a silent *g* in place of the dash. Say which:

si–n	resi–n	campai–n	soverei–n	mai–n
desi–n	forei–n	rei–n	strai–n	pai–n
beni–n	fei–n	disdai–n	complai–n	mali–n

Some of these words begin with a silent *w*. Say which:

–rite	–rong	–rap	–rist	–rate
–rip	–rest	–retched	–rinkle	–ring
–reck	–root	–ran	–ren	–rope
–ry	–rote	–rath	–rut	–riggle
–rely	–rank	–rune	–rob	–run

Place a silent *t* OR an *s* in place of the dash in the following words:

fas–en	has–en	lis–en	whis–le	les–en
wres–le	tas–el	cas–le	les–on	mus–el
fis–ile	gos–ip	apos–le	pas–ing	chas–en
vas–al	ves–el	chris–en	fos–il	this–le
mis–al	rus–le	ris–ole	mis–letoe	kis–ing

Exercise No 196

The sounds [tʃ] and [dʒ] at the end of words have two spellings *ch* or *tch* and *ge* or *dge*. If the vowel sound is long, the spelling is *ch* or *ge*:

> reach, brooch, huge, siege

If the vowel sound is short the spelling is *tch* or *dge*:

> ridge, lodge, match, stitch

Exceptions: college, which, rich, attach, detach, and words of two syllables ending in -*age* [-idʒ].

Now add a *t* or a *d* where this is necessary:

ra–ge	ba–ge	le–ge	e–ge
a–ge	lo–ge	bagga–ge	lugga–ge
porri–ge	delu–ge	subterfu–ge	gou–ge
sie–ge	ha–ch	wi–ch	broo–ch
approa–ch	cou–ch	pou–ch	slou–ch
pa–ch	pea–ch	bee–ch	fe–ch
wre–ch	gau–ge	ma–ch	besie–ge
di–ch	refu–ge	knowle–ge	cotta–ge
sti–ch	ca–ch	hu–ge	sta–ge
tea–ch	ju–ge		

Exercise No 197. Words with Greek Roots

Words using Greek roots often contain certain characteristic letters or groups of letters which are not usually found in words of English or Latin origin:

ps—psychiatry [s]   *ch*—archive [k]   *ph*—philosophy [f]
y—cycle [ai] or [i]   *ae*—haematology [i:]   *rh*—rheumatism [r]

The teacher will dictate these words to the students:

typography	psychology	alphabet	photography
microscope	physics	oxygen	anaemic
hydrophobia	bicycle	character	rhyme
choir	psalm	rhythm	chorus
pseudonym	analyse	chloride	aesthetic
hydrogen	chronicle	cylinder	thermometer
pharmacy	pyramid	rhetoric	philanthropic
crystal	phonetic	phrase	physical

Exercise No 198. The Hyphen

1. The hyphen is always used in the compound adjectives practised in Exercises Nos 208, 210:

    Blue-eyed, long-nosed, third-floor, two-foot

2. It is usually used in making new words with the Latin prefixes practised in Exercises Nos. 224, 233:

    Anti-Semitism, pro-Belgian, un-American

3. In the making of compound nouns the use of the hyphen is less regular. There is no fixed rule. The tendency is:

    (*a*) To join the two parts if they are short and if the thing is common and we no longer think of it as a compound word—

    teapot, bedroom, bathroom, bookcase

    (*b*) To use a hyphen if we still think of the thing as a compound word, particularly if one part is a gerund—

    drawing-room, walking-stick, market-place

    (*c*) To write the two parts separately if the combination is less common and the parts are long—

    insurance policy, history lessons, engineering faculty

SPELLING

Now combine the pairs of words or parts of words into complete wholes (*a*) by joining them together or (*b*) by joining them with a hyphen or (*c*) by writing them as two separate parts, according to instructions given above:

class room	arm chair	rain coat	book case
school teacher	reading lamp	tea spoon	head master
riding school	book shop	boot polish	boy scout
history master	house wife	waist coat	fore head
blue eyed	sauce pan	flag staff	horse racing
motor car	telephone box	water colour	post war
inter national	pro Belgian	co operation	co existence
bank note	hospital bed	pen knife	cup board
hand writing	sea shore	non sense	non intervention
post natal	flood lit	country man	pre Shakespearian
dining room	bath room	gas light	writing paper
note paper	milk jug	letter box	camp bed
sitting room			

(When in doubt, consult a good dictionary.)

SECTION 13

WORD BUILDING

Exercise No 199. Adjective Suffixes '-y' and '-ly'

1. The suffix -y is generally added to uncountable nouns indicating materials, to mean: *having the quality of* or *appearance of* that material:

    sand—sandy, grease—greasy, salt—salty

2. The suffix -ly is added to certain categories of persons, with the meaning of *having the quality or appearance of* that person:

    father—fatherly, scoundrel—scoundrelly

    also to certain periods of time:

    month—monthly (=*which occurs or appears every month*)

Form suitable adjectives from the following words:

night	elder	soldier	day
friend	ghost	daughter	year
scholar	sugar	woman	hour
rascal	God	oil	mud
cloud	sun	king	fortnight
maiden	wind	mist	snow
grass	beast	water	earth
silk	rubber	silver	rust

Exercise No 200. The Adjective Suffix '-ish'

The common suffix -ish is added to nouns and other adjectives.

1. Added to the names of animals or persons it generally means *having the bad qualities of*:

    girl—girlish   old maid—old maidish

2. Added to people of different nationality it forms the adjective of nationality:

    Swede—Swedish

3. Added to other short adjectives (adjectives of colour especially) it qualifies their meaning in this way:

    old: oldish (=*rather old*)
    green: greenish (=*having a slightly green quality*)

Now form the adjectives from the following words by adding *-ish* and then divide them into three groups according to the above classification and show exactly what they mean:

boy	strong	stiff	clown
swine	monk	Spain	long
Pole	grey	soft	young
Frank	Moor	tight	stand-off
poor	amateur	devil	slave
brute	sheep	mule	wasp
slug	kitten	self	Finn

Exercise No 201. Adjective Suffixes '-like', '-some' and '-worthy'

Here are three more adjective suffixes. These are slightly less common than those mentioned before.

1. *-like* is added to countable nouns, generally meaning people or animals (but sometimes objects) with the sense of *resembling* or *in the manner of* these things:

    box—boxlike; cat—catlike; God—Godlike

2. *-some* is added to verbs or nouns with a causative sense:

    to tire—tiresome (=*which makes one tired*)

3. *-worthy* is added to nouns with the meaning of *worthy of* or *suitable for*:

    praise—praiseworthy

Form adjectives from these words using the suffixes *-like*, *-some* and *-worthy*.

war	cumber	weary	trust
hand	full	whole	noise
irk	trouble	child	cow
love	lady	statesman	workman
seaman	Christ	fear	rod
blame	quarrel	dog	note
awe	respect	sea	air
road	paper	loathe	burden
meddle	life	business	lone

Exercise No 202. The Adjective Suffix '-able' ('-ible')

The suffix *-able* is extremely active * and can be added to a very large number of verbs and nouns to mean *able to be*:

    eat—eatable (=*which can be eaten*)

The form *-ible* is the one which is found already attached to words accepted into English direct from Latin. This ending can usually not be separated to leave a verb with any meaning:

    poss(ible)   indestruct(ible)

Now add the ending *-able* or *-ible* to the following words making any small changes in spelling which are necessary:

response	bear	reason	convert
consider	change	foresee	debate
access	defend	respect	suit
admire	read	divide	contempt
regret	value	permit	avoid

Exercise No 203. Negative Prefixes

The negative prefix *in-* is more often used with words of Latin origin whilst *un-* is more frequently found with words of English origin.

Make these words negative by adding the prefix *in-* or *un-*:

acceptable	reasonable	readable	comparable
admissible	thinkable	printable	accessible
defensible	believable	beatable	definable
bearable	eligible	desirable	dependable
usable	workable	teachable	digestible
palatable	different	pronounceable	climbable

Exercise No 204

Make these words negative by adding *un-*, *in-* or *dis-*. Some of them use both prefixes with slightly different meaning:

satisfied	approve	comfortable	trustworthy
appear	believe	trust	appoint
convenient	comfort	armament	agree

* An *active suffix* is one which we can still use in modern English to form new words.

please	oblige	cover	favour
grace	graceful	courage	honest
obey	order	soluble	applicable
fortunate	famous	appropriate	connected
efficient	frequent	considerable	equality
loyal	like	conclusive	equal
favourable	creditable	believable	kind

Exercise No 205. The Prefixes 'mis-' and 'dis-'

The prefix *mis-* can be added to verbs or their past participles and generally means that the action has been incorrectly or inadequately performed.

Misdirected (=*wrongly directed*), misused (=*incorrectly used*)

The prefix *dis-*, on the other hand, makes the meaning of the word the exact opposite:

like—dislike, contented—discontented

Compare: disbelief: (=*not believing*)
misbelief: (=*believing, but something wrong*)

Form adjectives by adding the prefixes *mis-* or *dis-* to these past participles. Some can take both prefixes:

taken	informed	applied	trusted
judged	continued	laid	read
inclined	affected	placed	shapen
translated	used	counted	led
liked	spelled	understood	covered
ordered	pleased	appropriated	inherited
directed	construed	leading	

Exercise No 206. The Suffixes '-ful' and '-less'

The suffix *-ful* (only one *l*) makes adjectives from nouns (and sometimes verbs) with the meaning of *filled with* or *having*:

faithful (=*having faith in*)

Some of these same nouns (never verbs) form adjectives of exactly opposite meaning by adding *-less*.

faithless (=*having no faith*)

Quite a large number of words may add one or the other of these two suffixes but not both:

frightful, but *not* 'frightless'
noiseless, but *not* 'noiseful'

(Note that this ending *-ful* must not be confused with the same ending as practised in Exercise No. 220, where it forms nouns not adjectives.)

Now make the following words into three lists, thus: one list of words which take both endings; and one list each of words which only take either *-less* or *-ful*:

Examples:

List I   Faithful—faithless
List II   Frightful—opposite: pleasant, nice, etc.
List III   Noiseless—opposite; noisy

harm	use	water	truth
colour	success	help	tree
purpose	child	sound	joy
thank	forget	cease	hair
eye	care	thought	regard
need	mind	heed	fruit
play	meaning	beauty	price
base	taste	sense	penny
sleep	rest	pain	time

(Note that the ending *-less* is still active:

sugarless tea, waterless desert, leafless tree

The suffix *-ful* is not active in this way.)

Exercise No 207. Comparatives and Superlatives

The following classes of adjectives form their comparatives and superlatives by adding *-er* and *-est*:

1. All adjectives of one syllable—

    longer, shorter, younger, older

2. Adjectives of two syllables ending in *-ow, -y, -le, -er*—

    hollower, simpler, rainiest, cleverest

3. A few adjectives of two syllables with the accent on the first syllable—

    common—commoner (or: more common)

SECTION 13　WORD BUILDING　193

The comparative and superlative of these adjectives can also be made with *more* and *most*.

More and *most* must be used to make the comparative and superlative of all other adjectives.

Give the comparatives and superlatives of the following adjectives:

young	late	pretty	brutish	wicked
fast	yellow	shallow	sunny	ample
beautiful	subtle	regular	elderly	interesting
able	capable	ugly	true	thorough
sudden	real	rapid	proper	polite
open	often	modest	unlucky	likely
humble	guilty	gentle	frequent	fierce
unfair	evil	even	correct	difficult
curious	cruel	content	bitter	worthy
lovely	childish	splendid	quiet	

Exercise No 208. Compound Adjectives Made with Past Participles

Compound adjectives are often made with past participles (or adjectives ending in *-ed*) joined to another word by a hyphen:

　　　hand-made (=*which has been made by hand*)
　　　red-haired (=*who has red hair*)
　　　well-watered (=*which has a good supply of water*)

Change the phrases and clauses in italics into a compound adjective in these examples:

　　Example:

　　A hat *with a broad brim* = a *broad-brimmed* hat

1. A plateau *swept by the wind*
2. A suit *which has been made by a tailor*
3. Ground *which is covered with snow*
4. A teacher *who has been trained in college*
5. A spoon *which has been plated with silver*
6. A dinner table *lit by candles*
7. Shoes *which have rubber soles*
8. An avenue *lined with trees*
9. A pullover *knitted by hand*
10. A cart *drawn by a horse*

11. Susan *with black eyes*
12. A young lad *with a quick wit*
13. A young fellow *with bad manners*
14. A dress *with the colour of coffee*
15. A man *with long hair*
16. A woman *who is well dressed*
17. A young man *who speaks well*
18. An enemy *with a hard heart*
19. A shop *with a good stock*
20. A chair *which is covered with leather*

Exercise No 209. Compound Adjectives with Present Participles

Compound adjectives made with present participles are less common than the previous type. They have an active meaning where the earlier examples have a passive meaning:

> A man-eating tiger (=*who eats men*)

Now reduce these adjective clauses and phrases to a compound adjective:

1. A conjuror *who eats fire*
2. A vehicle *which is moving fast*
3. An occupation *which consumes a lot of time*
4. A plant *which grows quickly*
5. An aeroplane *which can fly high*
6. A parent *who suffers a long time*
7. Machinery *for cutting grass*
8. A plant *for purifying water*
9. A machine-gun *which fires quickly*
10. A river *which runs slowly*

Exercise No 210. Compound Adjectives of Measurement with Numerals

A very useful sort of compound adjective is that which shows the dimension of something:

> a four-foot ruler, a ten-minute interval

The measuring word (foot, minute) is always singular because it is the unit of measurement.

SECTION 13   WORD BUILDING

Another sort of compound adjective which is very similar to this is made with ordinal numbers:

    a second-floor flat, a third-rate actor

Change the phrases and clauses in these examples into a compound adjective:

1. A walk *which takes three hours*
2. A journey *of three hundred miles*
3. A pamphlet *which costs 2½ pence*
4. A mountain *which is four thousand feet high*
5. Music *played by four hands*
6. A drum *which holds four gallons*
7. A house *with four storeys*
8. Exercises *for five fingers*
9. A book *with two hundred pages*
10. A man *who weighs fourteen stones*
11. A castle *built in the fourteenth century*
12. A railway carriage *of the second class*
13. A contract *which expires at the end of three years*
14. A class *which has reached the fourth year of studies*
15. A car *with the rating of 18 horse-power*

Exercise No 211

This exercise practises some common compound adjectives.

Put the correct word in the blank spaces:

1. The broadcast was made from a ...-proof room.
2. He is wearing a ...proof watch.
3. He escaped with his ...-gotten gains.
4. He continued speaking in a matter-of-... voice.
5. I shall always remember what happened in that never-to-be-... moment.
6. We have no time to listen to his ...-drawn-out argument.
7. He sells ...-to-wear suits.
8. The critics praised the books for its ...-thought-out argument.
9. She came in wearing a ...-fitting dress.
10. He was speaking to a sailor with a ...-beaten face.
11. Have you an up-to-... copy of the instructions.

12. He was driving the post in with a ...-called beetle.
13. I'm sure you wouldn't be interested in an account of our day-to-... existence.
14. I can assure you he's nothing but an out-and-... liar.
15. I regard your comments as entirely uncalled-...
16. Life in the jungle is very simple and down-to-...
17. You can imagine the relief of his ...-suffering employers when he left.
18. They caught the thief red-...
19. Are you wearing a made-to-... suit?
20. I should judge them to be ...-informed people.

Exercise No 212. The Prefixes 'Over-' and 'Under-'

The prefixes *over-* and *under-* can be added to adjectives and past participles with the meaning of *to an excessive degree* or *to an inadequate degree*:

> An overworked young man (=*a young man who has been given too much work*)
> An underprepared examination (=*which has been insufficiently prepared*)

Add the prefix *over-* or *under-* in the blank spaces according to the meaning of the sentence:

1. He has been working hard all week and is ...-tired.
2. It burst open like an ...-ripe tomato.
3. This meat is tough and ...-done.
4. As usual, she has come to the party hopelessly ...-dressed.
5. I can't make out anything in this photograph; it is very ...-exposed.
6. He has to work in the evenings at another job: he is seriously ...-paid by his employers.
7. Brazil is a very large country and still considerably ...-populated.
8. Murillo's position as an artist is frequently ...rated.
9. That child has a thin and ...fed look.
10. She is old enough to look after herself: I think her mother is ...-anxious about her.
11. He will come to trouble: he is far too ...-confident.
12. She lost her figure quite young: she was ...-fond of sweet things.

13. I am going to take you through the ...crowded slums of the city.
14. The ship nearly got wrecked because it was ...-manned.
15. You can't be ...-careful.
16. The government is planning aid to the ...-developed countries.

Exercise No 213. Noun Suffixes and Prefixes

The suffixes *-hood*, *-ship* and *-dom* are used to make abstract nouns from the names of people. These words usually have the meaning of *the state of being a . . .*

        priest—priesthood
        apprentice—apprenticeship
        earl—earldom

Note:

(*a*) The names for members of a family have the suffix *-hood*—

    mother—motherhood

(*b*) Words ending in *-er* and *-or* usually have *-ship*—

    dictator—dictatorship
    reader—readership

(*c*) Words ending in *-man* also have *-ship*; in this case the ending *-manship* means *the art or skill of a . . .*—

    workman—workmanship (=*the skill of the workman*)

Make new nouns from these words using the suffixes *-hood*, *-dom* and *-ship*:

wise	free	prince	librarian
lady	scholar	showman	lord
champion	girl	knight	maiden
relation	official	man	curator
brother	fellow	governor	sister
parent	seaman	mother	child
companion	salesman	woman	nation
likely	leader	partner	saint
spinster	lively	martyr	horseman
father	bachelor	hard	

Exercise No 214

The suffix *-ness* is so active in making new abstract words from adjectives of English and Latin origin that words are often invented which are not necessary, because another abstract word already exists made from the same root:

    great—greatness
    humble—humbleness (This word exists, but a better word is —humility)

Add *-ness* to the adjectives of List A, but give the correct abstract noun which corresponds to the adjectives in List B:

List A		List B	
short	full	beautiful	honest
sleepy	calm	courageous	certain
foolish	kind	generous	brave
straight	sad	dense	expensive
smooth	little	jealous	safe
weak	clean	dangerous	patient
rough	hard	difficult	proud
narrow		long	high
			intelligent

Exercise No 215

A small but very important group of words of English origin form (abstract) nouns by adding the ending *-th* or *-t*. They frequently change the vowel in the process:

    hale—health [ei—e]

Give the (abstract) nouns derived from these words:

fly	dead	wide	grow	thrive
young	long	broad		freeze
high	weigh	see	deep	steal
hot	true	give	foul	thieve
warm	bear	dry		

Exercise No 216. Agents: People who Do Things

The endings *-er*, *-or* and *-ar* are the commonest suffixes meaning the *person who does* or *who is connected with*. In spite of the different spelling, all have the same pronunciation, (ə).

    wear—wearer, Senate—senator, beg—beggar

SECTION 13 — WORD BUILDING

Add the correct suffix to these words, making slight changes in spelling where it is necessary:

liberate	lie	lead	law
sail	govern	visit	decorate
sing	donate	orate	translate
cater	dance	office	school
murder	war	Berlin	geography
golf	London		
New York	own		

Exercise No 217

The endings *-ist* and *-an*, *-ian* are also used for the person associated with certain things and places.

> violin—violinist, Rome—Roman, magic—magician

Add the correct endings to these words making slight changes in the spelling where it is necessary:

motor	piano	machine	bicycle
music	tobacco	tour	Christ
electric	mathematics	history	archaeology
botany	politics	Paris	terror
apology	accompany	Italy	cartoon
theology	science	art	Communism
Argentine	physics	psychiatry	
	physic	economics	

Exercise No 218

Here are two more endings used for people:

-eer is used as in the earlier examples for a person 'associated with something'—

> racketeer (=*a man associated with a racket (an illegal activity)*)

-ee is generally used for a person to whom something is done. It has a passive meaning:

> payee (=*the person who is paid*)

Add the ending *-eer* or *-ee* to these words:

employ	absent	refer	lease
auction	election	refuge	profit
mountain	pamphlet	engine	
chariot			

Exercise No 219. Feminine Forms

Feminine forms are usually made by adding the suffix *-ess*. There are some words we cannot add *-ess* to, and in these cases if we really want to show that the person is female, we put the word *woman-* or *lady-* before the noun:

    author—authoress, but: writer—woman-writer

Make the feminine form of these words:

adventurer	seamster	murderer	tiger
cook	shepherd	heir	host
lion	sorcerer	duke	prince
traitor	violinist	speaker	governor
emperor	singer	painter	waiter
master	teacher	mayor	doctor
dentist	lawyer	actor	conductor

Exercise No 220. The Noun Suffix '-ful'

This suffix *-ful* can be added freely to many names of things which can contain or hold something:

    mouth—mouthful (=*the quantity held by the mouth*)

Add the ending *-ful* to the following words and add a suitable phrase to show what is contained:

Example:

mouth—a mouthful of beans
spoon—a spoonful of salt

cupboard	saucer	cup	basin
house	eye	car	box
pocket	hand	shovel	spade
dish	fist	tin	crate
basket	jug	bucket	room

Exercise No 221. Verb Prefixes and Suffixes

The prefixes *under-* and *over-* are used to show that an action is excessive or insufficient. (See Adjective formation.)

Change the words in italics into one verb with the prefix *under-* or *over-*:

Example:

He has been *working too hard* for a long time
=He has been *overworking* for a long time.

1. As usual, he has *stated* his case *too strongly*.
2. If you continue *to wind up* your watch *to that extent*, the spring will break.
3. It is unwise *to rate* your opponent *too lightly*.
4. He died after *dosing* himself *too heavily* with sleeping pills.
5. George has *slept too long* again and missed his train.
6. He has *spent more* than his allowance and now the bank refuses him an overdraft.
7. She has *cooked* this meat *too long* and it's uneatable.
8. Be careful you don't *fill* that glass *too full* or it will spill all over the carpet.
9. I consider that the critics have *praised* that book *too highly*.
10. If you go on *eating too little* you won't be strong enough to come with us.
11. I suppose contractors frequently *give too low an estimate* of the building costs.
12. A shopkeeper who consistently *charges* his customers *too little* will soon go out of business.
13. They are the sort of people who always *put too much furniture in* their house.
14. You must give it at least two seconds if you want to avoid *giving it too short an exposure*.

Exercise No 222. The Suffixes '-en' and '-fy'

1. *-en*: this suffix makes verbs from adjectives and sometimes nouns with the meaning of *to make* . . .

    hard—harden, soft—soften, length—lengthen

2. *-fy* or *-ify*: a suffix of Latin origin which has the same meaning as *-en*. Sometimes it is used in a humorous or familiar way.

    pure—purify, saint—sanctify, French—frenchify (humorous)

Make verbs from these words by adding the endings *-en* or *-fy* and making any small changes in the spelling that are necessary:

strength	rough	short	horror	certain
deep	wide	peace	just	hard
loose	tight	solid	clear	saint
high	less	liquid	simple	false
light	terror	stupid	emulsion	mystery
sharp	beauty	identity	example	country
null	intense	thick		fat

Exercise No 223. '-ate' and '-ize'

These two suffixes have the same meaning: *to make* . . . :

1. *-ize* is very active and is added to adjectives and nouns—

    weatherize (=*to make proof against the weather*)
    tranquillize (=*to make calm*)

2. *-ate* is usually found attached to words of Latin origin which were taken into the language already combined and now inseparable—

    innocul(ate), specul(ate)

Make verbs from these words by adding the suffixes *-ize* or *-ate*, making any small changes in spelling that are necessary:

hospital	sympathy	circular	special	plastic
regular	captive	equal	pasteur	commercial
immune	pressure	active	apology	rubber
tranquil	domestic	familiar	satire	

Exercise No 224. The Prefix 're-'

1. The prefix *re-* is very active and can be added to almost any verb to mean a repeated performance of the action:

    read—re-read (*to read again*)   tell—re-tell (*to tell again*)

2. The same prefix is also found in a large number of words which were taken into the language from French with the prefix *re-* already attached:

    reduce, release, respond, recover

In these cases the original meaning of the prefix has been changed or lost.

SECTION 13 — WORD BUILDING

3. The active prefix *re-* is usually, but not always, joined to the verb by a hyphen. The hyphen must be used if there is any danger of misunderstanding:

   recover (=*to get back, to get well again*)
   re-cover (=*to cover something again*)

4. Note the pronunciation:

   recover [ri'kʌvə], release [ri'li:s], reduce [ri'dju:s]

   but in the active prefix:

   re-cover ['ri:'kʌvə], re-read ['ri:'ri:d], re-tell ['ri:'tel]

In this list, separate the verbs into two groups: those in which the *re-* has the meaning of *to repeat the action* and those in which the *re-* has to some extent lost or changed its meaning, as in 3. above:

recover	reflect	reduce	repair	rearrange
re-elect	rewrite	rewash	restore	refute
regard	rejoice	rehouse	rebuild	re-address
recount	remark	revolve	resist	react
remarry	re-organize	reconquer	rediscover	resolve
re-enter	re-establish	reopen	reconsider	rehearse
renounce	relax	reveal		

Note: Some of these words can be used both ways:

   reform [ri'fo:m] (=*to mend one's ways, to mend and improve*)
   re-form ['ri:'fo:m] (=*to form or shape again*)

Which other of the words in the list above can be considered in this way if a hyphen is placed after the *re-*?

Exercise No 225

The prefix *out-* is very active in forming verbs from other verbs and nouns with the meaning of *to surpass someone in any activity*.

   Example:
   He *out-talked* all his fellow members.
   =He *talked longer* than all his fellows.

Change the words in italics in these sentences into one verb with the prefix *out-*:

1. He *lived longer than* all his brothers and sisters.
2. He *played much better than* his own teacher.

3. Children *grow too big for* their clothes at an appalling rate.
4. The advantages *have more weight by far than* the disadvantages.
5. His competitors *offered a higher bid* than he did.
6. The trouble with shoes is that the uppers always *last longer than* the soles.
7. The visiting football team *completely beat their opponents by better manoeuvres*.
8. The thieves once again showed that *they had more wits than* the police.
9. So that you do not *do better than me*, I am going to practise hard. (Not to be . . .)
10. The Czech athletes *jumped far higher than* all other competitors in the recent meeting.

Exercise No 226. Adverb Particles Used as Prefixes

A number of words are made by adding adverb particles as prefixes to part of a verb:

an outlet	Compare: to let out
to overthrow	to throw over

1. Form verbs, nouns or adjectives, by adding the particles *up* or *down* as prefixes:

-bringing	-heaval	-keep	to -root	-cast
-hearted	-fall	-right	-pour	-trodden
to -holster		-roar		

2. Add the particles *out* or *in*:

-cast	-spoken	-break	-burst	-come
-set	-put	-born	-cry	-fit
-lay	-let			

3. Add the particles *over* or *under*:

to -flow	to -hang	to -take	-sight	to -stand
-wear	-growth	to -line	to -whelm	to -go
to -mine	-signed	to -come	to -write	to -look

SECTION 13 — WORD BUILDING

4. Add the particles *off* or *on*:

-set   -looker   -rush   -spring   -shoot   -print

(*Note:* The prefixes *over*, *under* and *out* are not to be confused with the same prefixes used in Exercises Nos 221 and 225, where they have only a figurative meaning.)

Exercise No 227. Prefixes on Verb Roots of Latin Origin

These are the principal prefixes of Latin origin which are found in English attached to verb roots also of Latin origin:

pro-, pre-, *con-, dis-, de-, ab-, *ad-, *in-, *sub-, re-, *ex-, *ob-

Those marked with asterisks may change a little when added to verb roots beginning with certain consonants.

Example:

ob + fend = offend, ad + cord = accord

Now add as many prefixes as possible to the following verb roots to form English verbs and their derivative adjectives and nouns:

Example:

-flect,	-flection	-flective
deflect	deflection	
inflect	inflection	inflective
reflect	reflection	reflective

	VERB	NOUN	ADJECTIVE
1.	-struct	-struction	-structive
2.	-ject	-jection, -ject	
3.	-ceive	-ception	-ceptive
4.	-tend	-tension, -tence	-tensive
		-tention, -tendance	-tentive
5.	-fine	-finition	-finitive
		-finement	
6.	-sign	-signation	
		-signment	
7.	-form	-formation	
		-formity	
8.	-sent	-sentment	
		-sent	
9.	-cord	-cord	

	Verb	Noun	Adjective
10.	-mit	-mittance -mission	-missive -missory
11.	-sist	-sistance -sistency	-sistant
12.	-voke	-vocation	-vocative
13.	-rect	-rection	-rectional -rect
14.	-volve	-volution -volvement	-volutionary
15.	-pose	-posal -position -posure -ponent	
16.	-fuse	-fusal -fusion	
17.	-verse	-versation -versal	-versational
18.	-vert	-version	
19.	-mand	-mand	
20.	-vide	-vision	-visional
21.	-pel	-pulsion	-pulsive
22.	-duce -duct	-ducement -duction	-ducive -ductive
23.	-flect	-flection	-flective
24.	-tribute	-tribulation	-tributory -tributive
25.	-lude	-lusion	-lusive
26.	-tract	-traction	-tractive
27.	-port	-port	
28.	-clude	-clusion	-clusive
29.	-sult	-sultation -sult	-sultative
30.	-vent	-vent	-ventative
31.	-scribe	-scription	-scriptive
32.	-serve	-servation	-servative
33.	-sume	-sumption	-sumptive
34.	-cede	-cession -cess	-cessive

SECTION 13　　　WORD BUILDING　　　207

35.	-press	-pression	-pressive
36.	-cline	-clination	
37.	-fect	-fection	-fective
		-fect	
		-ficiency	-ficient
38.	-plete	-pletion	-plete
39.	-fer	-ference	-ferential
40.	-tain	-tention	-tentive

Exercise No 228. Derivatives

Give the nouns or verbs with which these adjectives are connected:

Examples:

energetic—energy, critical—criticize, expansive—expand, convenient—convenience, exploratory—explore, humorous—humour, circular—circle

energetic	hypothetical	expansive	explanatory
athletic	mechanical	descriptive	compulsory
aesthetic	musical	intensive	illusory
hygienic	individual	attentive	sensory
public	central	explosive	inflammatory
diplomatic	regimental	defensive	confirmatory
historic	occasional	educative	derisory
prolific	colonial	distinctive	refractory
sympathetic	continual	deceptive	respiratory
lethargic	formal	nominative	defamatory
relevant	expectant	circular	peculiar
hesitant	militant	familiar	singular
obedient	penitent	regular	insular
sufficient	reluctant	similar	consular
	efficient	popular	rectangular

courageous	joyous	capacious	ferocious
curious	righteous	courteous	hideous
voracious	fabulous		

Exercise No 229. The Prefixes 'be-' and 'en-' ('em-')

These two prefixes have the same meaning: *to make . . .* or *to put into the state of . . .*

    bitter—embitter (=*to make bitter*)
    numb—benumb (=*to make numb*)

Make these words into verbs:

crust	courage	able	moan	
slave	bitter	close	tangle	
trust	friend	calm	force	
bold(en)	light(en)	title	little	
numb	siege	rich	rage	stir
witch	sure	joy	large	danger

Exercise No 230

Some verbs of one syllable have a noun made from them (also of one syllable) by changing a vowel or a consonant or both:

    tell—a tale, shoot—a shot

Give the nouns made from these verbs:

breathe	bathe	lose	choose	lend
believe	use	sell	strike	sing
relieve	sit	speak	feed	think
live	strive	advise	bleed	abide
halve	prove			grieve

Exercise No 231. The Suffixes '-al' and '-age'

These suffixes are used to make nouns from verbs with the meaning of *the act of . . .* or *the results of the act of . . .*

    remove—removal, post—postage

Make these words into nouns ending in -*al* or -*age*:

cart	refuse	arrive	dispose	disperse
reverse	approve	break	try	deny
bestow	pass	demur	propose	pack
haul	marry	recite	use	wreck
betray	stop	shrink	dote	post
renew	leak	waste	dismiss	store
bury				carry

SECTION 13 — WORD BUILDING

Exercise No 232. '-ment' '-ation', '-ance'

The endings *-ment, -ation, -ance* and *-ence* are all added to verbs to form nouns having the meaning of *the action of* or *the results of the action of*.

Add the correct ending to these verbs:

develop	select	confine	terminate
fulfil	revolve	discourage	imprison
forbear	assist	attend	govern
inform	combine	content	require
resent	acknowledge	confirm	deliver
reside	rely	resign	cancel
predict	refine	amaze	reveal
commit	invent	resist	disappear
ally	conceal	embark	define
separate	limit	present	postpone
interfere	confide	endure	remit
improve	invest	devote	enrich
arrange	situate	embank	occur
perform	inherit	hinder	

Exercise No 233. Modern Derivatives with Latin Prefixes

A number of Latin prefixes are still active in the formation of new words. The principal prefixes are these:

co- (=*together with*)
anti- (=*against*)
pro- (=*in favour of*)
pre- (=*before*)
ex- (=*former*)
sub- (=*beneath*)
inter- (=*between*)

counter- (=*in opposite direction*)
post- (=*after*)
bi- (=*double or twice*)
non- (=*not*)
semi- (=*half*)
de- (=*to undo the action of the verb it is attached to*)

1. Form derivatives by adding *semi-*, *bi-*, *non-*, *inter-*, to the following words:

official	detached	member	intervention
combatant	circle	existent	partisan
stop	aggression	monthly	weekly
college	continental	national	racial
civilized	final	university	

2. The same as above using these prefixes: *post-*, *pre-*, *anti-*, *counter-*:

war	date	graduate	natal
reformation	proposal	attack	act
charge	arranged	existence	Shakespearian
historic	climax	slavery	Christian
aircraft	semitic	body	operative

3. The same as above using these prefixes: *co-*, *ex-*, *sub-*, *de-*:

exist	operate	education	director
minister	President	incidence	service man
editor	way	committee	let
normal	tropical	mobilize	centralize
cipher	carbonize	populated	workers

(*Note:* The most common spelling of these modern derivatives is to join the prefix to the word with a hyphen:

non-conformist, anti-Prussian, post-Spenserian)

Many of these new words are international and are found in many other languages. Most of them are used in politics, science or commerce.

Exercise No 234. Compound Nouns

Nouns combine freely together in English to form compound nouns:

teapot (=*a pot for tea*), walking-stick (=*a stick for walking with*)

The first part of a compound noun shows which class the second part belongs to. Compound nouns usually answer the question, *What sort of?*

What sort of pot?—a teapot
What sort of stick?—a walking-stick
What sort of bag?—a paper-bag

Combine the words in capital letters with each word of the list below it, putting it either before or after according to the meaning. Explain the compound word you have formed in this way:

Example:

HOUSE
hen   Henhouse—a house for hens
wife   Housewife—the woman who runs a household

SECTION 13 — WORD BUILDING

House
- hold
- hen
- country
- wife
- work

Table
- land
- kitchen
- tennis
- bedside
- manners

Book
- case
- seller
- reading
- account
- stall

Music
- room
- stand
- chamber
- hall
- piano

Shoe
- walking
- horn
- maker
- horse
- lace

Horse
- towel
- cavalry
- man
- shoe
- race

Day
- break
- birth
- pay
- school
- time

Bed
- room
- hospital
- clothes
- hotel
- stead

Light
- night
- house
- ship
- lamp
- day

Hour
- glass
- dinner
- hand
- concert
- working

Ship
- merchant
- battle
- sailing
- yard
- builder

Paint
- oil
- brush
- water
- box
- shop

Master
- head
- list
- key
- school
- piece

Time
- bomb
- night
- dinner
- table
- keeper

Water
- rat
- way
- sea
- wheel
- drinking

Glass
- looking
- cloth
- eye
- paper
- wine

Man
- kind
- work
- police
- hole
- slaughter

Money
- box
- paper
- lender
- blood
- changer

Work
- day
- shop
- box
- needle
- stone

Side
- river
- bed
- table
- board
- view

Head
- office
- figure
- dress
- man
- mast

Paper
- news
- knife
- money
- writing
- bag

Land
- table
- father
- mark
- lord
- slide

School
- training
- day
- master
- grammar
- boy

Road	Shop	Factory	Floor
country	work	clothing	space
branch	book	whistle	board
cross	assistant	manager	covering
side	window	cigarette	dance
mender	hat	building	threshing

	Office	Knife	
	insurance	blade	
	boy	handle	
	hours	bread	
	head	paper	
	work	edge	

For the use of the hyphen in spelling compound nouns, see Exercise No 198.

Exercise No 235. Compound Words with 'Man'

The word *man* combines freely with a large number of other words to form compound nouns.

Using these words, complete the compound nouns in the sentences below:

fire	country	clergy	chair
head	horse	watch	sea
police	gentle	milk	fisher
railway	states	work	

1. He walked with the typical rolling gait of the ...man.
2. He was speaking to the ...man who was directing the traffic.
3. At what time does the night-...man come off duty?
4. This is the way in which no ...man would behave.
5. The ...man approached them at a gentle trot.
6. When travelling in this part of the country it is wise to be friends with the ...man of the village.
7. Roosevelt was always considered as a great ...man.
8. The ...man called the meeting to order.
9. The ...man has brought us two pints short today.
10. My brother is a ...man, famous for his long sermons.
11. Why is it that a ...man always exaggerates the size of what he has caught?

12. Madame Lebrun, I would like to introduce a ...man of mine.
13. This is the third week of the ...men's strike, so we shall have to go by bus.
14. The ...men were on the spot within a few minutes of the outbreak of fire.
15. I stood watching the ...men leaving the factory.

Exercise No 236. Gerunds in Compound Nouns

Gerunds are often used to make compound nouns:

> The writing of letters = Letter-writing
> The taking of drugs = Drug-taking

Change the phrases in italics into a compound noun with a gerund:

1. He was punished for *stealing sheep*.
2. *The smoking of cigarettes* has increased greatly in recent years.
3. This farmer has always specialized in *the breeding of cattle*.
4. Parts of Turkey are famous for *the growing of tobacco*.
5. Are you interested in *the making of films*?
6. *The climbing of mountains* is one of the finest of sports.
7. Young men in Spain are generally interested in *the fighting of bulls*.
8. Have you ever done any *fishing for trout*?
9. *The playing of the piano* is a technique which requires years of study.
10. She is an expert in *the making of dolls*.
11. Where did you put my *stick for walking with*?
12. Here is our new *college for training teachers*.
13. The art of *writing letters* was much cultivated in the eighteenth century.
14. I have recently bought a new pair of *boots for climbing*.

SECTION 14

WORDS

Exercise No 237. Sounds Made by Mouth and Nose

From these words choose the correct one to put into the blanks in these sentences:

puff	pant	blow	sigh	sob
snore	yawn	splutter	stutter	stammer
sniff	cough	sneeze	hiccup	

1. We ... and ... when we are out of breath.
2. We ... if we fall into the water unexpectedly.
3. We ... when we are bored or tired.
4. We ... and ... when we have a bad cold.
5. We ... or ... when we have difficulty in saying certain words.
6. We ... when we have no handkerchief and need to blow our noses.
7. We ... at night if we lie with our mouths open and on our backs.

Exercise No 238. Manners of Walking

From these words choose the right one to put into the blanks in the sentences which follow:

slip	slide	stagger	spring	linger
crawl	creep	hop	stumble	scramble
limp	steal	prowl		

1. Be careful you don't ... on this greasy patch.
2. Children love to ... when there is some ice on the road.
3. The drunken man ... out of the room.
4. He hurt his leg and ... for several weeks afterwards.
5. I saw a suspicious character ... round that dark corner.
6. They ... up the rough hillside.
7. He wasn't looking where he was going and ... over a stone.
8. The sparrow ... from branch to branch.
9. Babies ... before they walk.

SECTION 14　　　　　　WORDS　　　　　　215

10. It is foolish to ... behind the rest of the party if you don't know the way.
11. The lion ... at him with bared teeth.
12. The soldiers ... silently forward out of sight of the enemy.
13. A hyena was ... around the camp last night.

Exercise No 239

Match the animal to its sound. Some animals make more than one sound:

dog	pig	crow	low
horse	donkey	quack	buzz
cat	frog	hiss	cluck
hen	snake	cackle	croak
bee	duck	purr	mew
cow	cock	bray	neigh
sheep	sparrow	grunt	snarl
		bark	bleat
		growl	chirp
		howl	twitter

Exercise No 240. Words for Different Sorts of Light

From this list of words choose the right one to complete the following sentences:

shimmer	glimmer	gleam	flash	dazzle
sparkle	shine	twinkle	glow	
glisten	flicker	glare	glint	

1. It was difficult to see through the ... of the headlights.
2. A candle flame ... at the slightest breath of air.
3. A wet pavement ...
4. The middle of a fire ...
5. A star ...
6. Is the sun ...?
7. The diamonds at her neck ...
8. The darkness was complete between the lightning ...
9. We could see a light ... in the distance.
10. There was a ... of light through the mist.
11. The moonlight on the water ...

H

12. Their swords ... in the sunlight.
13. The driver was ... by the bright lights of the approaching car.

Exercise No 241. Words for Different Sorts of Sound

From the following list of words choose the right one to complete the following sentences:

squeak	hiss	thud	tinkle
peal	hum	rustle	roar
slam	rattle	clatter	squeal
crack	creak	crash	tick	rumble

1. She dropped the plates with a ...
2. The chair ... as he sat down.
3. The stick ... as he broke it.
4. The brakes of the car ...
5. The old cart ... over the stony road.
6. The wind made the door ...
7. We could hear the ... of the waterfall from a distance.
8. The leaves ... as the wind blew.
9. All that we could hear was the quiet ... of machinery.
10. A clock ...
11. The church bells ... in celebration.
12. The glasses ... as she carried them on the tray.
13. The thunder ... in the distance.
14. He sat down on the floor with a ...
15. The steam escaped with a ...
16. Can you hear the mice ...?
17. His boots ... as he ran downstairs.

Exercise No 242. Wind and Movement of Air

Explain these words which mean different sorts and intensities of wind:

breath	puff	gust	blast
draught	breeze	squall	gale
	storm	hurricane	

SECTION 14 — WORDS

Exercise No 243

Here is a list of words connected with the growth and death of plants. Place them in the order in which they happen and explain each stage. Some are nearly synonymous:

bud	droop	wither	shoot up
blossom	flower	flourish	bloom
sprout	fade		

Exercise No 244

Here is a list of words which all have the meaning of moving objects from one place to another. Distinguish between them:

shove	shift	push	haul	
drag	heave	jerk	toss	
fling	pitch	hurl	tow	pull

Exercise No 245. Heat

Here is a list of words connected with the effects of heat and fire. Explain the meanings:

sweat	simmer	boil	burn
singe	scorch	scald	smoulder
blaze	flame	thaw	melt
roast	fry	toast	

Exercise No 246. Liquids

These words are all connected with the movement of water or liquids:

spurt	squirt	spout	trickle
gush	stream	drip	dribble
pour	spill		

Choose the right one to fit into these sentences:

1. The hostess ... out the tea.
2. Drops of sweat ... down his cheek.
3. A thin stream of water ... out of the hole in the pipe.
4. Children enjoy ... water at each other on a hot day.

5. The oil ... out of the well in large quantities.
6. This tap always ... because it needs mending.
7. The sailors saw a whale ... in the distance.
8. Babies ... down their chins when they are getting teeth.
9. The rain ... down the window panes.

Exercise No 247. Verbal Expressions

'To take fright'

In the following lists the verbs on the left-hand side form one of these expressions with an object on the right-hand side. Find the right object for the verb and then make a sentence to illustrate the expression:

pay	a trumpet	break	a promise	keep	a train
work	a child	catch	one's mind	catch	in love
bear	a miracle	change	conclusion	use	one's word
beg	a visit	draw	one's nose	wear	force
blow	pardon	blow	a cold	fall	a look
keep	one's temper	put	a stop to	pay	a compliment
serve	a habit	catch	a prayer	lay	a meeting
fly	a trick	reach	fire	throw	the table
waste	free	save	a hand	drive	a tyre
set	time	strike	trouble	blow up	the piano
play	a flag	lend	a match	play	a bargain
break	a purpose	say	an agreement	call	a glance
pay	sight of	earn	an exam	lose	mercy on
set	asleep	send	a corner	hold	one's respects
keep	to death	have	the time	pay	a lie
fall	sail	tell	occasion	tell	a meeting
put	count of	turn	word	have	heart
catch	attention	pass	a living	ask	questions
set	a business	miss	the truth	keep	an example
speak	hands	strike	a chance	lead	a risk
shake	touch with	fall	an end to	run	a secret
run	the truth	put	fault with	lose	a busy life
lose	light on	tell	the hour	set	confidence in
throw	fire to	find	ill	throw	suspicion on

SECTION 14 WORDS 219

Exercise No 248. 'Make' and 'Do'

Many languages have only one verb for *do* and *make*. These two verbs are found in a number of more or less fixed expressions:

>To do a favour
>To make a difference

Divide the following words and expressions into two lists: those found with *do* and those found with *make*:

wonders	a good job	a kindness	excuses
haste	fun of	room for	money
a mistake	a favour	one's apologies	work
a service	a sum	damage	peace
war	certain	friends	harm
business	a choice	a face	repairs
trade	one's best	a complaint	a confession
enquiries	homework	wrong	duty
justice to	good	use of	welcome
way	an escape	right	an offer
a discovery	one's way	an injury	one's worst
a journey	a trip	love	fast

And then make sentences to illustrate them.

Exercise No 249. 'Take' and 'Give'

These verbs are found in a number of more or less fixed expressions.

Examples:
>to take place, to give rise to

Divide the list of objects below into two groups: those which are found with the verb *take* and those which are found with the verb *give*:

shape	place	a cry	a shout
an explanation	an interest	root	a photograph
thanks	a laugh	fright	an answer
notice of	one's word	hold of	consideration to
breath	examinations	care	a liking to
pleasure in	a holiday	flight	steps to
leave of	pains	offence	pity on
rise to	pride in	turns	charge of

And then make sentences to illustrate them.

Exercise No 250. 'Become'—'Grow', 'Get' and 'Go'

In spoken English we often replace the word 'become' by the words *get*, *go* or *grow*:

> He is becoming old. =He is growing old.
> I became angry. =I grew angry.
> They are becoming impatient. =They are getting impatient.

go is used with such adjectives as:

> mad, blind, deaf, lame, bald

which mean that the condition is getting worse:

> He became mad. =He went mad.

also with all colours:

> John went red in the face.
> Mary went blue with cold.

Replace the word *become* in these sentences with *grow*, *get* or *go*:

1. It has become quite cool outside.
2. Our horses are becoming rather tired.
3. The leaves become red and gold in Autumn.
4. I'm afraid Mr. Collins has become quite blind.
5. It was becoming quite late while we discussed our plans.
6. The poor fellow became lame after his accident.
7. Just see if that water is becoming hot, will you?
8. He became quite bald in his old age.
9. This iron has become quite rusty in the rain.
10. If you drink any more, you'll become drunk.
11. She became frightened at the sound of the thunder.
12. He became red in the face from his exertions.
13. The rope became loose when the tension was relaxed.
14. We must get home before it becomes quite dark.
15. That student is becoming lazy; he rarely comes to class now.
16. John became deaf as a result of the explosion.
17. The sugar is becoming used up too quickly. Use less!
18. Mary is becoming clever at sewing.
19. I'm glad to say that she is becoming well again.
20. The telephone line has become quite dead again.

Exercise No 251. 'Bring' and 'Take', 'Carry' and 'Fetch'

The milkman brought the milk to her house.
She took away the scissors from the baby.
She carries her own suitcase from the train to the taxi.

Bring means to carry to the place where the speaker is.
Take means to carry from the place the speaker is.
Carry means only to transport without any relation to the speaker's position.
Fetch means to go from the place of speaking, find something and bring it back to the place of starting.

Now add the right verb in these sentences:

1. ... me my spectacles, dear.
2. Waiter, ... this steak away; it's underdone.
3. You can't possibly ... all those things. They're far too heavy.
4. You are not permitted to ... more than 25 lb. on the plane with you.
5. He offered to ... her bags to the car.
6. Don't let him ... that book. I'm still reading it.
7. Wait a moment, while I ... my pen.
8. ... another chair for Mrs. Robinson, there is one short.
9. Did you remember to ... your exercise books with you to class today?
10. Oh, dear! I do believe Johnny forgot to ... his pen with him to school.
11. Finish your lunch and then help me ... the dishes into the kitchen.
12. Go and ... your coat immediately!
13. The postman has just ... a big parcel. Let's open it straightaway.
14. When did he say the tickets could be ...?
15. All the materials had to be ... on mule-back over the mountains.
16. ... these papers to the manager, Miss Smith.
17. There is scarcely time to ... the books before the class.
18. Who ... your papers in the morning?
19. ... these clothes to the bedroom. All right, I'll help you ... them.
20. She ... the dogs for a walk every evening.

Exercise No 252. 'Raise' and 'Rise', 'Lay' and 'Lie'

Raise and *lay* always have an object. They are regular verbs:

> raise, raised, raised: He raised his hat to the lady.
> lay, laid, laid: She laid her hat on the table.

Rise and *lie* do not have an object. They are irregular:

> rise, rose, risen: The sun rises every morning.
> lie, lay, lain: He lay on his bed all day.

Choose the correct verb in the brackets for the following sentences:

1. He tried to (raise, rise) the lid of the chest.
2. He (rose, raised) from his seat.
3. The patient tried to (raise, rise) himself up on his elbows.
4. The rocket (rose, raised) into the sky.
5. They have (raised, risen) the level of the water in the reservoir.
6. His hopes (raised, rose) as the day drew near.
7. I don't wish to (raise, rise) false hopes.
8. If you know the answer, (raise, rise) your hand.
9. Prices have (raised, risen) sharply in the last few months.
10. How long have those books been (lying, laying) on the floor?
11. She told her dog to (lay, lie) down.
12. Mary (lay, laid) her head on John's shoulder.
13. This pottery has (lain, laid) buried in the earth for a thousand years.
14. He found his papers (laying, lying) on the floor when he came in.
15. They let him (lie, lay) where he had fallen.
16. These bricks have been (lain, laid) very badly.
17. The prisoners were ordered to (lay, lie) down their arms.
18. The mayor (lay, laid) the foundation stone of the new school.
19. They told the doctor that she had been (lying, laying) motionless for three hours.
20. (Lay, lie) your hand on the book and say . . .

Exercise No 253. 'Say' and 'Tell'

This exercise is not concerned with the use of *say* and *tell* in direct and indirect speech, but with the more or less fixed expressions in which these verbs are used.

Basically, *tell* means *to give an account* or *to distinguish between*. *Say* means *to speak words*.

Now put the right verb into these sentences:

1. Can you ... me your name, please?
2. He was ... his prayers when we came in.
3. Will you lend me some money; ..., about £5?
4. I should be glad if you would ... me your opinion of these plans.
5. I dare ... what you ... me is true, although it seems improbable.
6. Let's meet in the square, shall we ... at six o'clock?
7. She's only five and can't ... the time yet.
8. Twenty-five students, that is to ..., three-quarters of the class, passed the exam.
9. There is nothing to be ... for his proposal.
10. I...! Just look here a moment.
11. The children begged her to ... them a story before they went to bed.
12. She had a feeling that they were not ... her the truth.
13. How can you ... which is the right one to use?
14. I can never ... those two brothers apart.
15. Come a little closer and I'll ... you a secret.
16. I wasn't allowed to do that when I was young, I can ... you.
17. Any country, let's ... Turkey, would follow a similar policy in the circumstances.
18. Don't ... me you haven't brought it after all?
19. That he is intelligent goes without ...
20. You never can ...! It may be true.
21. Can you ... the difference between these two colours? I can't.

Exercise No 254. Verbs Which can be Used With or Without Objects

Some common English verbs can be used with or without an object (transitively or intransitively):

> We begin *the lesson* at six o'clock.
> *The lesson* begins at six o'clock.
>
> They are selling *cars* abroad in large numbers.
> *Cars* are selling abroad in large numbers.

Note that these sentences do not necessarily have the same meaning.

Change the following sentences in the same way as in the example. It will be necessary to leave out the subjects and use the words in italics as the new subjects:

> *Example:*
>
> They spread *false rumours* throughout the country.
> =False rumours spread throughout the country.

1. The lightning started *fires* in many parts of the town.
2. He is improving *his knowledge of English* every day.
3. The new headmaster will meet *his staff* next week.
4. He dropped *a stone* into the well.
5. The pilot flew *his plane* low over the city.
6. She leaned *her baby* against the side of its cradle.
7. The bicyclist stuck *the patch* firmly on to the inner tube.
8. The explosion shook *the whole house* for several seconds.
9. They shut *the door* behind them.
10. He bent *the metal bar* at its weakest point.
11. They are hanging *the pictures* on the studio wall.
12. John broke *his pen* when he dropped it on the floor.
13. You must not wake *the children* too soon.
14. Leaders should divide *their parties* into three for the attack.
15. The captain sailed *his ship* eastwards for three days.
16. The students increase *their English vocabulary* every year.
17. I have hurt *my hand* badly.
18. When is the priest going to marry *John and Mary*?
19. The baby's mother is rocking *the cradle*.
20. Roll *the ball* to me along the ground.
21. The player swung *his bat* through the air.
22. The crowd waved *flags* when the President arrived.
23. John opened *the door* and walked into the room.

24. The teacher collected *all the children* into one group
25. The policemen kept *the crowd* moving along.
26. I asked him if he would work *the projector*.
27. She stretched *the rope* from one side of the garden to the other.
28. She poured *the water* onto the grass.
29. She kept *the children* dry by putting up an umbrella.
30. She never changed *her opinion* of him.
31. The mechanic turned *the engine* over and it sprang into life.
32. The soldiers are gathering *all the people* together in the main square of the town.

Exercise No 255

Change the following sentences from an intransitive to a transitive construction as in the example, using the subjects supplied:

Example:
The letter dropped into the letter-box. (John . . .)
John dropped the letter into the letter-box.

1. Vegetables grow in Mr. Smith's garden. (Mr. Smith . . .)
2. The rifles were standing in the corner of the barracks. (The soldiers . . .)
3. The ship sank in shallow water. (The captain . . .)
4. The business ran very efficiently. (The manager . . .)
5. The water must freeze before they do the experiment. (They must . . .)
6. The paper in his hand burnt quickly. (He . . .)
7. The lesson will begin at six o'clock sharp. (The teacher will . . .)
8. The water must boil before you make tea. (You must . . .)
9. Has the meat cooked yet? (Has the maid . . .)
10. The wine passed round the table. (Please pass . . .)

Exercise No 256. 'Wait for', 'Hope', 'Expect', 'Look forward to'

These verbs need careful distinguishing:

1. *Wait for:* I am waiting for a friend. He will be here in ten minutes.
   This verb means to pass time until something which we believe certain happens.

2. *Hope:* I hope he will come today, but I have heard nothing.
   In this case we want something to happen but there is no certainty.

3. *Expect:* I expect it will rain this afternoon.
   In this case we believe something will happen, but we do not necessarily want it to.

4. *Look forward to:* The children are looking forward to the holidays.
   In this case we are not speaking about probability or certainty, we are thinking only of the pleasure that we are going to have.

Now supply the right verb in these sentences:

1. I do ... he will not get hurt.
2. I had a telegram yesterday and am ... him at three o'clock.
3. I am definitely not ... to the examinations. I have had no time to study.
4. I ... very much that you will agree to these proposals.
5. I ... he will stay to dinner, but I know he's a very busy man.
6. Oh, dear! I ... she will stay to dinner, she always does.
7. They are always ... to win the lottery, but I don't ... they will.
8. The doctor came a few minutes ago and she is ... there is nothing wrong with the children.
9. 'Can he mend the car?' 'I ... so. He's a very good mechanic.'
10. Who are you ... for? The others all left some time ago.
11. She ... for ten minutes, because she was ... her boy-friend to come.
12. Are you ... to your birthday?
13. Please ... for me, I shan't be long.
14. We ... him yesterday, but he never came.
15. I am ... them at ten o'clock. But I certainly shan't ... for them, if they're late.
16. We ... for him for three hours, but he never came.
17. I think she has given up ... he will return, but she still ... he will.
18. Do you mind ... a moment while I get my things?
19. I ... I shall have to go to the dentist again soon, but I'm certainly not ... to it.
20. Joan is ... to being married. I ... she's not disappointed. However, her future husband is a good fellow and I ... it will turn out all right.

Exercise No 257. 'Avoid' and 'Prevent'

Both these verbs have the meaning of *keep away from*.

1. *Avoid* is often reflexive in sense: *to keep oneself away from*.

    Mary avoided talking to strangers.
    =Mary kept herself away from talking to strangers.

    In this case Mary has the temptation to do something.

2. *Prevent* is transitive: *to keep someone else away from*.

    Mary prevented her daughter (from) talking to strangers.
    =Mary kept her daughter away from talking to strangers.

    In this case the daughter has the temptation to do something.

    Avoid, therefore, means *to prevent oneself doing something*.

Now supply the correct verb in these sentences:

1. Children should ... walking in the mud.
   The mother ... her children from walking in the mud.
2. It is difficult to ... making mistakes.
   It is the teacher's duty to ... his students making mistakes.
3. You ought to ... drinking that water; it's unsafe.
   Nobody shall ... me drinking what I like.
4. ... Mr. Robinson. He has a bad reputation.
   She could not be ... from seeing Mr. Robinson.
5. Accidents cannot be ...
   The authorities are doing their best to ... accidents.
6. How did you manage to ... getting wet in the rain?
   You can ... yourself getting wet by carrying an umbrella.
7. Part of a doctor's work is to ... people falling sick.
   But you can ... falling sick, if you are careful.
8. You can ... the heat of the sun, by staying indoors.
   But you cannot ... the sun shining.
9. She ... his eyes, but she could not ... him looking at her.
   You can ... walking under a ladder, but you can't ... people using them.
10. We can generally ... getting dirty ourselves, but it is not easy to ... children doing so.

Exercise No 258. 'Rob' and 'Steal'

A thief or robber robs a person or a place of a thing. Cf. *to deprive*.
A thief steals something from a person or a place. Cf. *to take*.

The difference between these two verbs is one of construction.

Change the following sentences by substituting the word *rob* for the word *steal*, making the necessary changes of construction:

Example:

They stole all her jewels from her.
=They robbed her of all her jewels.

1. They stole a valuable ring from my wife last night.
2. Some thieves stole Mrs. Jones's handbag in full daylight.
3. They stole all the ready cash from my house.
4. The burglar stole £25 from the grocer's.
5. £5,000 were stolen from the bank last night.
6. From which house in the street did they steal those papers?
7. Who had his wallet stolen at the races?
8. She had her last penny stolen.

Exercise No 259. Vegetables

Here is a list of fourteen common vegetables found in England. The student must find out what they are and their name in his own language. These words should form part of his passive vocabulary, at least, so that when he meets them in his reading or in conversation he can identify them.

It is probable that in his own country there are vegetables which are equally, or even more, common than those on this list. If this is so, he should learn their English names, if they have any, and add them to this list.

potato	cabbage	cauliflower	spinach
pea	bean	carrot	beetroot
celery	tomato	onion	parsley
lettuce	cucumber		

SECTION 14 — WORDS

Exercise No 260. Flowers

Here is a list of the commonest wild and garden flowers in England. See instructions to previous exercise.

rose	carnation	lavender	poppy
pansy	primrose	tulip	daffodil
violet	daisy	buttercup	dandelion
bluebell	lily	lilac	forget-me-not

Exercise No 261. Fruit

See instructions to Exercise No 259.

apple	pear	cherry	plum
strawberry	raspberry	gooseberry	grape
orange	lemon	fig	date
banana		melon	

Exercise No 262. Trees

See instructions to Exercise No 259.

oak	ash	beech	birch
willow	poplar	elder	chestnut
walnut	palm	holly	elm
plane	fir	pine	

Exercise No 263. Birds

See instructions to Exercise No 259.

sparrow	thrush	robin	swallow
lark	crow	nightingale	woodpecker
eagle	hawk	owl	parrot
peacock	stork		

The foregoing lists have not been chosen scientifically according to the actual incidence in Britain, but according to the frequency with which students are likely to meet these words in reading and conversation.

Exercise No 264. Nationalities

The common endings for words of nationality are *-ian* and *-ish*.

> Italy—an Italian—Italian (adj.)
> Sweden—a Swede—Swedish

If the adjective ends in *-ish* (Swedish) the word for the man is different (a Swede), but if the adjective ends in *-ian* (Italian) the word for the man is the same (an Italian). Another ending is *-ese*.

> Burma—a Burmese—Burmese

Now give the man and his nationality connected with the following countries:

Russia	Poland	Switzerland	China
Ireland	Finland	Norway	Wales
France	Spain	Portugal	Greece
Turkey	Ceylon	New Zealand	Yugoslavia
Holland	Lebanon	Germany	Scotland
Hungary	Japan	Siam	Denmark
India	Brazil		

Exercise No 265. Professions

Give the name of the man who:

sells meat	paints pictures
cuts hair	makes bread
sells tickets on a bus	writes for the newspapers
administers the law	carves statues
obtains coal from the ground	investigates crimes
sells newspapers and magazines	cures sick people
looks after the sick	controls traffic
carries luggage	works on a ship
sells tobacco	travels for pleasure
sees something happen	cultivates the land
operates on sick people	sells metal goods
makes chairs and tables	sells medicines and drugs
sells fruit and vegetables	sells fish

SECTION 14 WORDS

Exercise No 266

What is the name of the chief person in:

a committee	an army	court of law	navy
newspaper	orchestra	Parliament	Republic
school	ship	football team	business firm
kitchen	aeroplane	household	party of climbers
workshop	University faculty	bank	party or reception

Exercise No 267. Masculine and Feminine

Give the masculine equivalent of the following persons and animals:

spinster	bride	nun	heroine
Madam	widow	witch	hen
duck	mare	headmistress	barmaid
landlady	queen	Girl Guide	cow
sow	niece	aunt	lady
maidservant			

Exercise No 268. Young Animals

What is the name of a young:

cow	lion	bear	dog
cat	pig	eagle	goose
duck	hen	sheep	horse

Exercise No 269. Homes

Where do these men or animals live:

monk	man	king	convict
lunatic	nun	soldier	peasant
horse	cow	dog	bee
bird	snail	spider	wasp
pig	gypsy		

Exercise No 270. Collective Nouns

Here is a list of the common nouns which mean *a group of* or *collection of* (collective nouns).

flock	swarm	pack	fleet	herd
shoal	mob	crowd	audience	congregation
bundle	bunch	staff	pair	flight
chest	stack	suit	set	clump

Now match the collective word to the one that belongs to each group:

flock	cattle	shoal	people in church
swarm	ships	mob	people in a theatre
pack	bees	crowd	people in the street
fleet	cards	audience	angry people
herd	sheep	congregation	fish
bundle	steps	chest	trees
bunch	scissors	stack	tools
staff	office workers	suit	clothes
pair	keys, flowers	set	drawers
flight	old clothes	clump	hay
crew	thieves	pair	grapes
gang	sailors and airmen	bunch	trousers

Exercise No 271. Units

We buy		by the	
	milk		ball
	beer		ounce
	butter		pint
	matches		bottle
	potatoes		sack
	coal		bunch
	eggs		yard
	flowers		pound
	ribbon		dozen
	toilet soap		box
	cigarettes		cake
	tobacco		stone
	shoes		pair

SECTION 14 · WORDS · 233

We buy	sewing cotton	by the	reel
	string		acre
	land		stick
	shaving soap		packet

Exercise No 272. Containers

What would you expect to find in:

a packet	a vase	a can or tin	a bath
a basket	a cellar	a cask	a flask
a trunk	a purse	an envelope	a satchel
a tank	a kettle	a jug	a wallet
a safe	a wardrobe	a suitcase	a compact
a tube	a briefcase	a barrel	

Exercise No 273 Reference

Where would you look to find:

Someone's telephone number
The date
Position of a country
The time of a train
Story of someone's life
Old letters in an office
Where a name is mentioned in a book
The meaning of a word
Information about a subject
List of goods and their prices
A daily record of personal events
A daily record of public events
A collection of family photographs

Exercise No 274. Tools

Here is a list of tools and what we use them for.
Which tool is used for which operation?

scissors	for collecting together dry leaves
saw	for cutting wood into planks
hammer	for putting in screws
chisel	for digging in the garden
file	for cutting down trees
spade	for making metal smooth
axe	for making wood smooth
plane	for carving wood

screwdriver	for driving in nails
rake	for holding and bending wire
pliers	for making holes in metal or wood
drill	for cutting cloth and paper

Exercise No 275. Things and Materials for Joining and Fastening

Here is a list of materials and things which are used in fastening, joining and attaching. Say which material or thing in the first list is used to join or fasten the words in the second list:

handcuff	thread	criminals	cloth
chain	nuts and bolts	woodwork	door
nails and screws	clip	metalwork	paper
string	strap	trunk	parcel
mortar	laces	dress	bricks
zip	button	anchor	brooch
pin	glue or gum	shoes	jacket
hinge			

Exercise No 276. Diminutives

These words all have diminutive endings. Explain their meaning:

booklet	sapling	globule	chicken
bracelet	seedling	molecule	maiden
coronet	darling	particle	kitten
eaglet	duckling	lambkin	hillock
pocket	nestling	napkin	bullock
rivulet	gosling		
Johnny	Tommy	Willie	Lizzie
piggy	baby	dolly	

Note that the only active diminutive ending in modern English is: *-y* or *-ie*.

Exercise No 277. Small Quantities

Match the quantity to the substance:

A grain	A chip	of bread	of air
A speck	A scrap	of rain	of paper
A drop	A lock	of food	of hair

A crumb	A breath	of grass	of pottery
A morsel	A puff	of salt	of dirt
A blade	A fragment	of wind	of wood

Exercise No 278. Abbreviations

Here are the most common abbreviations in English. Say what they are short for and describe exactly where they are used:

A.D.	etc.	R.N.	Dr.
h.p.	U.K.	Esq.	P.S.
B.C.	i.e.	U.S.A.	Ltd.
P.T.O.	Co.	M.P.	v.
Messrs.	R.S.V.P.	do.	No.
a.m.	p.m.	Mr.	B.B.C.
Mrs.	e.g.	U.S.S.R.	U.N.O.
St.	Rd.	c/o.	TV.

Exercise No 279. Abbreviations

Give the usual abbreviations of:

1. The days of the week
2. The months of the year
3. Penny, pound (sterling)
4. Second, minute, hours, years
5. Miles, yards, feet, inches
6. Ounce, pounds (weight)

Exercise No 280. Words with Similar Meanings

Real synonyms are rare in a language. There is nearly always some slight difference of meaning between two words which are usually called synonymous. Often the only difference is that we prefer to use one in circumstances where the other would be perfectly correct but not so common.

For example: *to start* and *to begin*. Their meaning is truly synonymous in modern English, but we have a preference for *start* when we are thinking of movement:

        To start a race, a journey, walking
but: To begin reading, to think, to understand

The words in this exercise are in pairs. They are not synonymous, but their meanings are close and it is useful to distinguish between them. Do this by a short explanation and then give an example of each one in a sentence:

Example:

to hinder and *to prevent*

To hinder means to make it difficult for someone to continue an activity:

> The rain hindered our progress but we finally arrived.

To prevent means to stop someone from carrying on with some activity:

> The rain prevented us from going out and so we never arrived.

It is important that you make an example in which only one of the two words could be properly used:

fold, wrap	attain, obtain	borrow, lend
defeat, overwhelm	acquit, pardon	spend, waste
hesitate, delay	undertake, perform	deny, disprove
abolish, destroy	follow, pursue	trot, gallop
relieve, cure	share, divide	chew, bite
spoil, destroy	introduce, admit	accompany, attend
anger, annoy	forgive, excuse	seize, capture
acknowledge, confess	suffer, bear	stay, remain
copy, imitate	heal, cure	compare, contrast
flatter, deceive	rule, govern	earn, gain
warn, advise	discover, invent	hear, listen
hurt, harm	bore, tire	test, examine
betray, show	look, see	achieve, finish
tie, fasten	spread, stretch	surround, enclose
disappoint, deceive	confess, admit	catch, take
tolerate, permit	stare, gaze	origin, beginning
pluck, pick	rent, hire	lack, want
despise, condemn	learn, find out	attend, assist
shiver, tremble	pretend, claim	convince, persuade

SECTION 14 — WORDS

Exercise No 281. Adjectives with Similar Meanings

Distinguish between these pairs of adjectives:

dense, thick	idle, lazy	effective, useful
wet, damp	cold, cool	exact, accurate
human, humane	gracious, graceful	last, latest
wild, savage	remarkable, curious	same, equal
quick, fast	regular, frequent	thankful, grateful
wholesome, sound	stale, old	abrupt, sudden
beastly, brutal	legal, lawful	alone, lonely
righteous, sacred	anxious, eager	stubborn, persistent
suitable, convenient	fat, stout	glad, happy
old, elderly	young, youthful	clever, skillful
quiet, noiseless	capable, clever	audible, loud
separate, distinct	various, variable	healthy, sound
sincere, earnest	uneven, rough	dumb, silent
flat, level	high, lofty	chilly, cool
alert, aware	crooked, curved	ready, finished
slim, thin	feeble, weak	countless, numerous
acute, sharp	continuous, continual	essential, important
proud, vain	frank, sincere	tidy, neat
remote, distant	permanent, eternal	incurable, fatal
childish, childlike	sincere, genuine	jolly, merry
even, smooth	intimate, personal	
present, actual	old, antique	

Exercise No 282

In the case of nouns there is generally less danger of confusion, since nouns, in many cases, are the names of objects or materials which can be easily identified.

It is among the abstract nouns that there is a possibility of confusion. The majority of the nouns in this list are of this sort. Distinguish between them:

merit, quality	refuge, shelter	evidence, proof
career, profession	prejudice, opinion	courage, bravery
liking, preference	rumour, report	version, account
error, fault	fiction, lie	mood, temper
species, kind	job, task	errand, message

leisure, idleness	traitor, rebel	period, age
manners, behaviour	envy, jealousy	attendance, service
providence, fate	mercy, pity	compensation, reward
customer, client	custom, habit	event, accident
error, defect	pain, distress	noise, sound
verdict, sentence	consolation, pity	mind, brain
worth, value	co-operation, assist-	confidence, assurance
acquaintance, friend	ance	scent, smell
preoccupation, worry	marriage, wedding	power, force
	possibility, opportunity	

Here are some examples of a more concrete kind:

ground, earth	pair, couple	earth, world
house, home	student, pupil	shore, bank
salary, wages	tool, implement	present, gift
specimen, sample	hedge, bush	twig, branch
partner, companion	boundary, frontier	line, row
jug, jar	shade, shadow	lid, cap
spectator, witness	heap, pile	target, shield
can, tin		

Exercise No 283. Collocations

Many collocations are introduced by a preposition (see Exercise No 112).

Here are the most important collocations of this sort, introduced by prepositions and not included in the previous exercises. Make sentences to show their meaning:

for my sake	for instance	for a start	for a change
for one thing	for the present	to some extent	until further
of course	before long	at all	notice
above all	after all	at your convenience	of one's own
	of one's own accord		

Exercise No 284. Collocations

Here are a number of the most useful collocations of all types. Make sentences to show their meaning:

that is to say
so to say
inside out
once more
every other day
sooner or later
all things considered
the other day

more or less
as it were
upside down
no doubt
all right
all the better
as follows:
next door

so much the better
as a matter of fact
never mind!
all at once
and so on
all the same
as a rule

Exercise No 285. 'All' and 'Whole'

These two words have the same meaning but cannot always be used interchangeably.

Whole is used only with singular and countable nouns.
All is used with both singular and plural nouns.

Look at these examples:

All the world is waiting anxiously for the results of the conference.
The whole world is waiting anxiously for the results of the conference.

Now change *all the* into *the whole* in these sentences:

1. All the family enjoyed the picnic.
2. He didn't stay to see all the film.
3. The headmaster promised all the school a holiday.
4. It has been raining all the day.
5. Must I read all the book?
6. Look, Mother! John has eaten all the cake.
7. She was sick during all the journey.
8. Those students have wasted all the term.
9. You must do all the exercise.
10. What have you been doing all the time?
11. All the room was in disorder.
12. All the week has been spent in making up the books.
13. All the fleet steamed towards the enemy.
14. We were unable to collect all the party together at one time.
15. All the house was soon in flames.

Exercise No 286. 'All', 'Everybody', 'Everything'

In modern English the pronoun *all*, unless it is followed by some phrase or clause which restricts its meaning, is rather stiff and formal:

> I told him all. =I told him everything.
> All signed their names in the book. =Everybody signed his name in the book.

but:

> *All of them* agreed with me.
> *All who say* that are liars.
> I gave him *all I had*.

Now change the rather formal *all* into the more usual *everybody* or *everything* (with a singular verb) in the following sentences:

1. He has lost all.
2. All were surprised at his ability.
3. There is not sufficient here for all.
4. His skill was admired by all.
5. We may begin since all are present.
6. You can safely confess all to me.
7. Let me speak! I can explain all.
8. I am giving a party to which all are invited.
9. This is a place where all can feel at home.
10. Here is a programme which all can enjoy.

Exercise No 287. 'Fairly' and 'Rather'

Both these words have about the same meaning. *Fairly* means *moderately* but *not as much as we should like*. It shows that we are a little disappointed. We usually use it with favourable or pleasant ideas:

> This essay is fairly good, but I think you can do better.
> The food in that restaurant is fairly good, but it is much better in this one.

Rather also means *moderately*, but we usually use it with words which have an unpleasant or unfavourable meaning:

> That is rather a nasty thing to say.

Only *rather* can be used with comparative adjectives:

> The weather has turned out rather finer than we expected.

You must remember that the same word can have a favourable meaning in one sentence and an unfavourable one in another:

> This house is rather big for our small family.

but:

> This house is fairly big. I suppose it will have to do.

Add *fairly* or *rather* in the following sentences according to the sense:

1. I showed him the book and he was ... interested.
2. It's getting ... late. We ought to go home.
3. Don't you think that chair is ... high for a little boy?
4. This hill is ... high. You should get quite a good view from the top.
5. I'm afraid you'll have to walk ... quickly if you want to catch your train.
6. This boy is ... intelligent. The work shouldn't be too difficult for him.
7. I must say that I'm ... surprised at your behaviour.
8. Be careful. That knife is ... sharp.
9. This pencil is ... sharp. I expect you could write with it.
10. It's ... cold today. I should put on an overcoat.
11. You'll find Mary is ... better today.
12. She was ... disgusted to find the dirty plates still on the table.
13. I think you'll find this exercise ... simpler than the other.
14. Poor old Jane! She is really ... plain, isn't she?
15. I found his latest book ... more interesting than the earlier ones.

(*Note:* The student will, however, meet *rather* used with adjectives of favourable meaning also. This use is highly idiomatic and depends for its sense on a special intonation.)

Exercise No 288. 'Quite'

Quite has two different meanings. Which meaning it has in a sentence will depend on the meaning of the word it is used with and the intonation we give it:

> (1) quite useless, quite irregular, quite wrong, quite unique quite finished

In these examples it means *completely*. The words it is used with have a falling tone and are either negative in meaning or are words which do not have relative values (i.e. We cannot say *more unique* or *more finished*: a thing is either unique or not. There are no degrees of uniqueness.)

> (2) quite interesting, quite pleasant, quite useful, quite pretty, quite heavy

In these examples it means *moderately, but not very*. The words it is used with have a rising tone and are words which do have relative degrees of value (i.e. we can say, *more or less interesting, more pleasant* or *heavier*. It is clear that *quite* cannot mean *completely* in these cases, because *completely pretty* or *completely heavy* are nonsense).

Make two lists from these words: those with which *quite* means *completely* and those with which *quite* means *moderately*:

terrified	wrong	sour	extraordinary
good	interesting		useless
illegal	helpless	useful	a large number
difficult	unusual	helpful	inexperienced
tired out	sweet	original	black
white	amazed	nice	desperate
right	difficult	amusing	hopeful
different	quickly	hopeless	outrageous

SECTION 15

DICTATION PASSAGES

1. The moment / she had been waiting for / had come at last. / The loudspeakers / in the waiting hall / announced her flight. / Gripping her handbag firmly, / she made her way / to the exit gate / and out into the bright sun / to the aircraft standing there / like some great silver bird. / After handing in / her boarding card / to the hostess, / she climbed up the steps / into the cabin / and looked around her. / Above a door / at the end of the passage / she saw a notice: / NO SMOKING. FASTEN SEAT BELTS.

2. Deep snow / lay on the track / as the doctor struggled slowly / against a biting wind / to the lonely farmhouse. / It must have been two hours / since he left / the cosy warmth / of his consulting-room / in the small town / to visit the old woman / who lay sick / in this deserted spot. / He wondered, / as he had so often done before, / why he had chosen / this remote district / to practise in.

3. It was clear / that autumn had come / at last. / The long days of summer were over / and already / the trees were changing / from green to gold, / while here and there / a dry leaf rustled / as it was swept / by the breeze / along the garden path. / On the telegraph wires / one or two swallows perched / impatiently waiting for the day / when they would turn their heads / to the south / and fly to a warmer climate.

4. The children's playroom was empty. / Scattered on the floor / lay the toys / they had been occupied with / before they were called away / to bed. / A model train / lay on its side / where it had run / off the rails / in its last accident. / Two dolls sat motionless / at the table, / their meal half-finished, / while in the corner / stood the rocking-horse, / gently swaying / backwards and forwards / deserted by its young rider.

5 As the traffic lights / turned to red, / the bus drew up / with a squeal of brakes. / Pedestrians began / to cross the road, / glancing anxiously / from time to time / to see whether the lights / had changed again / and whether it was still safe / to step off the pavement. / It was at this moment / that a dog chose / to wander slowly out / into the roadway / and, / although the lights were green, / not a vehicle stirred.

6. It was five minutes to nine / and in the distance / the tolling of a bell / could be heard. / Small figures, / carrying bags, / could be seen / hurrying round corners / leading into the main road, / which went / in the direction of the bell. / The minute hand of the clock / on the church tower / gradually moved up / to the figure twelve, / and the ringing ceased / abruptly. / Only one solitary figure / remained in the street. / There was no need / for him to hurry now; / he would be late for school / anyhow.

7. As the day went on / and darkness fell / in the streets outside, / the number of Christmas shoppers / seemed to increase. / The assistants in the store / were kept so busy / all the time / that they did not have a moment / to exchange / more than an occasional word / with their friends / as they attended / to the never-ending stream / of customers. / Their legs ached / and they longed / for the moment / when the doors of the store / would close / and they could have / a cup of tea / and a cigarette / before catching the bus home.

8. For a moment / he stopped outside the door / to make sure / he had come / to the right place. / Yes, / there was the sign: / FISHER'S RESTAURANT. / He pushed open the swing-doors / and stepped / into the warm atmosphere. / The room was crowded with diners, / and waitresses darted / backwards and forwards / to the kitchen / with trays of food. / A quick glance around the room / told him / that his friend was already there / and, / greeting her / with a wave of the hand, / he made his way between the tables / to where she was sitting.

9. Although the factory stood / some distance / from the main road, / the hum of machinery / could still be heard / quite clearly. / Black smoke belched / in great clouds / from the chimney, / blotting out the sun / from time to time / from a group of workers / standing at the bus stop. / Then the midday whistle sounded / and gradually / the whole building fell silent / as the remaining workers / poured out into the sunlight.

10. The old shepherd sat / in the warm parlour / of the inn, / and looked out of the windows / at the hills / he knew so well. / Ever since he was a boy / he had climbed these slopes, / tending his sheep. / In winter / he would collect them / to bring them down / to the shelter of the valleys; / he would stay up / all night / during the lambing season, / and in summer / he would drive them / to the farm / for the annual shearing. / But now those days were past, / and another walked / on those hills / in his place.

SECTION 15   DICTATION PASSAGES

11. The village main street, / usually busy with buses, / farmers' carts / and tradesmen's vans, / was transformed. / It was now the fairground. / For one misty November day / it glowed / with the lights / of shooting booths / and cheap stalls / where the farmers' wives / were buying / lengths of cotton material, / aluminium pans / and floor brushes / while their children / shouted and screamed / as they swung / on the round-abouts.

12. A small boy / stood watching the goldfish. / It swam round and round / in its tiny glass bowl, / and every movement / of its tail / made the water / flash in the sunlight. / The boy put his hands / in his pockets / and reluctantly / brought out a coin, / which he held tightly / in his fist, / still watching the fish. / Then, / with a deep sigh, / he handed the money / to the shopkeeper / and, with bowl and goldfish / firmly clasped in his arms, / he walked out / into the street.

13. The whole family / were sitting in the drawing-room / watching the television. / You could see / by the look on their faces / that they had settled down / to an evening / of easy entertainment / and would stay / in front of the set / until bedtime. / A faint click, / as the kitchen window / was forced open, / did not reach their ears; / nor did the stealthy footsteps / of the burglar / as he quietly and unhurriedly / gathered all the silver / in the dining-room / before silently creeping away / once more.

14. The castle had stood / on its little hill / for over six hundred years. / It had been built there / to guard the entrance / to the valley / at a time when / attacks by lawless men / from the north / were frequent. / But with the coming / of more peaceful times, / it had been abandoned, / had fallen into ruins / and was now no more / than a few crumbling, / ivy-covered walls / and empty windows / staring at the sky. / By night / it was the haunt of owls / and by day the tourists wandered / through gates and doorways / where formerly / knights in armour / had ridden out to war.

15. The woman was sweeping / the kitchen floor / when the postman arrived. / Hearing his knock, / she dropped her broom / to the ground / with a loud clatter, / rushed to the front door / and threw it open. / The postman held out to her / a small bunch of letters / and bills. / Scarcely bothering to thank him / and without turning back / into the house, / the woman anxiously looked / through the letters / she now had in her hand / and with a little

cry / tore open the envelope / of the one / which she had been expecting.

16. The party had been climbing / for some hours / when the clouds / that had hidden / the mountain peaks / before them / lifted for a moment. / A shaft of winter sunlight / momentarily illuminated the path / they were following / and showed a solitary climber / several hundred feet above them. / They were at a loss / to explain his presence there / since they had thought / that they were alone / on the mountain-side / that day, / until one of the party / recalled / that a traveller had arrived late / at their inn / the night before.

17. One of his favourite pastimes / was collecting clocks. / He already had / a most remarkable collection, / which was admired / by his friends / and envied / by his fellow-collectors. / The most valuable piece / was an old Dutch clock, / which had been made / in the seventeenth century / and, so he said, / had been in the possession / of his family / for several generations. / He used to make a round / of all his clocks / every morning, / winding up those / that were running down / and adjusting any / that were going fast or slow. / There was nothing he loved more / than to hear the different ticks / of his treasured possessions / as he performed / this daily task.

18. There is nothing more satisfying / after a cold busy day / than to settle down / in an armchair / in front of a fire / with your feet / stretched towards the blaze, / a good book on your lap, / friends to chat with / and no need / to do anything / but watch the glowing coals. / It is when / you are comfortably settled / in this way / that the telephone rings, / that there is a knock / at the front door, / or that the baby upstairs, / who is meant to be asleep, / wakes up / and begins to cry.

19. The museum was almost empty / of visitors / at this hour of the morning. / A few bored travellers, / forced to spend / a few hours in the town / waiting for their train, / wandered aimlessly about. / The guard, / sitting in the main hall, / wondered how long / he must wait / till he could smoke a cigarette. / Suddenly / the silence was shattered / by a mob of schoolchildren, / all shouting and screaming / in the excitement / of having a short holiday / from lessons, / and, / at their head, / the poor distracted teacher.

20. The village green / is an open stretch of grass / between

the duck pond / and the Norman church. / Here / on fine summer evenings / the schoolchildren gather / to play cricket / until it is too dark / to see the ball / any more. / Then one by one / they turn reluctantly / towards their homes, / leaving the old men / smoking their pipes / under the great oak tree / and talking of their youth.

SECTION 16

PASSAGES FOR COMPREHENSION AND PRECIS

1. A short puff of wind extinguished the candle I was carrying. Laying it carefully down at my feet, so that I could easily find it again in the dark, I quickly *went through* my pockets to see if I still had the box of matches which I had *thoughtfully* put there that morning, when I set out to explore the cave. But a thorough searched revealed nothing with which to re-light the candle and left me desperately trying to recall how the matches could have *gone astray*. I then remembered that half an hour before, I had taken a short rest and eaten a bar of chocolate. While doing so, I had rested the candle on a convenient rock in order to leave my hands free to unwrap the chocolate, and, just as now, a breath of wind had made the candle *flicker* and finally go out. It was then that I had had occasion to use my matches and I can only suppose that I had thoughtlessly left the box on the rock where the candle had been standing. I reckoned that I must be about half a mile from the entrance and that *the only thing for it* was to grope my way back again. About an hour later, bruised from my frequent collisions with projecting rocks, I stumbled into the daylight. The first thing I thought of was a cigarette. Instinctively I drew out my lighter from my trouser pocket. It was only when I had it in my hand that I realized what a fool I had been.

(*a*) Answer the following questions with a single sentence:

1. Why did the writer take a box of matches with him?
2. Where and when did he leave his matches behind?
3. In what condition did the writer return?
4. Why did he realize that he had been a fool?

(*b*) Indicate in your own words the meaning of the words and phrases in italics.

(*c*) Describe in not more than 150 of your own words what happened in this passage.

2. The group of tired dusty riders arrived at a fork in the road.

SECTION 16 PASSAGES FOR COMPREHENSION 249

Their leader immediately sprang to the ground after first throwing his horse's rein to one of the others, and began to examine *minutely* the sandy track. The problem was simple: if the fleeing enemy had taken the left turning, *there remained little hope* of catching them, since he knew that it led back to a small settlement of native huts where they would be sheltered by the friendly inhabitants. If, on the other hand, they had branched to the right, they would have before them the *open desert*, not a flat expanse of sand such as they had just crossed, but country broken by a series of ridges, behind any one of which a whole army could hide.

He turned to his companions to see if he could read any solution in their faces. But they were too occupied by their aching limbs and several were taking a quick drink from the flasks which hung at their belts. He realized that every minute's delay *lessened their chances* of overtaking their *adversaries*, so, with a rapid glance at the sun to estimate what daylight still remained, he jumped once more into the saddle and with his whip indicated the way they were to go.

(*a*) Write a short account in not more than 120 words imagining that you were one of the group of riders. Only material in the passage should be used.

(*b*) Indicate in your own words the meaning of the words and phrases in italics.

(*c*) Answer the following questions with a single sentence:

1. Why did the leader examine the track?
2. Where did the two tracks lead?
3. What difficulties did the pursuers expect if they took the right-hand track?
4. Why were the leader's companions not helpful?
5. Why did he look at the sun?

3. I had already waited three and a half hours and knew the airport waiting-room as well as my own drawing-room. I had already consumed three glasses of beer, a packet of cigarettes and *I don't know how many* sandwiches, when, with a sharp click, the loudspeaker once more came to life. I scarcely *bothered* to listen to the announcement as I had so often been disappointed that day, but I caught the words 'announce the arrival of their flight number 457 from . . .' and I *strained my ears* to hear the next word.

At that precise moment a loud argument broke out between two porters and I failed to hear the end of the announcement.

A couple of minutes later the roar of aircraft engines again *drowned all other sounds* and I strolled over to the arrival gate to watch the passengers walk in across the tarmac. One by one they came down the steps and I counted fifteen before I caught sight of what I thought must be John. I *shouldered my way* through the crowd and stationed myself directly beside the door he was to come through. Eleven, twelve, a woman and her little son. Yes, there he was. I stepped forwards and touched him lightly on the shoulder. 'Hello, John,' I said, holding out my arm to shake him by the hand. He turned his face towards me with eyes that showed no recognition. It was then that I realized that he was a complete stranger, whom I had never in my life seen before.

(*a*) Answer the following questions in one sentence, using your own words as far as possible:

1. How did the writer spend his time waiting?
2. Why did he not hear the announcement?
3. When did he first see 'John'?
4. How did he greet 'John'?
5. When did he realize that he had made a mistake?

(*b*) Imagine that you are 'John' and describe in not more than sixty words what happened from the moment you stepped out of the aeroplane.

(*c*) Indicate in your own words the meaning of the words and phrases in italics.

4. The crouching position which the restricted space of his hiding-place had forced him to assume and the pain he still felt in his ankle made it seem like hours that his pursuers searched the area where he lay concealed, although it was probably not more than a matter of minutes. He dared not move; nor dared he *give way* to his overwhelming desire to sneeze *for fear of revealing his presence*. When eventually the voices became fainter in the distance he allowed himself to shift his position and finally, when he could hear no more, to crawl, half-paralysed, from between the two rocks in whose shelter he had managed to escape capture. Cautiously he *peeped out* to see if it was safe for him to continue

SECTION 16 PASSAGES FOR COMPREHENSION   251

his escape, and, discovering no sign of life about him, he started to creep painfully in the direction he had come, hoping in this way to deceive his pursuers. He had not gone *above* a hundred yards when a movement in the undergrowth near by made him stand *stock-still*. Could it be that, after all, some of his enemies were still searching the neighbourhood? A few seconds passed and then, from behind a stump of a tree, there appeared a small black and white dog. Man and dog eyed each other suspiciously for a moment, until, to the man's immense relief, it rushed up to him wagging its tail.

(*a*) Answer the following questions in your own words using only material given in the passage:

  1. Why did the writer crouch in his hiding-place?
  2. Why did it seem like hours that the pursuers searched?
  3. When did he decide that it was safe to continue his escape?
  4. What did he fear when he heard the movement in the undergrowth?
  5. Why was he relieved when the dog rushed up to him?

(*b*) Give a short resumé in not more than sixty-five of your own words of what happened from the time the pursuers went away.

(*c*) Indicate in your own words the meaning of the words and phrases in italics.

5. Legend tells us that about three thousand years B.C. a Chinese Empress, while taking her tea, *out of curiosity* dipped the cocoon of a silk-worm into it and learnt how to unwind the fine thread of silk of which it was composed. It was nearly five thousand years later that a Frenchman, experimenting with the crushed leaves of the mulberry tree, on which the silk-worm feeds, found out how to produce a fine *silk-like* filament which we now call artificial silk. His discovery stimulated other scientists to search for new fibres, and it was not long before several more were produced; but all of them had as *their starting-point* some natural organic material, such as: cellulose, casein, etc.

It is only in the last twenty-five years that man has succeeded in *synthesizing* new fibres from inorganic materials. Everyone has heard of nylon, and scarcely one of us can say that he does not use something made from this valuable product every day. But nylon was only the first of an *ever-lengthening* list of new synthetic fibres Orlon, Dacron, Acrilan, Terylene—all bearing some *Greek-sounding* name. Hardly a year now passes without some new fibre making its appearance and some unfamiliar name finding its way into our everyday speech. Is it not natural that the producers of silk, cotton and wool are alarmed?

(*a*) Answer these questions in your own words:

1. How is silk said to have been discovered?
2. What is the principal difference between artificial silk and the modern synthetic fibres?
3. Why did the Frenchman experiment with the leaves of the mulberry tree?

(*b*) Give a concise account in not more than 100 words of the passage under the title 'Fibres, ancient and modern'.
(*c*) Give the meaning of the words and phrases in italics in your own words.

6. SMITH, ROBERTS & Co.

oOOo

North Street, London, S.E.2

November 17, 1957

Dear Sirs,

Re: Accounting Machinery

Having read your advertisement in the 'Daily News' of November 6th, in which you offer your advisory services *free* to firms who have *problems of accounting procedure*, we should be most obliged if you would arrange to send a representative to our Head Office at the *above* address for consultation.

We give you, *herewith*, a short account of the problem we wish to solve: Our firm employs a large number of *part-time* workers and, although our wages bill, which is *made up* weekly, does not reach a very high figure, it involves an unusually large amount of

SECTION 16 PASSAGES FOR COMPREHENSION   253

our accounting staff's time to prepare. We are anxious *to lighten the burden* on this department and believe that by using one of the accounting machines made by your organization, suitably modified to meet our special requirements, we might be able to effect considerable economies in time and money.

Yours faithfully,

p.p. Messrs. Smith, Roberts and Co.

The National Office Machine Co. Ltd.,
National Buildings,
London, E.C.23.

(*a*) State briefly in your own words:

1. What did the National Office Machine Co. say in their advertisement?
2. What is Smith, Roberts and Co.'s accounting problem?

(*b*) Explain in your own words the meaning of the phrases and words in italics.

7. There are in the world some 3,000 different languages and dialects. This did not matter in the Middle Ages, when communications between different parts of the globe were slow and difficult and when, in Europe at least, all educated men spoke Latin. Things have changed completely *in our time*. While few men can now speak Latin, the telegraph and radio have made it possible to talk directly between continents, and a journey which might then have taken several *weary months* can now be achieved in a few hours by air. It is not surprising, then, that men have *increasingly* felt the need for a common language, and during the last century various solutions of the problem have been *put forward*. The first of these was the creation of a completely artificial tongue, quite unconnected with any existing language. Although such a tongue might be difficult for people to learn, it at least had the advantage that everybody started *on an equal footing*. The second solution was the invention of a synthetic language based on natural languages, but without their numerous irregularities. Such languages as Esperanto, Volapuk and Interlingua belong to this category and, since they are related to existing languages, are

easier to learn for European speakers. The two remaining solutions to the problem of international language are either to adopt as a world auxiliary some existing language already spoken by a large number of people or peoples (such languages as French, Spanish or Russian would be suitable), or to create a simplified version of one of these languages, in which the vocabulary and grammatical forms would be *reduced to a minimum*. An example of this is 'Basic English'.

It is most unlikely that the governments of the world will ever formally agree on an international auxiliary language, but meanwhile, whether we like it or not, there are signs that English is gradually becoming accepted as a second language by a majority of people all over the world.

(*a*) Answer the following questions:

1. Why was the need for an international language not felt in the Middle Ages?
2. What is the difference between ordinary English and 'Basic English'?
3. What has caused the recent demand for a common language?

(*b*) Explain the meaning of the words and phrases in italics.

(*c*) Write a short summary in your own words (ninety words) entitled: 'Four Solutions of the Problem of an International Language'.

8. From 'The Loamshire Evening Post.'

TWO DIE IN HOTEL BLAZE

BRIDGEHAMPTON. Friday. A disastrous fire broke out on the top floor of the Grand Hotel, Washington Road, in the *small hours* of the morning. The whole of the floor was *gutted* and damage estimated at £10,000 was done. Two of the guests staying at the hotel lost their lives. Only one other *casualty* is reported. John Green (43) and his wife Emily Green (38) of London Rd., Acton, were trapped in their room and were evidently overcome by fumes

SECTION 16 PASSAGES FOR COMPREHENSION   255

before rescuers could reach them. A third guest, John Wills (63), of Leeds, was taken to hospital with multiple burns. His condition is reported as being serious.

The alarm was given by the night porter, Robert Black, whose attention had been drawn to smoke issuing from one of the top floor windows by a group of young people returning late from a dance. Within five minutes the town Fire Brigade was on the spot. The work of fighting the blaze and evacuating the *by-now alarmed* guests was seriously *hampered by the non-operation of the lifts*. It is believed that the fire was caused by a short circuit in the lift machinery and had extended to the whole floor before it was observed. The flames were brought under control in two hours. The Manager, Mr. William Ramsey, interviewed by our reporter, expressed his deep regret at the loss of life and added, 'It was lucky that the hotel was half empty at the time or we might have had more casualties.'

Although it will be some months before the damage can be repaired, the hotel will remain open to guests as usual.

(*a*) Answer the following questions in your own words:
   1. Why was it difficult to get the guests out of the hotel quickly?
   2. Why were there so few casualties?
   3. Who first noticed the fire?

(*b*) Explain in your own words the meaning of the words and phrases in italics.

(*c*) Give a summary of the whole report in no more than 130 words.

9. From 'The Loamshire Evening Post'.

The announcement of the death last Friday at the age of seventy-two of Mr. John Henry Bingham, will have caused a widespread feeling of loss among his numerous friends and acquaintances. The details of Mr. Bingham's career are, we believe, generally known, for he had long been a familiar and respected figure in Oswell, where he spent the greater part of his life. He was not, however, a native of that place, having been born in the nearby village of Tanbridge.

Mr. Bingham's remarkable capacity for commerce showed itself early, when he left school at the age of fourteen to help his father in the family leather business. Within five years the number of his employees had doubled and some twenty years later the firm of Bingham's had become *a familiar name in county agricultural circles*.

The considerable wealth which his enterprise and ability brought him never affected his naturally simple ways, and he always *remained on affectionate terms with* the older employees of the firm who had served his father in the early days. The schools and hospitals of his home town had cause to be grateful to him for his generosity on numerous occasions, while his rare good sense was *frequently sought after* on their committees of management.

He was finally persuaded to enter politics and sat for five years in the House as Member for Oswell; but political life was never *congenial to him*, nor did his talents *lie that way*. At the General Election in 195- he decided not *to contest the seat* and shortly afterwards resigned his chairmanship of the company which bears his name in order to retire to his farm at Tanbridge. There he devoted himself to country life and to the development of his famous herd of pedigree cattle. He did not, however, lose touch with Bingham's Ltd., and it was after a visit to the factory in Oswell that he contracted the illness *to which he finally succumbed*.

(*a*) Give in your own words the meaning of the words and phrases in italics.
(*b*) Write a summary of the life of Mr. J. H. Bingham in your own words. (100 words.)
(*c*) Answer these questions:

1. What is the difference between 'friends' and 'acquaintances'?
2. What were Mr. Bingham's hobbies?
3. Name two ways in which his abilities and intelligence showed themselves.

10. DO-IT-YOURSELF

In former times when a window-pane in your house got broken, you would call the glazier to put in a new one, or if your lights fused, the electrician would be sent for to put them right. Nowadays *people are their own glaziers* and electricians.

SECTION 16   PASSAGES FOR COMPREHENSION

Before the war, when wages were *relatively* low, people did not think of doing these things for themselves, but during the war, when so many artisans were away in the armed forces, the master of the house had to undertake this sort of job himself. To his surprise he got to like sawing wood and gluing it, putting in new light fuses or new washers in running taps and all the *hundred and one* repair jobs there are to be done around most houses. By the time the war was over it had become a habit with him.

In the post-war period of full employment the number of artisans *available* is limited, many having found it more profitable to take work in factories, while those that are left are able to charge high prices for their services. Now that the householder has *got the hang of* mending leaking pipes and broken chairs, he sees no reason why he should pay someone else a lot of money to do something he really enjoys doing himself; and so in recent years the 'do-it-yourself' movement has grown rapidly. In the ironmonger's we can buy sets of 'do-it-yourself' tools which include everything we may need for repairs in the home, and in the bookshops, 'do-it-yourself' handbooks to tell us how to use the tools we have just bought. So clever have we all become that we are no longer satisfied only with mending things, we want to make them, too; and so, *to cater for this demand*, shops are now selling 'do-it-yourself' kits,* which enable the man-in-the-street to build anything he likes from a coffee-table to a sailing-boat.

(*a*) Explain in your own words the meaning of the words and phrases in italics.
(*b*) Explain in your own words why the 'do-it-yourself' movement has developed in recent years. (Seventy words.)
(*c*) Answer the following questions:

1. Why did people not think of doing their own repairs before the war?
2. Why does the householder nowadays not wish to call in an artisan to do repairs for him?
3. Why are people no longer satisfied only with repairing things?

*kit: a complete set of materials and tools.